About the Author

Da Chen, after graduating with top honours, served as an assistant professor at Beijing Language Institute. At the age of twenty-three, he came to America with thirty dollars in his pocket, a bamboo flute, and a heart filled with hope. He won a full scholarship to Columbia University Law School, in New York, from which, after graduation, he worked for the Wall Street firm of Rothschild, Inc. He lives in New York with his two children and physician wife.

Colours of the Mountain

Da Chen

ARROW

Published by Arrow Books in 2000

1 3 5 7 9 10 8 6 4 2

First published in the United Kingdom by
William Heinemann, 1999

Arrow Books
The Random House Group Limited
20 Vauxhall Bridge Road, London SW1V 2SA

Random House Australia (Pty) Limited
20 Alfred Street, Milsons Point, Sydney,
New South Wales 2061, Australia

Random House New Zealand Limited
18 Poland Road, Glenfield,
Auckland 10, New Zealand

Random House (Pty) Limited
Endulini, 5a Jubilee Road, Parktown 2193, South Africa

The Random House Group Limited Reg. No. 954009

www.randomhouse.co.uk

A CIP catalogue record for this book
is available from the British Library

Papers used by Random House are natural,
recyclable products made from wood grown in
sustainable forests. The manufacturing processes conform to
the environmental regulations of the country of origin.

ISBN 0 099 29800 7

Printed and bound in Denmark by
Nørhaven A/S, Viborg

Dedication

To Grandpa, for your smiling eyes;
to Grandma, for your big feeding spoon.
To my mother: you are all things beautiful;
and my father: you are for ever.

On the wooden door of the old Chen mansion, my grandpa had painted, with powerful strokes, a nostalgic couplet:

> Colours of the mountain will never leave our door
> Sounds of the river will linger for ever in our ears

Throughout Grandpa's life, Ch'ing Mountain, with its ever-changing colours, was his hope, and the Dong Jing River, with its whispers, thunderous shouts, or – sometimes – just its silence, was his inspiration.

COLOURS OF THE
MOUNTAIN

One

I was born in southern China in 1962, in the tiny town of Yellow Stone. They called it the Year of Great Starvation. Chairman Mao had had a parting of the ways with the Soviets, and now they wanted all their loans repaid or there would be blood, a lot of it.

Mao panicked. He ordered his citizens to cut down on meals and be hungry heroes so he could repay the loans. The superstitious citizens of Yellow Stone still saw the starving ghosts of those who had died during that year chasing around and sobbing for food on the eve of the spring Tomb-Sweeping Festival.

That year also saw a forbidding drought that made fields throughout China crack like wax. For the first time, the folks of Yellow Stone saw the bottom of Dong Jing River. Rice plants turned yellow and withered young.

Dad wanted to give me the name *Han*, which meant *drought*. But that would have been like naming a boy in Hiroshima *Atom Bomb*. And since the Chinese believe that their names dictate their fate, I would have probably ended up digging ditches, searching for water in some wasteland. So Dad named me *Da*, which means *prosperity*.

The unfortunate year of my birth left a permanent flaw in my character: I was always hungry. I yearned for food. I could talk, think, and dream about it for ever. As an infant, I ate with a large, adult spoon. I would open wide while they shovelled in the

3

porridge. My grandmother said she had never seen an easier baby to feed.

We lived in an old house that faced the only street in Yellow Stone. Our backyard led to the clear Dong Jing River, zigzagging like a dragon on land. The lush, odd-shaped Ch'ing Mountain stood beyond the endless rice paddies like an ancient giant with a pointed hat, round shoulders, and head bent in gentle slumber.

We rarely left our house to play because Mum said there were many bad people waiting to hurt us. When I did go out to buy food in the commune's grocery store a few blocks away, I always walked in the middle, safely flanked by my three sisters, as we hurried in and out. Neighbourhood boys sometimes threw stones at us, made ugly faces and called us names. I always wondered why they did that. It was obviously not for fun. My sisters often cried, as we ran and dodged and slammed our door shut behind us.

I once tried to sneak through our side door and join the kids in the street, but Si caught me by the arm and snatched me back, screaming and kicking. She gave me quite a spanking for breaking the do-not-go-out order. When I asked Mum why we had to hide in our dark house all the time, she said that we were landlords, and that the people outside were poor peasants who had taken our houses, lands, and stores. They were making us suffer because the leaders were all bad. There was no fairness, no justice for us. We had to be quiet, stay out of trouble, and wait for better days to come.

When? I would ask. Some day, when you grow up, she'd answer. That will be a long time from now, I'd say. Mum would nod, her eyes gently studying my face as if looking for an answer herself. Then she'd take me in her arms and hum her favourite tune – a simple melody urging a boy to eat more and grow up faster so that he could help plough the land with his dad and harvest the grain.

Restricted to the house, I would silently wander into Grandpa's smoky room and practise calligraphy with him. Some days, when my sisters were in school and Mum was busy, and not watching me, I would wander out and wrestle with the neighbourhood

4

boys. This was a lot of fun, and I would come back all dusty, and tell Mum I had fallen, and she would make me change my clothes.

One day when I was about six I stood on the pavement watching a parade of Red Guards carrying their rifles and red flags and shouting slogans when a kid from next door, for no obvious reason, smacked me right on the face and kicked me when I fell. I picked myself up and charged like a bull into my smiling attacker. When he went down, I straddled him and hit him hard on the face and neck. Within half an hour, the Communist party secretary, a thin little man, stormed into our house with the kid's mother. He started shouting at my mum, demanding to see my father, who was away at labour camp. I hid behind a big chair.

'What have you been teaching your kids, to fight the world? To fright communism?' He shook his fist at my tiny mum. 'I could put you in a labour camp too, if you let one of your kids do this again. Do you hear me?'

Mum was too busy crying and being nervous. She didn't answer him right away and the secretary took this as an insult. He slapped her across the face, sending her whirling into a corner. I wanted to jump out from behind the chair and hit him with my fists, but fear held me back. I couldn't afford to bring any more trouble to our family. After spitting his dark phlegm on our spotless floor, the man stormed out. Mum sat there, crying. I spent the rest of the day watching her hold a wet towel to her face, where the humiliating imprints of his hand remained. She was quiet. She had nothing more to teach me about the cruelty outside.

Grandpa, who liked to drink a little – to calm his bones, as he put it – saw no future for us. In school, my sisters sat in the back, although, given their height, they should have been in the middle. They couldn't sing in the choir. They couldn't perform in the school plays. The kids could beat them, spit on them, and the teachers would not say a thing. Grandpa wished he would die soon in the hope that they might treat us better. Dad said that was nonsense. We were fine the way we were.

But everything wasn't fine. We had been stripped of all our property. Dad was fired from his teaching job, leaving a family of nine with no income. We relied entirely on a small food ration that went up and down with the harvest each year. A drought could wipe out half a year's ration and a wet season would rot the young rice in the fields. For months we would have nothing to eat but tree bark and the roots of wild plants. Even a good harvest would only get us through eight to nine months of the year. The remaining months were called 'the season where the green and yellow did not meet'. During those months, Dad would be out imploring for a longer grace period on an old loan, and begging to borrow more money in order to pay back the debt so that they wouldn't take away the tables and chairs. He had already sold the wooden doors and door frames inside our house to pay for food. Each door was replaced with makeshift planks of rotten wood. But never a day went by without Mum teaching us that we should have dignity in the face of hardship. She would point out to us which land and storefronts used to be ours, and we would feel quietly proud.

For those long months when there was no food, we ate anything that came to our table. One year, we ate mouldy yam three times a day for four months. Brother Jin summed it up well when he said, 'I'm sick of the yams, but I'm afraid they'll run out.' We learned to live with little and be content with what we had. Even the soupy yams brought laughter to our dining table when everyone was there. But most of the time Dad was away at labour camp, or Grandpa was being detained in the commune jail, waiting for another public humiliation meeting to be held in the market square, where he would be beaten badly.

Mum taught us to beg Buddha for his protection and help. This was easier than potty training. All you needed to do was wash yourself really clean, button your buttons, get on your knees, and bang your head on the floor before the hidden shrine of the big, fat, smiling Buddha. Ask all you want to ask and you will be answered, Mum told us.

I followed her to the shrine every day – the shrine that was hidden behind a window curtain in the attic, because religion was not allowed in Communist China. I knelt behind Mum and banged my head on the floor noisily, whispering my small requests. My list grew from two items to many. I asked for Dad not to get beaten by the Red Guards, for Grandpa to be well, for Mum not to cry as much. My last request was always for food – more of it, please.

Two

Grandpa lived the life of a mountain cat. He rose with the moon and dozed off in his small, wooden bed when the sun came out. Each midnight he would sneak into the kitchen, boil a pot of water, and brew some green tea. He said he was careful not to make too much noise, but he talked out loud to himself, and often dropped his plate or cup as he fumbled around the dark room. And when he bumped into something, you could hear him curse like a fisherman who had let the big one get away. Then there was his coughing. The foul, cheap tobacco made his lungs scream, and I had to stuff my ears with my thumbs until his nerve-racking coughs faded.

At midnight Grandpa had his first smoke of the day, then he was ready to start his secretive life as one who deserved, not the light, but darkness.

Since the beginning of the Cultural Revolution, the commune cadre in charge of landlord reform had set the following rules: Grandpa could not visit his friends, he could not leave town without advance permission, and he was to write a detailed diary of his life every day. This was to be turned in every week. He wasn't welcome in any public places, could not engage in any political discussions, and should look away if someone spat in his face. If they missed, he was to wipe the spit off the ground. There were more rules, but Grandpa forgot a number of them when he came home to tell us about them.

8

When he tried walking the street one day, children in the neighbourhood threw rocks at him, and he ran home with bruises all over his face. Dad was mad at him for being so reckless. He could have been beaten to death and no one would have cared. From then on, Grandpa woke up at night and crept out into the deserted street, breathing the air of freedom in darkness. He could have danced, tumbled, or practised kung fu and no one would have known. He'd come back before sunrise and tell us about his adventures. He'd talk about the addition to the Lius' backyard, the fight with the Dengs' mean dog, and the tasty fruits on the Changs' trees. Not your typical grandfatherly routine.

That same year, we lost our grandma to ovarian cancer. Grandpa was a changed man. He couldn't understand the order in which Buddha had called them to wherever dead people went. He had planned on going ahead of Grandma, and had even told her about the burial. Burn me to ashes, he said, and spread them on the farm as fertilizer. There was no will, no inheritance. He couldn't wait to leave this world. He was still hoping to join his gambling friends in the other one.

He was like a flimsy candle, flickering in the wind. He slept in short spurts, dozing here and there. And something changed in him. He became more daring, less afraid.

The diary he was required to turn in became cynical and sarcastic, filled with complicated puns and metaphors that confused the cadre, who had never gone to school. When the cadre told him to stop writing that way, Grandpa suggested that if he couldn't read what was written, then maybe it was time someone else did. The cadre slapped him across the face a couple of times and threw him out of the office. Back home, Grandpa laughed when he told us the story, wiping his face with a cold towel. He considered he'd won a victory.

He once slipped out of the house when we weren't watching and went to the market square to buy some bananas. He dawdled along, stopping at fruit stands and vegetable counters, having a grand time. He wasn't afraid of anything any more. People had spat in his face. Smiling, he wiped off the spittle. They had beaten him, and he'd been able to get up and ask for more.

He finally came to a banana stand and fished out twenty fens for two bananas. As he was paying for them, the cadre came up behind him.

'What are you doing here, you dirty landlord?' the cadre said.

'Oh, it's you. I'm doing what you are doing.' Grandpa smiled.

'Let's see if you can do what I'm doing now,' the cadre said, slapping Grandpa so hard that he fell down on the muddy ground. Rolling in the dirt, he struggled to get to his knees, but he kept slipping. The cadre just watched him. A large crowd had gathered, but no one offered to help the old man. They threw rotten vegetables and rocks at him. Grandpa got less sympathy than a street rat being beaten by a gang of wild children.

Just as Grandpa steadied himself, the cadre kicked his head and brought him down again. This time he was quiet. His thin, hunched body stirred a little. His hands reached out. He wanted to get up, but he couldn't. He moaned weakly and stared at the crowd. The people dispersed and the cadre sauntered off like a hero.

A kind old woman came to our house and told my dad what had happened. Dad quickly found Grandpa and carried him home on his back. Grandpa was in bed for two weeks, and before he was fully recovered, the cadre ordered him to go to a construction site to watch the lumber at night. Every night at nine, he would bundle up in his torn cotton coat, a cane in one hand and a lamp in the other. I'd stand by the door and watch him disappear into the darkness. We all worried about him, but he was as happy as a monkey. He couldn't wait to go to work. He wanted to walk the new frontier, watch the stars twinkle, and enjoy the sunrise.

One morning, he came back limping badly. Grandpa wasn't one to fake illness. He had tripped over a rock and had fallen while chasing a bunch of hooligans trying to steal the lumber. A doctor gave written testimony and the cadre temporarily let him off night duty.

When summer came, Grandpa was ordered to chase the birds, thousands of them, off the fields that were strewn with seeds. By then, he was getting weaker and weaker every day. His lungs were failing, his kidneys were failing, and so was his liver.

On a bad day, when every organ in his body seemed to be aching and alcohol couldn't ease the pain, Grandpa asked Dad to write an excuse. I ran with it to the cadre's office. The cadre glanced at it and asked me how serious it was. I said Grandpa could die. The cadre pounded his desk, which startled me, and said that maybe I could go in his place. I said I would be happy to. So that was the deal.

The next day, I waited at our door for Grandpa's friend, a fellow landlord, to come and pick me up. Mr Gong wasn't really a landlord. Dad said he had only owned a little bit of land, but had been unluckily mislabelled. He had been jailed, and looked like a shell of a man, with high cheekbones, a tall forehead, and a black beard. He had kind but shifty eyes, which Dad said was from the fear he felt. When he arrived, I followed ten yards behind him. I was afraid of being seen with a landlord. I was only seven, and had a long life before me. The kids might start throwing stones. They could do anything they wanted and no one would defend us. Landlords were open game. We separated and walked quietly at the edge of the street.

The field we were to watch was five miles away from the town of Yellow Stone. The Dong Jing River slithered like a serpent along the fields. The mountains on the horizon blurred in the summer heat. The insects sang their songs, hidden among the rice plants. The soil smelled like summer. The young seeds were spread over ten acres in the middle of nowhere. The commune was growing rice for the next season, and had sowed the seeds as soon as the ripened rice was harvested and the field ploughed.

Mr Gong asked me to cover the south end. He would watch the north. When we got there, I was amazed by the number of sparrows picking at the seeds. They were having a free breakfast, and were undisturbed by the two humans. From the bushes, where they'd been hidden, Mr Gong took out a huge bronze gong, and two long bamboo poles with some shreds of red cloth attached to the ends.

I decided to do something drastic for a change. I took the gong and started beating it while running along the field. The birds flew furiously away and I stood before Mr Gong, waiting for him to praise my youthful energy. He smiled and asked me how long I could keep running like that. I said every ten minutes. He shook his head mildly, not at all impressed. He said that the farmers deliberately sowed ten times more seed than they needed – they had already thought about the birds, and knew that we couldn't keep running for ever.

I asked him what we should do. He pointed vaguely at the river nearby and asked if I wanted to fish in the river to kill some time. I asked him if that was all right. Who was around to say it wasn't? he asked. The cadre couldn't come here to count how many seeds were missing. Mr Gong would keep an eye on the road, and if I heard him beat on his gong three times, I was to jump out of the river right away.

That first day I swam for three hours, then napped for two. In between, I beat the gong for fun. The second day I was bored, so I sat next to Mr Gong and chatted about my school. During the lulls, I would quietly play with his beard. On the third day, he started talking and I couldn't get him to stop. He talked about language and how he loved the beauty of words. He used to write poems and prose. It was his prose that had made his wife fall in love with him at a college campus up north. His father had owned a little land, so he had come back after college with his wife and had volunteered to be a landlord. His wife had died an angry woman, but he was very proud of his sons because they were all writers who wrote better than he did. He had high hopes for them as poets. Then he recited some of their favourite lines, moved at times to tears. I forgot about the scorching sun and the boring, quiet, deserted fields, where we saw only an occasional fisherman sailing by in his bamboo boat.

I was getting so tanned that Mr Gong fondly called me 'Eel'. We set a nice routine for ourselves. I fished in the morning, while he napped at noon. Then I napped for two hours. Afterwards, I would run around for half an hour scaring the birds, then we would talk and watch the sunset while waiting for the last bird to fly off. Soon we no longer separated out when we walked down the street. Going to and coming back from work, I walked right behind Mr Gong like his shadow, no longer afraid of being associated with

12

him. We joked and laughed. He kept his shifty eyes alert, and, knowingly we shut up when there were people around.

When my time of substituting for Grandpa was over, I missed the swims in the cool water, the naps in the vast quiet of the rice fields and the conversations we had while watching the beautiful sunsets. I wished I were a poet like Mr Gong, able to immortalize those moments in words.

Yellow Stone Elementary School sat a mile away down the street. It was an old Confucian temple with tilted roofs and lots of wood-carvings on the walls. Ancient trees shielded the buildings from the sun, and there was a pond full of lotus blossoms.

When registration day came for the new school year, I got up early and studied my appearance in front of a piece of mirror, broken off from my brother's bigger one. I was as dark as charcoal and as thin as sugarcane. My crew cut, Mum's handiwork, had uneven furrows left behind by rusty scissors and a not-too-experienced hand, as though a clumsy farmer had ploughed the fields. I didn't mind too much. The hair would grow again and the pain of having your hair yanked out by blunt scissors was soon forgotten. My sisters cut each other's hair and Mum took care of the four men in the family. We saved a lot of money that way. The only time I had my hair cut by the barber was on the day of my grandma's death.

My forehead was peeling like a snake casting off its skin in the springtime. I rubbed hard, and pulled off the larger pieces of skin. But I finally gave up. I would grow out of this terrible tan when the scorching summer changed to a mild, breezy autumn, with deep blue skies and thin white clouds that chased each other like lovers.

I put on a white shirt – a hand-me-down from Jin – and ran to school. The red poster in the schoolyard said that Mr Sun was to be our new teacher. The tuition was three yuen, a staggering amount on the Chen economic scale. I checked the information twice, wrote it down for Mum to read, and parked myself by the window, watching parents take their kids by the hand and march happily to the teachers to register. It was an all-cash deal. They came out laughing, the kids jumping up and down with a bunch of new books in their hands. It was all cosy for them, but I had to find some resources for my education. I knew well enough that we would be out of rice and yams in a matter of weeks. Dad was away at camp and the food ration kept going down each day. Mum was saving every fen for food. There was no money for tuition. The three yuen I needed would buy us ten pounds of rice, or a hundred pounds of yams. How much knowledge could it buy?

I went home with a lump in my throat. I knew the routine well. I would go to Mum and tell her about the tuition. She would tell me how much money she had left for the whole family, a few yuen at most. She would say to go and ask for an extension or a waiver of tuition. Then I would have to go to meet my new teacher, begging on my knees. Even if an extension were granted, the teacher would mention the tuition fees every day in class until everyone would know how poor I was. He might even keep me after school, lecturing. It had happened to my siblings, and all the while they would be going to school without textbooks. Kind students would let them copy from their books. Now it was happening to me.

I went home, feeling defeated, poor, and pathetic. Mum knew why. She wiped her wet hands on her apron and gave me fifty fens and told me it was a stretch for the family already. I didn't need to be told. A poor child knew what it meant to be poor. We didn't ask for much, and sometimes we didn't even ask.

She said that I should beg for an extension. I asked her just how long would the delay be. She said until the piglets were grown and sold to the buyer from the south. That was something to hope for, but the mother pig was still pregnant. I took the money with a heavy heart. It was a pound of flesh off the family fortune, but only a small piece of the tuition.

I pinned the fifty fens to the inside of my pocket lest I lose them, and ran back to school. I parked myself below the window again and had a good look at the teacher. He was a thin man with short, curly hair like feathers. He seemed your regular, boring, stiff-necked young educator who had read some books. He was shaking hands with the parents of my classmates, smiling and smoking.

I slumped against the wall, feeling depressed. The world was unfair. Everyone in my class seemed to have young parents with money. They chatted, laughed, and socialized with the new teacher. Their manners were smooth, their clothes were nice. It was a very special occasion for them, and a milestone for the kids. Some of the parents were so influential in the little, deprived town of Yellow Stone that being the teacher for those kids could mean a lot of back-door favours.

Take that fat butcher from the commune with his fat boy, who now sat with the teacher. He was so rich that he took out a thick wad of large bills and casually pulled out two large notes. The teacher had to clean out the drawer for change. I could imagine what they were saying.

Cute kid.

Thanks, but he's naughty.

Can't be that bad.

Needs a good teacher like you to discipline him.

No problem, pal, I'll take care of it. What line of business are you in, by the way?

Oh, I sell meat. Come by any time. I'll give you some real lean meat through the back door.

Deal.

The butcher put out his greasy hand and the teacher took it. No doubt the fat boy would be well taken care of in class. He would act like a spoiled brat with the teacher's blessing. He was the one with the meat daddy so he would win each time. And good meat would be forthcoming on holidays, the New Year, and special occasions. The teacher would be sorry when the fat boy finally graduated. That was how it went.

And what did I have to offer? Nothing. Grandpa was dying, sick in bed. The doctor said he might live a few months with the proper medication. Tough luck. Medicine was expensive. No money, no life. Dad was digging in the mountains somewhere, camped in an old, windy temple. And I had only fifty fens in small coins. My personal appearance was shocking – a pumpkin head and a ten-year-old patched shirt. And personally I hadn't eaten any meat since New Year's Day.

The thoughts tortured me and I squirmed in shame and

humiliation, but I had to face reality. The teacher could throw me out with a sneer on his face. That was fine, I had thick skin. A poor child couldn't afford to have thin skin. Only rich boys and well-to-do girls with cute little butterflies in their hair could afford to have thin skin.

I adjusted my belt, made sure my pee hole wasn't open and gingerly stepped into the teacher's office. I would go there and beg the hell out of him, though I was prepared for the worst. The window looked reasonably large and there was a patch of soft grass for landing.

'So you are Chen Da,' he said, to my surprise.

'Yes, sir. I have a problem.'

'Don't we all.'

'Excuse me?'

'I meant, we all have problems.' He was smiling.

'Yes, well, you see, I only have fifty fens for the tuition.'

'And you want to register?'

'If I could.'

'What's your story?'

'We're waiting for the piglets to grow.'

'How big are the pigs?'

'Young.'

'How young?'

'Not born yet.' I waited for him to grab my neck and toss me out.

'Okay, write a note down here about the pigs and I will register you.'

I looked at him in disbelief. A wave of gratitude swept through my heart. I wanted to kneel down and kiss his toes. There *was* a Buddha somewhere up there in the fuzzy sky. I took his pen and wrote the promise on a piece of paper.

'But I cannot give you the textbooks now. It's a school rule.'

'That's fine. I can copy them from others.'

'Well, if you don't mind, I was thinking maybe you could use my last year's copy, but it's messy, it has my handwriting all over the pages.'

If I didn't mind? Who was this guy? A saint from Buddha's heaven?

16

I was overwhelmed and didn't know what to say. I kept looking at my feet. I had rehearsed being thrown out of the window, being slighted or laughed at, but kindness? . . . I wasn't prepared for kindness. I nodded quickly, and ran off after saying a very heartfelt thank-you and bowing so deep that I almost rubbed my nose on my knees.

Mr Sun, the new teacher, came from a village at the foot of the Ch'ing Mountain. He had a sunny personality and was an outdoors kind of a guy. In the mornings, he and his wife watered the vegetables, then he walked to school. I soon began to tag along behind him like his shadow every morning. He told me many stories during those walks.

He elected me to be the monitor of the class, a bold political decision on his part, and had me lead the revolutionary songs at the beginning of every lesson. I was that 1-per cent exception in our harsh reality. I was never supposed to be a leader among other students. I was born with a political defect that no one could fix. But once in a while they threw a bone out to us, a bone that we chased around with enthusiasm. I was grateful for this bone. I played with it, poked it with my snout, and cherished every moment of being tempted before I sank my teeth into the juiciest part.

I'd arrive early with the teacher and hit the books. In my spare time, I helped the slower students catch up. I was the captain of our basketball team and a formidable singer in school-wide competitions. Once I sang so loud that I was hoarse for the next three days. I read classical stories to the whole room, while my teacher sat in the back and graded the homework, stopping occasionally to nod with approval.

Late in the afternoons, my new friends – Jie, Ciang, and a few others – would urge me to tell them some more stories. We would climb over the short wall at the back of our school and throw ourselves into an ancient orchard. It was a little paradise.

Our spot was a huge lychee tree with low-hanging boughs. Each of us had a favourite sitting spot. Mine had a back support and a small branch to rest my feet on. The comfort helped the flow of the story. Sometimes Jie would rub the soles of my feet which was good for another twenty minutes. And each time I threatened to end the story they would beg for more and more, and I would have to stretch my imagination and make a short story longer and a long story go on for ever.

My popularity went unchallenged till one day a big-eyed boy showed up at our door for late registration. I hated to admit it, but he was good-looking. He was there for five minutes and the girls were already giggling at his sweet smile and nasty winking. During break, I sat in my seat, heaving with anger and contempt for this sudden intruder. I contemplated the proper step to take. I thought of going to him and introducing myself as the leader of the class. It was, after all, my territory, and I deserved a certain courtesy and respect from him. You can't just walk in and ruin everything. If he was a decent man (my keen observation of him during the last hour made me feel this was unlikely) then I would give my blessing, offer my protection, and help him settle in on our turf. I was, after all, a nice guy with a big heart. I welcomed any bright man as my friend, but no way was I going to walk up to him and shake hands. He was surrounded by a fan club, admirers who were fawning over something he was wearing. The girls lingered and giggled. The place was out of control.

As I burned with jealousy, a negative feeling that as a leader I tried hard to suppress, the hotshot kid broke through the crowd and walked over. He looked straight at me with those attractive, intelligent eyes of his. At that moment, my heart softened. No wonder the girls had lost their minds. I couldn't help being impressed by the clarity and sense of purpose in his eyes, that straight nose, so tall and defined, and that square, chiselled jaw. Had he been a general, I would have followed him into battle and fought until the end.

I stood up with what little dignity I had left and extended my hand to meet his. We shook hands. That was when I saw the buckle. He had this shining buckle the size of a large fist that he wore around his waist. There were five stars carved on it. It shone in the morning sun, obviously the result of a lot of polishing by a proud hand.

18

'I heard you're the *Tau-Ke*.' The top man. His diction was imaginative.

'Hardly, hardly.' High praise called for a humble response, but I was flattered nonetheless.

'I think this would look really good on you.' He took his belt and buckle off and handed it over to me, just like that.

'No, no. You wear it.'

'I've been wearing it since my dad came back from the Vietnam War.' He had the casual art of name-dropping down pat.

'Your dad was in the war with the Americans?'

'Sure, he has lots of medals and was at Ho Chi Minh City. White Americans. Okay, okay, okay.' He even spoke English.

He studied the buckle carefully. A wall of classmates had gathered behind me, watching the exchange.

'That belt has a little history to it,' he continued.

'What history?'

'My dad wore it in the war. It's been hit a few times but it's so strong and tough you can't even see a dent. I'm talking the super-bullets from the American weapons.'

I was sold on the spot. He became my best friend and we named him 'Mr Buckle'. He took the nickname in stride.

I showed him around the seedy part of town, the bushy burial grounds where the ghosts roamed, named all the dogs he should watch out for, and warned him about the dangerous spots to avoid. I pointed out fruit trees that were safe to steal from and helped him with his homework as part of my duty as the class monitor. He, in turn, let me use his buckle. Then he took to wearing his dad's army uniform to our house in the morning, and we would exchange our clothes. I wore his green jacket with the neat cartridge pockets, his dad's oversized boots, and a marvellous army hat. I tromped around the school like an idiot, feeling great. I imitated the nasal accent of a general and talked with my head high and hands resting on my belt. The afternoon stories in the woods soon all had something to do with the Vietnam War. It was much easier to create a story wearing the right costume. I told the stories, spoke the lines, and acted at the same time. My friends, including Mr Buckle, laughed, cried, and cheered until they peed their pants.

But I still felt small twinges of jealousy. He was the only boy who dared cross that invisible line, and spoke openly to girls in class. They squirmed in his presence. They loved to be with him, but were shy, a sign of captivation. But as our friendship deepened, my admiration for him grew. I watched his moves closely. He looked moody in class, and had this way of focusing on your eyes when he talked to you. He walked tall, his eyes looking straight ahead. Confidence emanated from him. When he smiled, he didn't open his mouth from ear to ear like an idiot, but tantalized you with a glimpse of white teeth. When you asked him a question, he knotted his brow into an intelligent frown. The guy wrote the book on proper body language.

One day Mr Buckle formally invited me to visit his home. I tagged along and found myself standing before the threshold of a grand town house near the hospital. His dad was a retired hero from the war and was now the party secretary of the hospital, enjoying a hero's retirement at an early age. The door of the house opened suddenly, and there stood Mr Buckle, senior. Tall and handsome, a man's man. He had a big smile, large eyes, and thick eyebrows, a picture-perfect hero. It was obvious where the son had got his good looks.

'Come on in, Da.' The father even knew my name.

'Thank you.' I extended my right hand but he didn't take it. Instead, he smiled and said, 'Sorry, I got no hands left to shake yours. Hey, why don't you shake my shoulder.' He leaned over, letting his two empty sleeves dangle, and waited for me to shake his broad shoulder.

I was so shocked at his armlessness that I stood there unmoving.

'That's okay, Dad. I don't think they practise shoulder-shaking in Yellow Stone.'

'All right, then. Let's cut the ceremony and have some cookies and candy.'

'Dad, we're not babies any more. Let me show the guy around, okay? I think he has seen enough of you.'

Father and son bantered back and forth like a couple of drinking buddies, while I stood by in deep shock. For Buddha's sake, the perfect hero had no arms. My heart was saddened. Like a lost soul,

I followed Buckle around the house and the hospital. He took me on a tour, but my mind was still on those arms. I had no appetite when I went home. My jealousy was gone. From then on, I quietly watched out for Buckle.

Before long, Mr Sun was bidding us a sad goodbye. He was heading for a re-education camp for teachers. I gave him a small notebook as a gift. The school would be taught by the militiamen and women from the commune. There was a directive from the central government that from now on all schools would be governed by poor farmers; all teachers – a class made up of dangerous and stinking intellectuals – would be reformed and instilled with revolutionary thoughts before they could return to teach China's younger generation.

School wasn't the same. Our teacher was a sleepy young man, a distant nephew of Yellow Stone commune's party secretary. He had never graduated from elementary school; he misspelled simple words and twisted pronunciations so badly that they hardly sounded like Chinese any more. The first day he came to class he was shaking, and there were long lulls while he searched through his notes and tried to think of something to say. In the evening, these farmers played poker and drank at the same tables where real teachers used to grade homework. The zoo was being run by the animals.

To say the least, I was disappointed. I searched outside school for books to entertain myself, and yearned for the farmers to leave, to have the real teachers come back from the camp. Although the earliest that could ever happen would be the following year, I nonetheless believed that, like the spring, it *would* happen.

Three

In September 1971, I entered third grade. Dad had come back from the camp in the mountain and was at another reform camp ten miles away from our town. They made him dig ditches from morning to night to expand an irrigation system that eventually failed to work, while continuing to press for more confessions about my uncle in Taiwan, which had always been China's sworn enemy.

Sometimes I was allowed to visit Dad and bring him food. I would stand on the edge of the work site, searching for signs of my father among the hundred or so other people being 'reformed'. Tired, curious faces would look at me, word would pass on down the line, then eventually out would come my dad from the ditches, his back straight, head held high, and a dazzling smile on his face for his son as he busily dusted off his ragged clothes. I would have nothing to say and could only look at his blistered hands, while he asked how everybody was and how my schoolwork was going. Then it was time to leave; if I delayed, the foreman would chase me off the site with his wooden stick.

Grandpa was suffering all the time now. An expensive medication was bought to cure him, but he was outraged when he heard its price, since he knew that what it cost could have bought the whole family some decent food for a month. Despite his frail condition, he was still ordered to go to the rice fields every day to chase the birds. After he had had an especially bad night, I brought in another petition. The cadre ripped it to pieces in front of me.

'The stinking dogshit!' he screamed, and spat on the floor. 'Tell your no-good grandpa to wake up. I've already given him the lightest job and he doesn't appreciate it. What does he want, to sleep in his warm bed all day and plot his revenge against our Communist system? Well, that's not going to happen with me in charge.' He thumped his chest. 'Do you hear me? And as for you, you little shit. I don't want to see you this often. You'll be in trouble yourself one of these days, running all these errands for your no-good family.'

I ran home angrily and told Grandpa the answer was no.

My eldest sister, Si, had graduated from junior high school. Brother Jin had had to stop one year short of completing it, and Ke and Huang were asked to leave before finishing elementary school. The Red Guards took over the classroom and put some teacher on a humiliation parade. They had made the lives of landlords' children and grandchildren miserable. Si's classmates had hacked at her hair with scissors, which made her look like a mental case, and Jin, while he was still in school, had been constantly hassled and beaten by his classmates.

One day we received a notice from the local authorities. It read, 'Due to overcrowding in our school system, it has been decided by the Communist party that the children of landlords, capitalists, rich farmers, and the leftists will no longer be going directly to junior high or high school. This new policy is to be implemented immediately for the benefit of thousands of poor farmers.' The curt notice didn't explain the logic behind such a decree. But we understood that they considered us the enemy and a danger to their world. Education could only further our cause and threaten theirs.

Thus I became the last student in our family. Every day Mum would whisper to me before school that I should cherish this precious opportunity. I should work hard and be a good student, or I would have to stop school like my siblings and become a farmer or a carpenter, with no hope for a better future. She said the more they wanted you out of school, the more you should show them how good you are. She admonished me to behave myself and not give them reason to throw me out.

The pressure weighed heavily on me. The idea of being a farmer for the rest of my life, working in the fields unceasingly, rain or shine, chilled my bones. I saw my sisters and brothers, still so young, getting up before dawn to cut the ripened rice in darkness before the biting sun made work unbearable. They came home by moonlight after labouring a full day, their backs cramped and sore, cuts on their fingers, blisters covering their hands. Sometimes they were humiliated because the older, more experienced farmers in the commune trashed them for making mistakes. And sometimes they were angry because they were made to work the heaviest jobs, like jumping into manholes to scoop up manure. At night, my sisters often cried in Mum's arms. They were no longer children.

I looked at school in a different light. It was still a fun place, but now it was much, much more. It was the key to a bright future. I knew if I could somehow stay in school, I would do well. There was hope. I arrived at school early every morning and volunteered to sweep the classroom and clean the blackboard. I still managed to have my morning reading assignment done before the others arrived so that I had time to play and help those who needed some tutoring. But the new teacher wasn't the least impressed with me. I sometimes became aware of him staring silently at my back as I sat alone in class doing my work. He was cool and abrupt and seemed disgusted with the little boy who wanted so hard to please him.

My third-grade teacher was a young man about twenty-five years old. He had icy, protruding eyes, and thin lips that squeezed out his words slowly and deliberately. His nose was pointed, with long black hairs sticking out of both nostrils, and a receding chin that melted into his long neck. He had a habit of looking at his reflection in the window, preening and combing his hair before entering the classroom. His name was La Shan.

La Shan invited many of his students to his dormitory on campus, where they played chess and talked long after school. He also organized basketball games among the students, but I was never included. I stood at a distance, watching them play with the energetic young teacher, laughing and shouting. When I sometimes quietly inquired about what they did in his dormitory, my friends Jie and Ciang would tell me that they played and listened to La Shan talk about politics, about things like the class struggle and what to do with bad people like landlords and American special agents.

I became quieter and less active in his class. He continued to act as if I didn't exist, and I became more and more isolated, but I still carried on my work with pride and always scored the best in quizzes. I missed my teacher, Mr Sun, terribly.

In the back of each classroom there was another blackboard on which the best poems or compositions by the students were displayed. It was an honour to have your work posted and mine used to appear there every week. Many years of my grandfather's tutelage had made me the best calligrapher in the entire school and I had won school-wide competitions against older students. But since La Shan had become my teacher, my work never appeared on the blackboard. He also deprived me of the task of copying the poem on to the blackboard with chalk, a task only students with the best calligraphy were allowed to do.

I was no longer the head of the class. In my place stepped the son of the party chief of Yellow Stone Commune, the most feared man in town. La Shan also made him the head of the Little Red Guard, a political organization for children. I was the only one in class who was not a member. I coveted the pretty red bands worn on their arms and had applied to join, but La Shan told me I needed to make more of an effort, that he wasn't sure I was loyal in my heart to the Communist cause like other children from good working-class families. Whenever a Little Red Guard meeting was held, I was asked to step outside. I would hang around the playground by myself until they finished.

My whole life seemed to be drifting away from the crowd. It puzzled me and kept me awake at night as I stared up at my mosquito net. I didn't tell my family about any of the changes; they already had enough to worry about. At home, I pretended to be cheerful and told them how well I was doing in school. Once a cousin of mine mentioned to my brother that I was no longer doing the blackboard copying. I made up a story, telling my family that I needed a change, so was giving my fellow students a chance.

Because I was driven and still confident in my abilities, I worked even harder and volunteered even more for tasks before and after school. It was like throwing myself against a stone wall. The harder I tried, the more the teacher disliked me. He even criticized me in front of all the students about my overzealous attempts to win his praise. This upset and confused me. What more could I do to try and fit into the place that I once used to love?

My first real brush with La Shan came when he was collecting the weekend homework. The assignment had been to copy a text of Chairman Mao's quotations, but my work had been soaked in the rain on the way to class and I had thrown away the smeared, useless paper, intending to redo it in the afternoon. When he found out I had nothing to turn in, La Shan called the class to attention. 'Students, Chen Da has not done his homework, which he knew was to copy the text of our great Chairman Mao. It is a deliberate insult to our great leader.'

'I did the homework like I always do,' I protested loudly, 'but the rain got it all wet.'

The whole class looked at me quietly.

La Shan turned red, the muscles in his cheeks twitching. He had lost face because I had answered back.

'What did you do with it?' he demanded.

'I threw it into a manhole on my way to class because it was all messy.' The students laughed.

'*What* did you say?'

'I said I threw it into a manhole,' I screamed back. I knew I was acting irrationally, but couldn't stop.

'You threw Chairman Mao's quotations into a stinking manhole?' His face flamed and spittle flew from his mouth with each word. 'Do you realize how severe an offence you have just committed?'

A deadly quiet came over the class. Everyone looked at me,

waiting for my reaction. In that split second, I glimpsed the possible serious trouble he could make if he chose to. Mum's words, 'Stay out of trouble,' rang in my ears.

I felt dizzy, as if I had been hit with a club. I already regretted my actions and wished I could take everything back, but it was too late, the damage had been done. I thought of Mum and Dad and the trouble I might have just brought to my family if the teacher blew this thing up. My head began to pound.

'I am sorry, honourable teacher. I will redo my homework and hand it in as soon as possible.'

He stared at me silently with his icy eyes, looking like a wolf that had just caught a rabbit in a trap.

'You think it's going to be that easy?' He shook his head slowly. 'Everybody!' His voice cracked out. 'Let's have a vote. Those who wish to have Da thrown out of our classroom, raise your hands.'

There was a moment of silence. Then, slowly, the son of the party chief raised his hand. A few more hands from the La Shan club went up. Next the whole class raised their collective hands, even my friends Jie and Ciang.

I felt trapped. I felt half-dead. I couldn't understand how even my best friends could vote against me.

'Please, I don't want to leave this class. I would like to stay.'

'We'll see about that. Class is over for the day,' La Shan said, slamming his book closed and walking out of the room, his disciples trailing behind him.

I walked home in a daze. Nobody talked to me. I redid my homework and turned it in right away. I waited for La Shan to throw me out of school, but nothing happened. I sat in the back corner of the class by myself. No one talked to me, not even my friends. Occasionally, La Shan would throw disgusted glances my way. The worst thing was when he disparagingly called me 'that person in the corner' without looking at me. Why did he take the whole thing so personally, as if I had desecrated his ancestor's tombstone?

Then one day during the morning exercise break La Shan called my name and asked me to stay behind while the others noisily poured out of class.

'I have received reports about you,' he said, pacing in front of the classroom. 'Really bad reports.'

My heart began to race. 'What kind of reports?'

'You have been saying anti-revolutionary and anti-Communist things to your classmates, haven't you?'

'No, I haven't.' He was trying to paint me as a counter-revolutionary, just as they had done to Yu Xuang, a fifth-grader whom they had locked in the commune jail for further investigation. It was a dangerous situation.

'I have never done anything like that! You know that!' I said, using the best defence a nine-year-old could muster.

'I have the reports here' – he waved a thick sheaf of paper – 'and I can ask these people to testify against you if necessary.'

'The people who wrote those reports were lying. I have never said anything against our country or the Communist party.'

'Shut up! You have no right to defend yourself, only the chance to confess and repent,' he spat out angrily. His voice deepened. 'Do you understand what kind of trouble you are in now?'

'I have nothing to confess!' My throat dried up and my arms began to tremble. I was losing control again.

'I said, shut up! You have today and tonight to write a confession of all the treasonous things you have said, to explain the motivation, and to state who told you to say these horrible things. Like perhaps your father, mother, or your landlord grandparents.'

He was trying to involve my family. They would put my dad in prison. They would take Grandpa out into the street and beat him to death.

'They did *not* tell me to do or say bad things against the party! They didn't!' I cried. I couldn't afford to have my family dragged into this. I was scared and began to sob helplessly. The sky had just caved in and I felt that nobody could help me. I would be a young counter-revolutionary, a condemned boy, despised by the whole country. I would be left to rot in a dark prison cell for life. That was what had happened to Shi He, another high school kid, who was caught listening to an anti-Communist radio programme from Taiwan, and worse, to the banned Teresa Deng's love songs. His prison sentence had been twenty years.

I don't remember how long I cried that morning. When I walked home alone in the afternoon's setting sun, I felt the weight of shackles already around my ankles.

A condemned man at the age of nine! Confession tomorrow! The thoughts played over and over in my mind.

When I got home, I told Mum what had happened and she started sobbing, hitting her face and chest and pulling out her hair. She mumbled hysterically, in broken sentences, that their generation had brought the curse to the next generation. After a while, she sat down quietly, weak and limp like a frightened animal. Finally, she got up and sent Si and Jin to Dad's camp to ask for advice. They got to talk to him by using the excuse that Mum was very sick again.

It was after midnight when, breathless, they ran back. I was still sitting in my room, staring at a piece of blank paper. I had not eaten anything. For the first time in my life, I had absolutely no appetite.

The message from Dad was simple. There was nothing to confess. Go back to school tomorrow and tell them that, he instructed. What were they going to do to you? Nothing, if you did not confess. Everything, if you did. If school becomes too hard, then quit. Dad's words gave us power and courage even from afar, allowing me to feel hopeful again that everything would be fine. But I dreamed that night of the teacher's face and smelled the dank odour of a dark, wet prison.

The following day, I dragged myself along the cobbled street, my eyes fixed on the ground, wishing I were as tiny as a mosquito. When I entered the classroom, there were silent stares from the other children. The lesson was on fractions, but nothing sank in. My mind kept wandering to the piece of paper I carried with me. What would the teacher say? What were they going to do to me? Each hour of class crawled torturously by. I couldn't wait to hand in the confession and run back home to my family.

Finally, the day came to an end. My classmates filed out as I put my books in my schoolbag and prepared to face the teacher.

'You're not going anywhere, are you?' La Shan questioned sternly, not looking up from the homework he was grading.

'I was just going to give you this.' I pulled out the piece of paper. 'May I come up to your desk, please?'

'You have your confession?' he asked sharply, arching his eyebrows.

'I thought long and hard, and all that I have to say is here, honourable teacher.' I put the 'confession' on his desk and turned to walk away.

'Stop!' His voice was so angry and disgusted it startled me. I stopped and stood there with my head down, afraid to look at him.

'You confessed nothing?' He screamed at me. 'Did your parents tell you to write this?' He crushed the paper into a ball and threw it at me.

'No, it is all from me and it is the truth. I swear upon my ancestors' graves that I am honest and innocent.' Tears trickled uncontrollably down my face. I was so nervous that my head began to feel hot again. Desperately, I felt myself losing my logic and calm.

'You are a liar, Chen Da! I am going to refer your counter-revolutionary acts to the principal and party secretary of the school. I wished to handle your case here, but you are not co-operating, so now you force me to go to higher authorities.'

His threats were working. My knees felt weak. I wanted to kneel before him and beg him not to report this to the principal, who was also the commune's party secretary. Today I was the outcast in my classroom, but tomorrow the whole school would know about it. I would be finished.

'Please!' I cried. 'Can you please just let it go, honourable Teacher Shan? I'm very scared. Please help me?'

'Help you? How can I help you if you don't help me?' His tone softened. 'Here, take this paper back and promise to write something useful on it and bring it back tomorrow.'

I saw it as a gesture of kindness. I took the crumpled paper gratefully and quickly left school. As soon as I got home, Mum asked me, 'What are you still doing with the paper?'

I told her how the teacher had softened and was giving me a second chance instead of sending my case to the principal.

'He's tricking you again, that snake!' Mum began to sob. 'Do as your father said. Confess nothing! Do you want to go to prison? Do you want to see the rest of your family in prison?' she screamed at me, trying to make me understand what was at stake. But all the tricks, threats, and political subtleties were beyond my grasp. I felt lost, but I believed in my parents' wisdom and vowed to do as they said.

I lay in bed that night staring at the ceiling, wishing desperately that my parents were a couple of poor young farmers with no political burdens to worry about, only their wrath over the mistreatment of their young son. Then they could have gone with me to school, punched out that snake of a teacher's teeth, thrown him to the floor, and kicked the shit out of him until he begged for mercy and swore not to lay a finger on me any more. But Dad was burdened with political troubles of his own, my tiny mum was in no shape to perform such an act, and my landlord grandpa would be thrown into prison for even thinking such a thing.

A trick it had been. As soon as I walked into school the following day, the teacher stopped me in the hallway and personally marched me to the principal's office.

Thoughts about running into the fields, hiding in the woods, and never returning to the damned place passed through my mind, but I didn't have the will to do anything. They would catch me and put me in the slammer in no time. I admired the students who passed by us, so carefree, laughing and joking. They were just starting another day of fun and learning while I was being escorted to a political questioning session, just short of wearing handcuffs.

The teacher dropped me off in the principal's office and left. The principal didn't even bother to look at me. He was cleaning his huge wooden desk as I stood nervously in the corner.

The principal, Mr Gao, was a frog of a man. He had bowed legs and walked with a wide side-to-side swing. His face was bland despite a moustache. He was about fifty and, in addition to being the school principal, had recently been promoted to the position of party secretary. Older students once told me that he loved fondling little girls' hands and shoulders and enjoyed having young female teachers iron his clothes in his dormitory room late at night, while he conferred his seasoned political wisdom on them. He was the most zealous objector to romance among the young teachers because, it was said, he couldn't bear the idea of anyone else having his way. His wife was a heavy smoker, with yellow teeth and ugly wrinkles on her face. They were a well-matched couple.

He asked me all kinds of questions and urged me again to make a confession. I declared my innocence over and over.

For the entire week that followed, Mr Gao met with me daily, either in between classes or after school. He went on mumbling his advice and making threats to stop my schooling. I sat quietly during those sessions, much more alert and logical than in the presence of the teacher. Though Mr Gao was the top dog, he somehow didn't scare me. He muttered rather than talked and he was an incoherent speaker. He would start a line of argument then totally lose himself in it until he had to ask me blankly, 'Where were we?'

In the beginning, I would tell him where we had left off. Then, gradually, I told him I also forgot and he would stare at me and scratch his head. He seemed quite bored with these sessions that were getting nowhere. All I confessed to him were some minor infractions, useless garbage like stealing chalk, letting classmates copy my homework, and taking fruit from the neighbour's fruit trees. One thing seemed clear throughout the week-long questioning. He asked a lot of questions about my family. I was very careful not to say anything stupid that could implicate them. They were going out of their way to try and get my dad.

Finally, one day he said, 'If you do not confess, I am sending you to the police.' This time, his face was deadly serious. 'You have left me no other choice. In fact, the police chief asked about you the other day and recommended that you appear on the public humiliation platform with Yu Xuang during his confession in front of the whole school.'

The mention of Yu Xuang terrified me. He had confessed to making counter-revolutionary statements and was already condemned to sweeping the dirty street of Yellow Stone. Sometimes he was sent to the same labour reform camp that my dad was in.

This was the end of me. Standing next to Yu Xuang on the platform, facing hundreds of students shouting threats and throwing bricks at me, would ruin my future for ever, if I survived the session. In the people's eyes I would be branded a counter-revolutionary like Yu Xuang. I might as well be dead already.

Gloomily, I headed for home, hoping there was a god who could turn the whole world around, send me a new, bright day full of colours, but it was hopeless. Families were registered at a certain commune. You couldn't move anywhere else unless the government reassigned you. There was no escape.

As the day of Yu Xuang's public denunciation approached, Mum quietly said to me, 'Go pack. You are leaving tomorrow.'

'Where am I going?'

'To Wen Qui's home.' He was a distant cousin who lived in Ding Zhuang, another tiny town about twenty miles west of Yellow Stone.

'They will catch me.'

'No, they won't come after you. They were just threatening you.'

'What about school?' It was my future.

'We will worry about that later. You can still be the best student after missing a few lessons.'

I went into her arms. 'I'm scared.'

'Don't be.' She held me tight. 'Wen Qui has already been secretly informed of your coming.'

The next day, as the sky shed its first ray of light, I crept out of our back door, crossed the wooden bridge that swung and squeaked in the wind, and started my half-day's journey on foot. I carried a bag of clothes, a small bag of dried yams to contribute to Wen Qui's household when I got there, and two pieces of sweet rice cake, which were my favourite treats, and which Mum had stayed up late preparing for me. As soon as I crossed the Dong Jing River, I followed Mum's instructions: ducked low, and disappeared into the lush, mile-long fields of sugarcane to avoid bumping into anyone. The morning dew still kissed the sharp leaves that innocently scratched my face and arms.

33

Beyond the sugarcane field lay a narrow dirt road winding into the mountains. Though I had walked this scenic path a few times before, it was scarily quiet in the early dawn, so I sang out loud and whistled as I ran along, my bag bouncing on my back. When I was halfway to my destination I sat down to rest by a large pond. I leaned against an old pine tree and unwrapped my first piece of rice cake. As I sank my teeth into the sticky sweetmeat, I was reminded once more of how good life could be if one weren't a political fugitive running for his life.

I took off my shoes and waded into the shallow edge of the pond, scooping up a handful of the fresh spring water to drink. It tasted as sweet as the mountain itself. Everything was so peaceful I couldn't help skipping a few rocks and watching the ripples spread out gently. I remembered the time my dad and I had often competed at this very pond to see who could skip a rock the farthest. I once had thrown a stone so hard that I had skidded and fallen into the soft young wheat, and now, again, I could hear Dad's hearty laughter at my antics.

When I got to the Qui's home, it was lunchtime. Wen's sister was the wife of my uncle. The family had been forced to move to this small mountain village remote from Yellow Stone because his father had been a wealthy fabric merchant. Wen once said his father could judge the quality of a fabric by blindly feeling it behind his back. The Quis lived in the house of a former landlord, a man whose family had all been executed by the Communists.

Wen was no more than twenty-eight and was really fun to be with. He played the *er hu*, a two-stringed instrument that sounded like a violin, as well as a bamboo flute. He sang beautifully, and could write wonderful prose. He was a handsome, carefree, romantic artist condemned to farming in the village. He was also the first man I knew who had not found his wife through a matchmaker, but on his own. I had known them during their courtship several years ago, when he had been our neighbour in Yellow Stone. He and his future wife would play and sing in their backyard in the moonlight. His wedding was the saddest one I ever attended. The bride's family had tied her to her bed in an attempt to prevent the ceremony, because she was from a worker's family, a politically good family, and had been promised to a distant cousin who was a rich Hong Kong businessman. Wen was from a politically bad family. Her brothers and father had caught Wen and beaten him severely. But later that evening the bride escaped to Wen's house and they were married beneath a kerosene lamp with a few close family members in attendance, and with a meal of fried noodles to celebrate.

Wen and his lovely wife met me at the door and invited me in.

'Da, this is your home. We want you to enjoy your stay here,' Wen said, relieving me of my sack. 'Don't be afraid here.'

'Thank you,' I said. 'Do you think they will find me?'

'No,' his wife said firmly. 'We will not let anything happen to you. You're only a child. Who are these damned, heartless people?' she exclaimed, her eyes misty. 'They won't find you. If they come looking, I will hide you in a safe place. They can't do anything to me. I'm the daughter of a worker's family, remember?' She laughed and wiped away her tears. 'Besides, Wen is the personal bookkeeper and fortune-teller of our commune's party secretary. He wouldn't do a thing without checking with Wen first.'

They fed me and gave me a bundle of old books to read. At night, they were the same hopeless romantics I had known from before. They read each other poems, shared old photos, and sang songs, while the candlelight danced in the mountain breeze coming through the window. Wen's parents, who lived upstairs, called them crazy, but their love for each other warmed my heart in that lonely and remote village so far away from home.

I stayed there for a week before it was deemed safe for me to return. I did not go back to school for the rest of the semester. I heard that at the public humiliation meeting Yu Xuang was sentenced to four years of labour reform in a juvenile prison. He was beaten unconscious after being thrown off the stage. No one had come to inquire about me. Mum said later that she had spent the entire day on her knees in front of Buddha, praying for my safety.

Four

I quit school after I came back from hiding. I kept expecting the teacher, the principal, or the police chief to show up any day for my capture. I asked Jie and Buckle, who still talked to me occasionally, whether they had heard anything about a public meeting to be held soon in the school. They said no.

Every morning at eight-thirty I climbed up to our attic, which was the highest point of our house, and sat on the window-sill, looking out of the large window and listening to the melody of the distant school bell ring from afar. *'Ding, dong. Ding dong . . .'* It was time for classes to begin. A skinny teacher nicknamed 'Monkey' threw his entire weight on the rope, pulling the giant bell and grinning like a buffoon each time it tolled.

In the afternoons, I sat behind our closed front door and shelled the fresh fava beans that my brother and sisters had harvested in the fields. I was working to justify my existence. On a good day, I could pick three large baskets with only a ten-minute break for lunch and a few pee runs in between. At four, I would crack our door open just enough to peer out at my classmates as they made their way home from school. They were so happy and carefree. None of them felt like a criminal in hiding, condemned to petty labour. They all went to school and learned wonderful things about the world.

I missed school terribly, and would ask Buckle what lesson they were on, and who was sitting in my seat. But deep inside, I was sick of being such a weak person. If Dad knew I was being so nostalgic about a place that had treated me like dirt he would think me a wimp. So I looked away from the door and continued shelling my endless baskets of fava beans.

One day Dad came home on a short leave, sat me down beside him. 'Maybe you should go and apprentice as a carpenter or a blacksmith,' he said. 'They make a decent living. But they have to work their balls off.' I remembered seeing our town blacksmith's balls swinging in and out of his loose shorts as he hammered away at his anvil. I smiled at my dad's humour, which was meant to cheer me up, but I wasn't too keen on those options. They weren't my choices. I had watched carpenters at construction sites, dangling dangerously from rooftops. Blacksmiths made good money, but I wasn't sure I wanted to spend the rest of my life swinging heavy hammers near a blazing fire.

'How about learning to play a flute or something?' I suggested.

'Those are nice jobs,' he agreed, 'but you have to go to music school and I don't think they would take anyone from a landlord's family.'

I nodded with understanding.

He sensed my lack of enthusiasm. He suggested we wait a while before sending me off to a carpentry shop somewhere in the mountains, where young apprentices not only did the most menial tasks, but also washed the teacher's feet, brewed his tea, fed his babies, and paid a huge tuition. At the end of three years, the qualified student had to work for the teacher, free of charge, for one additional year.

The following month I spent my time weeding the sweet potatoes in the fields, building a dirt wall in our backyard, carrying lunches and dinners to my brother and sisters in the fields in little bamboo baskets slung over my shoulders, and spreading wet hay to dry before storing it in the evenings. Bugs crawled everywhere and the moist hay's sharp, blade-like edges made my skin itch constantly.

As I settled into the routine of a young farmhand, part of me was dying inside. I felt old and rejected, a misfit. The people I worked with were all older farmers who could no longer work the fields. One was a toothless mute, who yelled at me like an animal, made obscene gestures behind young women's backs, and laughed like a hyena when I repeated his gestures back to him. I was merely keeping him company.

I no longer played out in the street. I had aged and had become an outcast. By now, everyone knew the reason why I had quit school. Sometimes the kids shouted outside my house calling me the 'little counter-revolutionary,' daring me to come out and fight them. I would clutch a sharp spade and wait behind the door in case they burst through and attacked us. A few times, stones were thrown against our windows. One morning Mum found a dead bird in our backyard, headless. I suspected the teacher had urged his gang to come after me. Whenever Mum asked me to run out to buy some soy sauce, I checked the street first, then darted out and back. The last thing I wanted to do was cause any more trouble.

But every night before I went to sleep, I wrote in my diary, trying not to forget the words I had learned. I made up a lot of signs for the words I didn't know. There was nothing good to write about. Often I found myself drawing a picture of La Shan, the chinless skunk, and adding a huge bullet hole on his forehead. Some day I wanted to avenge all the things that had been done to me. Maybe when I grew up or maybe when the world changed.

Then one day a kindhearted teacher named Mr Lan from our neighbourhood dropped by to have tea with us. He casually mentioned that he had brokered a deal with the school to allow me to enter group eight of the fourth grade. He said, smiling, 'It's better than being a farmer and genuine pearls shine even in darkness.'

I remembered that line for a long time.

With mixed feelings of joy, fear, curiosity, and suspicion, I dusted off my books and prepared for the frightening ordeal of going back to face the very same people I had tried to avoid.

On Monday morning, shock hit me as I stepped into the classroom of the fabled group eight. The kids hooted at me. It took me a second before I noticed the seating arrangement was unlike that in any other classroom. The desks were separated into two corners. One was for eight girls in the front. The other was in the far back corner for the boys. There was a large, empty space in the middle of the room where trash and paper planes were piled up.

The teacher gestured with his cigarette in the direction of the boys' group and absentmindedly said, 'Pick a chair for yourself over there.'

'Which one?' I asked. The dirty faces from the boys' corner looked dangerously back at me.

'Any seat, I said.' The teacher, whom I came to know as Mr Chu, swiped his arm in the general direction again.

I nervously walked down the open space in the middle, and took a seat at the edge of the group next to a fat, ugly little guy.

'Whaddya doing here, big shot?' my new neighbour shouted, stretching his arms to mark his territory line on the desk we shared. Somehow, I had a feeling they knew I had been kicked out from group one, where all the brightest students and the snobs were.

'Why didya send him in here? We ain't no garbage can here,' another wise guy asked the teacher. The whole class erupted with laughter like a bunch of drunks in a rowdy bar.

Mr Chu had a puffy face with big pouches under his eyes. The bags seemed to drag his eyelids down with their weight.

'Shuuut up,' he screamed. 'You rascals don't deserve better, and for your information, you are a garbage can.'

Laughter.

'And . . .?' a few boys teased.

He took a long drag on his cigarette, breathed heavily, and continued as if in a play, 'No, no, no! You're worse than that. You're a bunch of animals that belong in a zoo! You have no discipline . . .'

'And . . .' the class chanted.

'No willpower . . .'

'And . . .'

'No brains . . .'

'Huh . . . and . . .'

'No manners, no hygiene . . .'

'And . . .'

'Stop interrupting me!' He stomped on the floor and threw a

wooden ruler in the boys' direction. It landed on top of the pile of paper planes. 'And no future!' Finally he ended his tirade. My neighbour, the fat boy, picked up the ruler and threw it back to the teacher.

'Hey, hey, hey, Mr Chu. You might wanna be careful there,' a calm, deep voice said from behind me. I turned and saw an older boy with a big square face, a nose like a fat bulb of garlic, and a nasty cut across his forehead. His eyes twinkled with mischief. A wicked smile creased his face. 'My dad wouldn't like hearing that part about there being no future for me. You got to be careful there.'

'Don't you mention your dad again. I'm not scared of him.'

'Yeah? Well if that's the case, how come you weren't around when he showed his face here last time he was mad at you?'

'He was lucky I wasn't here that day. I could have your dad and you arrested if he were trouble. Let's turn to page twenty and waste no more time.'

More laughter and grunts. Slowly the class moved along, like an old freight train going up a hill. Mr Chu kept shouting and screaming and the students kept laughing and teasing. It was like a circus where everybody was a clown. Even the girls cursed like mean old bitches at boys who didn't know to stay out of their corner.

By the second class, I was able to answer 80 per cent of the maths questions, and by the third, the class had found a new star. At the end of the day, the big guy with the nasty cut, who was known as 'the King', walked over and patted my shoulder, announcing, 'From now on, ya can sit next to me and do my homework whenever I feel like it.'

I was flattered by the intimacy and readily agreed. It wasn't as if I had any choice. The boy was a head taller than me and was surrounded by all his lieutenants, each more devilish than the other. They seemed to be the class Mafia. I later came to know that he had been in the same grade for the last three years and that his father, whom he often used as a shield, was a high-ranking officer in the Chinese navy, captain of a huge ship that cruised the Pacific, guarding against a Taiwanese invasion. He carried a gun around Yellow Stone, even on home visits.

That night, lying in bed, I was convinced that I couldn't have found a more nurturing environment to revive my student career. My classmates were animals, but they couldn't care less where I had come from. They respected me.

Our school was like any town. It had its fancy parts and seedy corners. Our side of the playground was the Wild West, complete with hooligans and hustlers, where the law was written by the biggest fists and guys such as the King moved around with supple, pantherlike ease, calling the shots. It was a world away from the intellectual ivory tower of group one. The windows on our side had broken glass that had remained unrepaired for years, weeds that had long since strangled all the flowers, and mud that pooled at the classroom door as though nature had favoured the other side by tilting the surface of the earth a little and letting us have the soupy muck when it rained. Nonetheless, I was proud to walk on this frontier. To me, this was a place to begin, not end. Among these tough but simple kids, I had space to breathe. All my new friends in school had to help their families on the farm as soon as they got home. They were kids from distant villages without a school of their own and had to walk an hour each way to come to Yellow Stone.

It was here that I learned to hit people with my fists for the first time. One day, as I sat at my desk doing homework, my neighbour, Yian, the fat, ugly boy, ran by and snatched my rubber ball. I chased him around the classroom, demanding he give it back to me. He teased me by sticking the ball up his crotch. All the boys laughed while the girls turned their faces away in disgust. I jumped at him, but missed. He suddenly stopped. 'Fight me, fight me,' he taunted. His fat face turned into a meatball as he pushed his chubby chest against mine. The close body contact made me nervous and angry, but I was too afraid to punch him. I had never done it before. His nose kept coming closer and closer. He started pushing me.

'Fight him or I'm not speaking to you,' the King said in my ear.

I closed my eyes to calm myself and tried to smother my fear of getting thrown out again. I had to do it. I swung my arm back and smashed my fist into his face. It felt good. He fell and rolled a few

41

yards into a corner. I cracked my knuckles and bent down, waiting for him. As soon as he found his feet, he charged like a buffalo. I dodged to one side and he banged his head against a desk and fell again. I turned and kicked him on the backside. The crowd cheered excitedly. By then, all the fear was gone. I just wanted to keep hitting and hitting him until it was officially over.

He suddenly stood up, raised his arms, and said, 'You won, all right. You can have your ball back.' Then he laughed and dusted off his clothes.

I was left hanging and felt cheated. I wanted to continue fighting. How could he treat a fight so casually, like a cup of tea he could just pick up and put down whenever he wanted? There was no emotional attachment.

'You won. Now sit down before the teacher catches you,' the King said. 'You know, you're not bad. I should arrange more of these fights. You'll come to like it.' He laughed and slapped my shoulder, then pressed hard and made me sit down. I threw his hand off, tossed my books into my bag, and went home early.

'You'll get over it, virgin,' the King said and laughter rang in my ears all the way home.

One day an announcement was made through the crackling school loudspeaker. There was going to be a meeting in the playground for the entire school. A new directive was to be read. As I started to follow the rest of the class outside, Teacher Chu stopped me and said, 'You are to remain here by order of the principal.'

'Why?'

'Because of the document's contents. You're not politically ready yet.'

'If all the others can listen to it, why can't I?'

'You're not like them,' he said.

I was insulted and hurt, and wanted to ask, what kind of shithole is this? Again, the fear of isolation and pain gripped my heart. When was this bullshit going to end? If there had been a bomb in my hand right then, I would have brought it to the stage and blasted the fucking principal, teacher La Shan, and his little groupies into tiny pieces.

42

I stayed in my classroom, depressed and disillusioned. When the class returned, they questioned me with their eyes and left me alone for the rest of the day. I prayed that my new friends would not desert me as my last ones had done. But, thank Buddha, they didn't. The whole thing was forgotten the next day. I was still King's counsel on academic matters, and I like to think that I played no small role in finally pushing him through to the fourth grade. Though he didn't exactly answer the questions on his paper, his bigshot Navy father should be proud of him, if not for his work, then for his ability to get his work done for him.

I considered it a tragedy when group eight was dissolved at the end of the term. A school closer to the villagers reopened and the students happily went back to their own school. I got placed in group two, next door to the hateful faces I tried to erase from my memory for ever. Each day I ran past the doors of group one as fast as possible, for fear of bumping into them and getting into trouble. In the new group, I soon became the recognized top student. I began to hear some good words from a few of the teachers. But a gang of students in my new class was organized against me. It was headed by a sneaky boy called Han, whose father had fallen out with mine after a bee-raising business they had started together failed. The others in the gang were Quei, the son of a local politician, and Wang, whose father was a carpenter and an enemy of some of my father's good friends.

Inside the class, they made up silly songs to humiliate my family, revived the old accusations, and discouraged others from being friends with me. After school, they spied on me and made up a story that I had picked up an expensive ballpoint pen and didn't return it to the school as I should have. It got me four hours of questioning in the same principal's office that was a living hell to me. Outside the window, they smiled and made faces. The next day, I ran after Han with a rusty iron space when he passed our house going back home. I whacked and whacked his head and back until a bystander stopped me. Han cried and reported me to our teacher, Mr Lan. But I had already written and turned in my side of the story and the teacher believed my version.

What really made me mad was these kids also demanded that I

43

share my homework with them while doing everything they could to make my life miserable. In the beginning, I complied, thinking I could convert them into my friends by sharing a little with them. Instead, they turned on me and told Teacher Lan about it. Of course, he lectured me and I had to clean the blackboard for a week as punishment. Later, in retaliation, I deliberately gave wrong answers for them to copy, then reported this to the teacher. This time they were trapped like rabbits and Han lost his chance to become the best Communist student that year.

During this time, Grandpa was slowly dying. He was seventy-seven years old. Almost every day, I found writings on the blackboard that debased and humiliated him.

On the day he died, we carried him in a wheelbarrow about twenty miles away to the city of Putien for cremation. I wore a white shirt and spread pieces of paper money over the bridges we passed and chanted sayings like 'peaceful passing' to the imaginary soldiers guarding the bridges. In the crowd that watched the procession, I saw the three ugly mugs of Han, Quei and Wang, smiling without pity or sympathy. They even made faces at me. I bit my lips trying to control my sadness and hatred. Tears poured forth as the strong voice of revenge cried out within me. I wiped away my tears and walked on with my family pushing Grandpa's body along the dirt road to Putien for two more hours.

When we got there, four young monks were hired to carry Grandpa up into the mountain to the cremation site. I knelt before his body with my family like a pious grandson, sobbing farewell as an ancient monk torched the wood pile beneath Grandpa's flimsy coffin. Flames shot up against the setting sun. My beloved Grandpa was no more.

Five

Even in wintertime Yellow Stone was laced by the greenness of the surrounding wheat and fava-bean fields. Yellow wild flowers were scattered across the green carpet like solitary souls still searching for their destiny. The water of the Dong Jing River lay calm and pensive, as if quietly dreaming about the coming spring.

Farmers flocked to the market square to trade goods for the New Year, a week away. The narrow street of Yellow Stone became filled with mules carrying food and vegetables. Bicycles strained beneath the double weight of two riders, and noisy tractors fought their way among crowds of people carrying sacks of produce slung over their shoulders.

One morning, Teacher Lan visited our home with the results of our first countywide exam. I had scored 100 per cent in all four subjects. He and Mum couldn't stop smiling and my sisters swarmed, fighting to get a glimpse of the report card.

'Only two students made that score in the whole county of Putien,' Lan said, beaming happily, for my distinction had made him one of the teachers of the year.

I became an instant star among the neighbours. There were some warmer glances and sweeter greetings for me. It was both liberating and a little intoxicating. I felt glorified. I was no longer just another one of those hopeless descendants of the old ruling class, who ended up becoming a carpenter, a blacksmith, or a nobody, buried in the guilt and shame of their fathers. I shone, despite their efforts to snuff me out.

Grandpa's passing only hardened my will to succeed, to beat the odds. I wanted to honour this man, who had died poor, sad, and broken. The image of his body, reduced to eighty pounds of yellow skin and old bones, lying in that rough wooden wheelbarrow like some discarded dead animal, would never leave me. He had wanted to be burned because he knew we couldn't afford a burial plot for his tiny body, which had been dressed in a newly tailored black robe made from coarse material. My dad's words, as he carried Grandfather's ashes home, still echoed in my ears: 'Now you can join your drinking buddies again, and gamble for ever,' he said, brushing his wet face against the jar of ashes.

It was decided that I would go with my cousin Yan to the island where she taught, spend a few days there, and carry back some fish and shrimp for the New Year. The trip was meant to keep me out of trouble and away from the neighbourhood children, but I jumped for joy. I had always loved the ocean, with its blue waves and long, white beaches. Sailboats skimmed across the surface. A million possibilities lay hidden in the sea's depths, fuelled by stories told by old sailors.

When Yan asked me, 'Can you walk all day without complaining?' I bobbed my head eagerly.

Twenty miles off the mainland, Milon lay like a sapphire amid the blue Pacific. To get there before sunset, we started out early in the morning and walked all day along a winding path. We passed several brooks, plodded beside endless fava-bean fields, and walked under countless trees until the sun began to dip in the west. Long before we got to the coast, the land began to level and spread out. Grass thinned away and finally disappeared. There were no homes or dwellings in sight for miles around, nothing but an occasional lonely windmill, squeaking and grunting monotonously as the wind turned its sails.

As we drew closer to the coast, the breeze became stronger, pungent with the smell of salt and sea. I held tightly to the brim of my straw hat lest the wind blow it away. The stretch of land along the coast looked white and glistened under the setting sun. Yan told me these were the salt fields. The salt farmers pumped seawater into acres and acres of beachfront, then they built low walls to block the water from flowing back, and let the sun bake out all the moisture, leaving behind a field of salt in its solid form. This natural salt was exported to many foreign countries; the salt we used at home also came from here.

I knelt down and scooped a handful of the shining salt into my pocket when Yan wasn't looking, and ran off to see the coast.

Suddenly, the ocean loomed before us. At first it was a wide belt of dark blue water with glistening stars dancing on its surface. But as I ran closer and closer in my excitement to embrace it, the sea grew wider and longer until it seemed to engulf the little piece of land I was standing on. The vastness of the sea made me feel small and flimsy like a blade of grass in the wind.

As Yan caught up with me, a fragile old man waved to us and shouted my cousin's name.

'That's the boatman guarding the ferry from the island,' Yan said. 'His name is Old Mountain.'

'Old Mountain?' I laughed.

'Funny, huh?' Her eyes twinkled. 'Wait until you meet my pupils.'

We went to a lonely, creaky dock, where only two little sailboats bobbed in the water. Our ferry was small, its sails like a patchwork quilt filled with holes, flying in the wind. It wasn't much to look at, but it rocked sturdily as we gingerly crossed the plank and descended on to the deck. We were the only passengers. Old Mountain had a skinny young man helping him. Within minutes, we were on our way.

I held fast to the mast. Occasionally, waves spilled on to the deck, but the old ferry stayed upright and skipped forward with a taut sail. In the twilight, the sea was as scary as a dark night without stars. Yan told me that island people were extremely superstitious and did not want bad things mentioned on the boat, so all the way there I sat quietly, occasionally casting a glance at Old Mountain, who whistled a broken tune and narrowed his eyes, looking off into the distance.

Half an hour later, Yan helped me off the ferry and we said

goodbye to Old Mountain and his helper. The island of Milon was dotted with little houses. At the busy dock, we were suddenly surrounded by a dozen enthusiastic, noisy girls and boys who seemed to be around my own age. They grabbed our luggage, shook our hands, and even took my hat as if it were too great a burden for me to carry. The girls all seemed to have babies fastened to their backs; the boys wore only simple shorts on this warm winter day. They were all barefoot.

'These are all my pupils,' Yan told me proudly as she turned to the children. 'Here, I want you all to meet my cousin. His name is Da.'

'Good-day, Daaaa . . .' They said in unison, as if they were doing a class recitation. It was followed by giggling.

'Why was that funny?' I asked.

A girl with big eyes and long hair answered, smiling, while the rest peered at me.

'Because we never heard such a name before. It sounds like a grown-up's name.'

'A grown-up's name? Why?' I asked my cousin.

'None of the local children has a real name until they get to marriageable age, about fifteen. Then they are given one. Before that, they were named after animals or objects. For example, she is Piggy, he is Little Eel, the boy carrying your hat is Oyster Shell, and the pretty one with long hair is called Clear Moon.' Each blushed as his or her name was called.

'How do they get names like that?' I wondered.

'The fathers pick the name of the first thing they see after the baby is born.'

I shook my head and thought of Old Mountain. The poor dad must have seen his wife's tummy right after Old Mountain was born.

'Let's go,' Yan said.

Laughing, they lugged and dragged our bags as we started to climb the steep steps made from uneven slabs of stone, some of which still had oyster shells stuck to them. There must have been a hundred steps ahead of us.

'The school is right there.' Yan pointed to a small building

48

perched high up the hill. I felt a bit dizzy as I craned my neck to look.

The sun had dropped behind the sea by the time we finally climbed to the little school that was built on rocks. It had stone walls with a grey, clay-slabbed roof. While the surrounding sea was dark and forbidding, the whole island was dotted with lights that shone from the houses. One by one the schoolchildren bade us goodbye and ran off to their homes. We were both exhausted and retired early.

That night, I lay in a strange bed and thought about all the exciting things I would do the next day. Staring at the stars through a wide skylight, I heard the lulling of the ocean. The rhythm of its waters sounded like an old man telling an ancient legend as the waves lazily washed against the shore. I listened to the tale until I fell into a dreamless sleep.

The morning sun exploded in my eyes. Getting up I ventured into the next room, surprised to see a large crowd of girls surrounding my cousin, who sat on a tall chair. She was handing out colourful combs, plastic butterfly hairpins, and little ribbons that she had bought at Yellow Stone. She read from her roll-call book, making sure she gave the right gift to each girl. There was a smile of authority and contentment on her face. On this island of forty households, Teacher Chow, as she was respectfully addressed by the locals, was a woman of knowledge, wisdom, style, and wealth. She was probably the first person they had met who had been to the Paris of Asia, the great city of Shanghai, not once or twice, but every year, to visit her parents.

The women of the island sought out her ideas about everything – from their clothes and marriages to food and child rearing. Her students would not nod their approvals if Teacher Chow didn't seem to like their choices. Unhappy wives often came to her with domestic complaints. Like a civil judge Teacher Chow would go to their husbands and straighten them out.

Yan had a strong personality and handled the role well, but there was a downside. Family planning was being implemented in China. Her only colleague, a forty-five-year-old man, became quite jealous of her popularity and spread the word to government officials on the mainland that she was responsible for several marriages between fifteen-year-old youngsters. The truth was that it was the custom on the island to wed at such a tender age. Fifteen was ripe, while eighteen was rotten, as the saying there went.

During her five-year tenure, there was one especially unpleasant experience. A young son of the island's party secretary of the commune had proposed to her through a matchmaker. He was three years younger and a head shorter. Though the man's family occupied the fanciest building on the island, a ten-room house made from stone slabs, and the suitor was a skilled mason, Yan wasn't interested and politely turned the proposal down.

The rejection angered the party secretary, who came to the school himself. He slammed his fist on Yan's desk and delivered some thinly veiled threats about her future. Day and night, she cried alone, unable to come up with a solution. Finally, she visited my dad, who offered her a risky strategy.

The next day, she went straight to the party secretary. 'I was raised by my uncle who happens to be a very poor and greedy old man,' she said. 'He considers me his own daughter and treats me as such. He said that he would not mind marrying me off to your good son, if you will pay this sum.' Yan showed the eager man a slip of paper in Dad's writing. He read it with disbelief, left, and never came back again to bother Yan.

They told me later that the slip contained a long list of expensive items and conditions. A payment of twenty thousand yuen was demanded up front. Dad had actually calculated all the money he had invested in Yan and detailed his expected return income from her for the rest of her life. Dad called the strategy 'evil curing evil'.

That morning a muscular man showed up at the entrance of the school, smiled warmly, and took me out to his fishing boat down at the dock. The man, Ar Piao, was in his early forties and was the father of the school's class president. As we walked down the steep steps in silence, it seemed that even though he wanted to show me the island, he couldn't articulate very well. When he had something to say, his face went beet red. But the more silent he was, the more questions I asked him, for his tanned, leathery skin told me he had a vast knowledge of the sea. There was a story, a good story somewhere inside him. He answered in single syllables, with a nod, smile, or shake of the head. It seemed that the sea had made him think more and talk less.

The ocean was calm and blue and the sun gentle. The subtropical winter melted away on mornings like this. His boat was new, with tall sails and fishing nets hanging all over it. His son, whom he had named Monkey, waved to me with a broad smile and helped me on to the deck. Ar Piao said the boat was equipped with a motor and he could sail against the wind if he had to. Soon we left the busy dock, and skipped on the water with a breeze behind us as we set out for a fishing expedition off another tiny island. I leaned against the side of the boat, watching the waves part in our wake.

Monkey was twelve and was already quite muscular. He had the friendly look of a simple young man – much like his dad – but his eyes danced with excitement and curiosity as he gave me the once-over. I could see he wanted to chat but wasn't sure his quiet dad would approve of his forwardness. He kept glancing at me.

'Hey, you got a pretty good boat here,' I said to him, stroking the mast with my hand.

'You like it?' he asked. Monkey smiled, revealing two missing teeth. 'I'll show you the skeletons on the island later on.'

'No skeletons this time,' his dad said.

'What skeletons?' The subject definitely interested me.

'Some people slept on the little island,' Monkey said.

'And they died there?' I guessed.

He shook his head, stealing another look at his dad, who was handling the sails. 'Don't use that word on the deck, but you're right.'

'Maybe we can see them next time. Just fishing is enough, thanks.' I liked him already.

'What does your city look like? A lot of tall buildings?' he asked.

'I didn't come from a big city. Just a larger town than yours, that's all.'

'Any movies there?'

'Yeah, theatres, too.'

'I love movies, but we only see them once a year.' He looked quietly off into the distance.

'Been to the mainland before?' I asked.

He shook his head. 'But some day I'd like to go and live on the mainland like a city man.'

'What do you want to be?'

He thought for a moment. 'I'd like to build things.'

'You should come and visit me then,' I said. He laughed. He was a brave dreamer and I admired his frankness. This little island was too small for him.

Half an hour later, we arrived at a deserted island overgrown with lush vegetation. There was no sign of any human habitation. The boat slowed down.

Ar Piao's large hands coiled the fishing net into one big rope. Throwing it out into the clear water, he anchored the boat, fished out a pipe and started smoking.

'What are we catching today?' I asked.

'Mackerel,' Ar Piao said, puffing out a thick ring of smoke.

'Great, I love them.'

He nodded, looking at the net.

'Do you?' I asked.

'What do you think?' he said without moving his gaze.

'Maybe you hate them,' I replied.

'Why?' A smile quirked at the corner of his mouth.

'I know a butcher who never eats the meat he chops.'

With his pipe dangling from the corner of his mouth he chuckled. 'You're a smart kid, like they said.'

'Smart?'

He nodded. 'I want my son to grow up like you, to be a great student and maybe have a future so he could leave this little island and find a decent job. My life is over. All my hope rests with my sons now.'

I was surprised he could say so much at one time. Here on the sea, he was at ease. 'This is a good life here,' I said sincerely.

'From where you sit, perhaps. The boy only knows the boat and the sea, nothing else.' He looked at Monkey thoughtfully, who

52

smiled back at us shyly. 'I want him to know more than that. He should know science, art, and maybe business.'

'But he knows a lot more things than we do, just different things,' I said out of respect for his son, 'and he has a dream.'

'That he does. I just wish he had a better place to grow in, that's all.' He gazed at his son, and smoked quietly.

'Dad, it's time.'

Ar Piao shot out of his seat, knocked the unburned tobacco out of the pipe, and started cranking in the net. The net dipped deep in the middle, heavy with mackerel jumping at the bottom. It was a thrilling sight. Ar Piao and Monkey dumped the catch into a tank on board and cast the net again. There must have been more than fifty pounds of fish. Ar Piao let me help scoop up the jumping fish from the dripping net, but he wouldn't let me cast the net. He said I would follow the net down into the sea if I weren't skilful enough.

At noon, he docked his boat at the tiny island. We started to cook lunch on deck.

'Want some fish?' Ar Piao asked.

'Sure.'

'Go get some.'

I bent over the tank and grabbed three. They were fighting to get away. 'Should we dress them first?'

'We don't use knives on the boat.' He took the fish and dipped them in a bucket of fresh water, then threw them, live, into a pot of boiling water and quickly covered it with a heavy lid. His hands secured the lid for a few seconds before he said, 'Now they are quiet.'

'You mean boiled dead.' Another slip of the tongue.

'We don't use that word here on the boat.'

'Sorry.'

'That's okay. Here, son.' He gestured to Monkey, who came and sat closer to him. 'Take a good look at this guy. I want you to learn from him and score full marks in school, then you won't have to fish for the rest of your life. Do you hear me?' He lovingly pinched his son's ear and grabbed him into his arms. Monkey giggled happily.

53

I was a little embarrassed by the praise. Inside my heart, I would have traded anything just to have a friendly environment like this, not the daily battle I faced back home. But all my enemies in school – Han, Quei, Wang, the principal, and La Shan – seemed so remote and irrelevant here. I could have lived on the island for ever, just breathing the sea air.

'Hey, it's done,' Ar Piao declared. He handed me a pair of chopsticks and said, '*Chi ba.*' Dig in.

When he opened the lid, the tantalizing aroma of cooked fish and ginger rushed out. The three mackerel looked succulent and tender. My stomach rumbled. 'How do you eat it?'

'You city folk care about manners and all that stuff. We don't burden ourselves with any of that here in the middle of the ocean.' He picked up a fish with chopsticks and used his left hand to grab the head. Then, with the chopsticks wrapped tightly around each side of the neck, he slowly brought the wooden sticks down the length of the fish. Neatly filleted, the meat fell obediently down on to his plate. The head and spine were tossed into the sea. He grabbed a few chunks with his chopsticks, dipped them in soy sauce, and ate heartily. I followed suit. The fish was heavenly with the taste of the sea; the tender white meat melted in my mouth. When I was done, I licked my fingers like Ar Piao and Monkey. Even though I was stuffed, I could have had more, they were so good.

The next several days I spent playing with Monkey and his friends. They knew a game called Pirates, where, barefoot, they chased and threw one another on the beach. We told tales of our different towns. Some of the children even made necklaces out of big, colourful shells to give me as gifts. When it was finally time for me to leave, I said a sad goodbye to Monkey, his friends, and to the island. I wished I could have brought them home with me and let them be my friends for ever.

Six

'You've been hiding, haven't you?' said my enemy, Han, as he paced in front of our house with an angry face while I sat on the front porch. I had just returned from the island that morning.

'It's none of your business,' I answered angrily. I stood up and grabbed my chair. 'Get off our property!' I was wistfully thinking about Monkey and his friends and Han was like a buzzing fly spoiling my meal. I wielded my chair threateningly.

'Stop it!' Mum ran out to my side. 'What is going on here?'

'That son of a whore is bothering me.' I pointed at Han, who was flanked by his cronies, Quei and Wang. They had taken a step back at the sight of the chair.

'Look who is here,' Han said in a mocking tone, referring to my mum.

'It's Mummy.' Wang's ugly, fat face twisted jeeringly. The three of them laughed.

'Get out of here!' I shouted at the top of my lungs. My heart raced and I felt myself losing control.

'Stop it!' Mum said again, pulling the tails of my coat.

They bullied me cockily, not expecting any retaliation. I had never fought back in the past. But school was over and these bad boys still wouldn't leave me alone, even at home. What was I going to do? I wanted to smash their three hideous faces into pieces. Ignoring Mum, I picked up the chair and threw it with all my might. It startled them and they turned to run, but the chair caught Han's right foot. He screamed like a bitten dog running for cover as he limped away behind his friends. The chair was broken into pieces.

To my surprise, Mum wasn't angry with me, nor did she talk about it later. We picked up the bits of chair and closed our front door. Years later, Mum told me it was at that moment that they realized I was a strong boy who could stand on his own feet.

Later in the evening, Han's parents came to our house and loudly accused me of hurting their son and almost breaking his ankle.

'He started the whole thing!' I cried bitterly. 'Your son has made my life miserable in school. He hit me, cursed me, and set all his friends against me, but I had to help him with his homework. Go ask him how many times he made me let him copy my homework.' His parents were shocked at the outburst. I sobbed heavily.

'But you shouldn't have hit him with the chair,' Han's father scolded. 'I'm a carpenter and I know how heavy a chair is.'

'Then you better ask your hooligan son not to beat me up any more,' I said, doing most of the talking as my family looked on.

'Don't say that,' Mum jumped in.

'He *is* a hooligan!' I shouted. 'You don't know the bad things he does. He even uses money to buy things to bribe his friends against me.'

'Money? What money?' his dad asked.

I gauged the man's surprise. 'He has a lot of money. He buys cigarettes and smokes with his friends.'

'A lot of money and smoking?' his dad said, taken aback.

'Where does he get the money?' his mum asked. 'Do you know?'

'From home, I heard,' I replied, still crying.

'That rat!' His parents abruptly left.

I knew I was the winner of this match. It would do Han good to get a beating at home and taste the flavour of being ratted on.

Normally, my righteous family would have scolded me, telling me how wrong I was to fight, making me sit in the corner. But that night they didn't. At dinner, with the door closed, everyone laughed and chatted. There was tacit forgiveness, even a sense of victory in the air. They listened to my fishing stories and my version of life on the island. I demonstrated 'the right way' to eat the mackerel, and they laughed and relished the seafood I had brought home.

But in bed that night, I knew what lay before me during this New Year's holiday. The threesome wouldn't leave me alone. I couldn't hang out in the regular places where the children normally played. Nor could I skip town again. I just had to make do and fight as I went along. I tucked myself in, thought about the island and the kids a little more, then fell asleep with a smile on my face.

On New Year's Eve, money was traditionally handed out to children in small red envelopes called 'hon baos', which meant *red bags*. The good kids spent money on toys, candies, movies, and plays. The bad ones hit the gambling pits, where they cheated, hustled, and hoped to win enough money to lead a good life of bad habits. Smoking, drinking, and women were never far from their minds. I collected five yuen and thought about what weapons to buy to protect myself.

Early in the morning on New Year's Day, I helped Mum prepare all kinds of sacrifices before our makeshift shrine of numerous gods. There was Buddha, his Kitchen God, the Earth God, Rice God, Water God, and all our dead ancestors. It was pretty much like the administration of a government, Mum explained. There were local gods, provincial gods, and the big Buddha on top. She had designated a spot for each, with different displays of food as sacrifices. There was chicken, fish, shrimp, clams, crabs, whole piglets painted in red, greasy ducks, coloured eggs, wine, peaches, pears, bananas, rice, and a lot of incense and paper money to burn.

With incense clutched in her hands Mum knelt and said the prayers. I waited on the side and kowtowed as many as fifty to a hundred times before each god, doing extras for my sisters and brother. I couldn't remember how I had got into the business of kowtowing for my siblings. All I knew was that I was a little more religious than they were. I had always been afraid of ghosts, and believed in the power of good gods. I prayed like a monk and didn't mind bending down on my skinny knees to kowtow for as often as Mum thought appropriate, usually imagining a hundred to be her lucky number.

By the end of the ceremonies, though my back and knees ached, I was quietly content with the prospect of having bought my insurance with gods at all levels for the new year to come. I told my sisters and brother that I had also done favours before the gods in their stead and had them pay me back in monetary terms. They believed enough to pay me five fens each.

For breakfast on New Year's Day, long, thin, handmade noodles were prepared, served in elegant little bowls and decorated on top with slices of fried egg, marinated meat, fried peanuts, oysters, crispy seaweed, and lightly sautéed crunchy snow peas. Long noodles promised longevity. Oysters, in my local dialect, meant 'alive'. Eggs were round and perfect. Peanuts indicated countless offspring, and if you twisted the pronunciation of *seaweed* a little, it sounded a lot like the word that meant '*fortune*'.

I fought down the long noodles, donned a new jacket that Mum had tailored herself, and ran off to offer New Year's greetings to our neighbours. I clasped my hands, bowed my head, and wished wealth to the garlic-nosed Liang Qu, an old man with seven sons, who made a living selling cigarettes to children behind closed doors at a huge mark-up. He wiped his big, dripping nose and threw me a cigarette with dark tobacco in it. 'Thanks and happy New Year, young fella. Have a smoke,' he said.

'It's not one of those mouldy ones, is it?' I teased as I pocketed it. He was known to pass the kids rotten products. Since the children were smoking secretly, they never complained. Only on New Year's Day could I get away with a joke like that.

I crossed the bridge to greet the white-haired country doctor, who peered at me through his thick glasses, trying to figure out who I was. 'I'm the younger son of the Chens,' I said.

He nodded, pointed with his cane at the seat next to him, and offered some tea. I politely told him I had just had breakfast. He asked how my grandpa was. 'He's gone,' I said. I couldn't believe how forgetful the doctor was. Only half a year ago, he had been telling us that Grandpa didn't have long to live.

'Oh, I'm sorry. But the living has to go on, ain't that right?'

'Right, doctor. Happy New Year.'

He nodded in silence and watched me run off down the dirt road.

It was a tradition that for good luck you should greet as many as you could on New Year's Day. To me, it was the easiest way to score brownie points with people, for they were in the best of spirits then and you could get a lot of goodwill for nothing.

By noon, I had greeted no less than fifty people. There was the brigade leader, the neighbourly teacher, Mr Lan, the kind tailor who sometimes let Mum use his sewing machine, the blacksmith who made good farming tools for us, and the locksmith who stuttered when he became excited. His son had gone to Chinghua University in Beijing, the equivalent of MIT. He had the hardest time saying the name, and always ended up stuttering 'Chin . . . Chin . . . Chin . . . Chinghua University.' By the time he did the third *hap, hap, hap* of his unfinished 'happy New Year' greeting, I was long gone.

When I got home for lunch, our living room was already filled with well-wishers. Dad was holding court, busily pouring hot tea and lighting the water pipe for his visitors.

I often thought that if Dad hadn't been the unfortunate son of a landlord, he probably would have ended up being one of the Communist leaders. He was a big man who commanded attention the moment he entered the room. Dad loved laughing, and could charm your boots off, but when he was angry, his temper thundered and his tongue lashed out mercilessly. He was a natural, a dramatic leader in a sleepy little town like Yellow Stone.

The commune leaders put him down like trash; bad neighbours and ignorant militiamen spat in his direction when they passed him in the street. But villagers from the surrounding towns and remote farms still came to him for all sorts of advice. They came in groups of five and ten and treated Dad as if he were still the son of an old family that had once headed the local gentility.

He wrote persuasive letters for those whose relatives resided in rich places like Singapore, Hong Kong, and Malaysia, helping them to squeeze money from their rich relatives. Defenceless widows sought his aid in drawing up local complaints about neighbours who had encroached on their properties and families who had abandoned them. They paid Dad with money or a sack of rice or yam. But a lot of advice was offered free, with a smile.

Gradually, Dad's reputation spread, with villagers dropping by daily when they were in town to shop. They came here for a cup of hot tea, a puff on the water pipe, or just to rest their feet. If Dad wasn't away at a reform camp, by eleven every morning the living room was always full of all sorts of personalities. Dad felt comfortable in the role and presided over the affairs of others like an unpaid civil servant. The only rule was that there was to be no spitting on the clean floor that Mum scrubbed daily.

On this special day, all the friendly, familiar faces were crowded into our sun-drenched living room. In the corner was the mason. His son was a miner in the high mountains of Fujian; the illiterate mason depended on my father to write monthly letters to him. Next to him was Stone Knife, so named because of his shrewdness. He was one of those villagers who never went to school but who seemed to know everything. Dad was his idol. Stone Knife could play many traditional Chinese musical instruments and write prose, compose music, and direct plays like Dad, but he depended heavily on my father to get him his gigs.

Then there was the sugarcane man, who was literally the king of sugarcane. Each morning in the early hours he presided over the sugarcane market and set the local daily price for fresh sugarcane. At the end of each day, he always dropped off the leftovers and grabbed a cup of tea with us before heading for his village. And there was the widow from a village ten miles away. She had brought her second son to wish Dad a happy New Year. He was visiting his mother from his navy base in another province. The young man beamed with pride and handed out cigarettes with filters, a rare commodity he had bought at the navy post. The crowd bubbled with excitement as they lit their good cigarettes.

The young navy man gave me one also, which I sniffed with satisfaction and slipped into my coat pocket when Dad wasn't looking. I sat there, as I had for many years, listening to Dad's friends doing their New Year's version of a daily chat.

But on New Year's Day, I felt a need for something more festive and entertaining, only there wasn't much I could do. I could just see my enemies, Han, Quei, and Wang, chomping cigarettes and lurking among the crowds, plotting their revenge against me. And I couldn't fight today, it would be bad luck.

Mum, wearing her new apron, called me back to the kitchen. I slipped out of the living room and had a large bowl of rice with some delicious meat and fish. I had never seen our kitchen so full of good food, but I knew it wouldn't be there for long. The thought made me go for a second bowl of rice and two more chunks of Mum's famous well-roasted pork knuckles.

After lunch, when my brother Jin was out playing poker and my sisters had long since gone out giggling with their friends, doing whatever girls did, I told Mum I was heading out to a basketball game at school.

'I didn't hear about a game there,' Mum said.

'Yeah, well it should be starting soon,' I lied, and streaked out of the door. I walked cautiously along the small path meandering among the wheat and sugarcane fields, staying away from the crowded street that were now filled to the brim with villagers who had flocked to the town for the New Year. It was an event locally known as *Yu Chun*, or 'Spring Outing'. They came in groups of boys and girls nicely dressed in new and colourful outfits. They sang, laughed, flirted, and ogled each other. The spring, now ripening with flowers and blossoms, seemed to stir a nameless angst among the youngsters and to give an added lustre to the world. I envied the simplicity of their lives. Why was mine so damned complicated?

Soon I was alone, looking for a shortcut to the secret gambling pits somewhere among the tall sugarcane fields. Children my age whispered about them and raved over the heroism of some of the big-time winners whenever news mysteriously found its way out of the pit. But none dared venture near the place. A few really bad older boys from our neighbourhood were said to make their homes there during the whole New Year's holiday.

If I couldn't have fun in normal places, then I was determined to find something else to do, either watching the game or even running errands for those bad boys. I had only brought half a yuen with me, that way if they wanted me in the game, I wouldn't have too much to lose. I was mentally prepared for any roughing up that might occur.

I checked over my shoulder to make sure nobody was following me, then slipped into the sugarcane field. The leaves were thick and sharp. I ducked beneath them and walked with bent knees towards the heart of the field.

After ten minutes, I heard vague, hushed voices. Then I suddenly saw lights and a clearing ahead of me. Twenty yards of sugarcane had been felled and trampled down, and there were at least two dozen young people sitting at tables, squatting, and standing in clusters around the cleared area.

I jumped out quickly and they all froze. Their angry faces stared at me as if I had already overstayed my welcome. The only thing moving was the cigarette smoke spiralling over their heads. It was a perfect group picture of the local criminal elite in full swing.

'What the fuck are you doing here, you little punk? I thought you were a good mama's boy. This is no place for you,' Mo Gong, the local shoemaker's son, barked at me. His diction was crude, his tone menacing. His nostrils flared as he threw his cigarette butt against me. 'Get outta here.'

In the hierarchy of the local criminal elite, he easily took the top spot. He once cut his enemy's shoulder open with a sharp knife meant for trimming rubber-soled shoes.

'Yeah, get the fuck outta here or we'll kick your ass and make you eat shit before you go,' another elite roared.

I covered my head with my arms like a surrendered war criminal, and moved slowly around the edge.

Mo Gong took a few steps and threw me to the springy ground of crushed sugarcane. He sat on me, twisted my arms behind my back, and demanded, 'Who sent you here?'

'Nobody, I just wanted to see what's going on.' My nose ground against his muddy leather boots.

'Who told you where we were?'

'I found my way here.'

62

'Liar!' He forced my head harder against the ground. It smelled like the pig manure used as fertilizer.

'Wait, Mo Gong, let go of him,' I heard a calm voice say from above me. It sounded like Sen, the son of the local banker, the brains behind all the scandals in the recent history of Yellow Stone. Mo Gong did as he was told, but not before kicking me once more on the behind.

I got up and dusted the dirt off my new coat. Sen grabbed Mo Gong and pulled him aside.

'Don't hurt him too much or he'll tell the commune leader and we'll be in trouble,' I heard Sen whisper, then he turned around and grabbed my shoulder.

'I'll let you stay but don't come back tomorrow and don't tell anyone about this place. If you do, I'll have Mo Gong make you a useless cripple,' he warned, his eyes unmoving.

'I just want to watch, that's all.'

'Quiet! And I want your mouth shut while you watch, hear me?'

I remained gratefully quiet as I stood far behind the circle. Sen took his place at the head of one of the tables. It was a simple poker game played by four, two against two. The starting bet was half a yuen, which would only give me one shot if I were to jump in.

Two minutes into the game, Sen and his partner, Mo Gong, started making faces, blowing their noses and cracking their knuckles. They were playing against a couple of out-of-town village boys who didn't know their sign language. Soon the villagers were losing fast, and they wanted out.

'Can't do that in this town.' Mo Gong put his dirty palm on their money.

'Says who?' The villagers were a bit taller than they were. 'You guys don't play fair. We're leaving,' one of the villagers said as he pushed Mo Gong's hand away and grabbed the money.

'We said at the beginning that the game is finished only when you're empty. I don't think you're empty,' Sen said coolly. 'Sit down.'

'What's this? Are you guys trying to make us stay?' The villagers stepped together, back to back.

Sen and Mo Gong were also on their feet now. I saw Sen make

another one of his faces, then he and Mo Gong were on top of them. Fights must have been common in this place because the people at other tables didn't even turn around. 'Quiet, you guys. Keep it down,' they shouted.

The four wrestled on the floor, seemingly inseparable. They went on wrestling like that for five minutes until the pile of money was scattered all over the ground. Whenever Sen rolled over to face me, he winked at me, gestured towards the money, and went on fighting.

Finally, I got his message. I looked around and kicked the wads of money between the cracks of trampled sugarcane, where they were hidden among the dense leaves. When the villagers kicked off their shoes, I picked them up and threw them into the fields when they weren't looking.

It was over when they were too tired to fight any more. The two villagers stumbled around dizzily, looking for their money and shoes, finding neither. Bitching and cursing, they walked out of the pit, never looking back.

As soon as the villagers were out of sight, Sen and Mo Gong burst into laughter. Their faces were covered with mud and bloody cuts; their clothes were torn. They squatted down, looking for the hidden bills. They collected over forty or fifty yuen in total.

'Here, take this.' Sen stuffed a bunch of small bills into my hands.

'I don't want any.'

'Fine, then you don't get any.'

'You guys are ruthless,' I said.

'Fuck your ancestors, you little shit,' Sen said jokingly with a smile, and pinched my ear. 'Hey, you weren't too bad yourself. I saw you kick the money and throw the shoes away.'

'I saw it too,' Mo Gong said. 'Hey, Da, have a cigarette. It's Da, right?' He searched his pocket and came up empty. 'Got any, Sen?'

'Yeah, but they're all smashed up.' Sen held up a flattened pack.

'Boy, do I feel like a smoke after all that fighting,' Mo Gong said.

'Me, too.' Sen struck a match for fun.

'I got one.' I took out the filtered cigarette from my coat pocket and showed it to them. A smile appeared on their filthy faces.

64

'Well, well, well. A filtered one.' Mo Gong grabbed it, slipped it into his mouth, and was about to light it.

'Wait, let's split it.' Sen snatched the cigarette out of Mo Gong's mouth and they started chasing each other in circles. Finally, Sen took off the filter and broke the cigarette into two stubs, which they smoked with a vengeance.

I bade them goodbye. Sen nodded, smiling wickedly at me.

With a smirk on his clownish face, Mo Gong said, 'Remember, Da, more filtered ones next time.'

As I made my way home, I found myself smiling. Those guys were rough but likeable. They were natural and up front, no hidden emotions. It would be great to learn to smoke, drink, and gamble, and be their friend. I could imagine my enemies' faces. They'd look like spineless little rascals compared to these boys.

Seven

After my first encounter with the gambling duo, Sen and Mo Gong, I had to control the urge to go back and see them the next day. If I ventured out again so soon, it would arouse suspicion in my family and then my adventure would end prematurely. I looked out from our second-floor window, trying to get a glimpse of the gambling pit, but all I could see was the cold wind making the sugarcane leaves dance like the ocean waves.

Mum and Dad wanted us to grow up to be perfect kids so that our ugly political birthmark would be obliterated. They hoped one day that all those leaders would wake up and say, 'Hey, you guys are a bunch of wonderful kids. C'mon, let's get you into schools and offer you jobs.' If we fought against her belief, Mum would cite the example of a girl from our neighbouring town. Li Jun was also from a landlord's family, but she had recently been selected by the commune to work in a food-canning factory, a plum and juicy job that any child of a good family would kill to get. She left town on the back of the commune's tractor wearing a big paper flower on her flat chest as she rode down the street of Yellow Stone in all her glory. No one could forget the tears and smiles of joy on her pretty face. She was the one in a thousand that the Communist rulers used to illustrate their benevolent policy towards us. The message was that if you were obedient, a future might be handed down to you.

We all knew this was a lot of crap, and listened to it as though it were the western wind blowing in one ear and out the other. It made us want to puke. Children like us all over the commune were still getting beaten up and thrown out of school. Even those who had obtained good jobs and had been afforded a college education before the Cultural Revolution were sent back to the town of their birth to become re-educated. Sometimes they were even jailed if they rebelled against local ignorance. Zhu Eng, the son of a counter-revolutionary, was clubbed to death in the bushes by his college classmates at a Shanghai university. All his family received was a jar containing their son's ashes and a police statement saying he had taken his own life and had wasted the government's investment in him.

Mum still disciplined us strictly. Cynicism wasn't allowed in our family. Her belief was that we should do more and get less. When people spit at you, look the other way. When they curse you, pretend to be deaf. If she found out about my visit to the gambling pit, I'd be grounded for at least three days.

But boredom and the need to make friends got the better of me. The next day I took some cigarettes from Dad's drawer and sneaked back to the sugarcane fields.

Mo Gong and Sen treated me coolly, as if they had forgotten our united work such a short time ago. But they smoked my cigarettes and let me try some of theirs. It was the first time I'd smoked with the big league. Mo Gong showed me how to inhale without it hurting too much. Smaller puffs at first, he said. I felt the rush to my head, numb and soothing at the same time. I washed my mouth with handfuls of water by the river before heading home. Once I got home, I didn't speak until I had had some garlic, onions, and a lot of soup to mask the foul scent.

The second day, Sen let me sit next to him for good luck, and showed me the way he handled cards. I was so flattered by his trust I kept on nodding, feigning my ignorance of the game.

The third day, Mo Gong wanted me to sit with him and even let me pick the amount to bet. For the rest of the sessions, they coached me on their sign language. They had me standing at another table, opposite their other two friends, Yi and Siang, where I scratched my head and picked my nose to give away their competitors' cards. They kept winning.

The fourth day, I was late in coming to the field.

'Where the hell have you been?' Sen asked. 'Come sit here by me. I've been losing too much money without you being here.' He ruffled my hair, threw me a whole pack of unopened cigarettes, and let me cut the cards for good luck. As I lit my first cigarette of the day, I smiled. It was very satisfying to be missed by these hooligans.

That evening, after the four of them split their money, I went home, wrapped up some of Mum's sweet rice cakes, and shared them with my new friends. They fought like hungry dogs and ate with dirty hands. After they were done, they wiped their mouths with the corners of their jackets and ran their greasy hands through their unruly hair so that it would look shiny.

'No matter how shiny your hair is, you still look like shit, Sen,' Mo Gong joked.

'You look even more like shit,' Sen retorted, touching his hair.

'Okay, okay, you both look like shit.' Siang laughed.

They started hitting each other for fun. Yi grabbed my hair with his greasy hands and we started wrestling. Later, we took a stroll to the marketplace near the theatre and used some of the gambling money to buy candies and more cigarettes. We laughed, talked, and joked until midnight. Then, reluctantly, I told them I had to go home. In my household, it was way beyond bedtime even though it was still the New Year holiday period. They pushed me around jokingly and Siang lifted me up to his shoulders. Then they said goodbye.

I lay in bed and couldn't go to sleep for a long time. Their laughter, their faces, their way of saying things, and the way they had included me like a real friend replayed in my mind like a colourful film. They had never once mentioned that I was from a landlord's family. They called me 'little shit' because I was three or four years younger, weighed twenty pounds less, and measured a head shorter. Then again, they called everyone 'shit', including themselves. With them, I felt a freedom to say and do whatever I wanted without worrying that they might report me to the school authorities. My enemies at school looked conniving and petty in comparison. If they thought they were bad, wait till they saw these guys. I drifted off into a sound sleep, hoping tomorrow would come quickly.

As the holiday came to an end, the seasonal gambling activities also died away, once all the New Year's money had been won, lost, and spent. The five of us began to hang out at their usual spots. Their favourite was the stone bridge where the Dong Jing River crossed our narrow street. The thoughtful architect had built a row of stone seats along the bridge, where we would sit in the evenings, chatting and watching townspeople come and go. Mo Gong and Sen would make rude comments to passing females, then laugh like a bunch of monkeys when the girls scolded them and called them ruffians who belonged in jail. My friends seemed to take pleasure from anything that stimulated them, and in making fools of themselves.

Soon I came to know their personalities and the hierarchy that existed within the group. Sen, fifteen, was the lead dog. He had the brains and audacity. He was born the middle brother of five, who fought one another at home every day. His dad worked for a bank in a faraway town near the salt factory along the coast, sent money home once a month, and visited every third month. The whole clan seemed to have bushy eyebrows and upturned noses. His mum raised the five boys like a single parent. Each day she could be found chasing one of her unruly sons with a long wooden stick, cursing her ancestors for giving her these demons to torture her in this life. She was often busy in the fields doing farmwork, so Sen's elder brother would be in charge of cooking for the family. The cook often ate up most of the food, and whoever came home late got nothing.

Another reason for the fighting at home was that the five brothers shared one huge bed. Every morning, one or two of them would roll off the edge and end up on the cold floor. Sen got sick of home life, left school, and hit the road, where he had met Mo Gong, at whose home he sometimes stayed. Occasionally Sen would go home and steal things, and his mother would chase him around with the wooden stick. He started swiping other things like chickens and ducks, and sold them in the market, using the money to buy an ancient bicycle that he parked at Mo Gong's home.

Occasionally he used the bike to carry passengers around in exchange for a fee, since there was no public transportation in our area. If you wanted to travel, you used your legs. But more often, he would ride to other villages late at night with Mo Gong, and steal rice from a grinding mill, or poultry. When the fruit season was in, they rode to the orchards. One would wait at the road while the other climbed the tree and shook the fruit off. They never looked upon this as stealing, but rather as acts of necessity and as tests of courage. Mo Gong would challenge Sen over something, then they would make a bet and jump in. It was always about betting and about who was braver.

Once Sen was detained by the commune's police because someone had accused him of setting fire to a fruit watcher's little hut. When the police came to notify his mother and ask her to take him home, she said, 'He's not my son. Do whatever you want with him,' and shut the door in the cop's face. The poor officer, who was prepared to give a long lecture to the mother, left confused and disappointed. They let Sen out without a scratch.

Mo Gong, fifteen, distinguished himself by almost killing someone with a big knife when he was thirteen. Years later, the sheer size of the weapon still shocked people. He grew up in a family of entrepreneurs. His mum and dad secretly made shoes behind closed doors and sold them in the black market. Mo Gong was born a rough kid, and couldn't stay out of trouble. His mouth said the wrong things and his hands were always out of control. He had an endless need to touch and hit things. No matter how hard his parents tried to discipline him, it never worked. They had hung him up by the wrists, locked him up, and whipped him till his butt was red and swollen. He always went back to the old ways. He stole money from home to buy cigarettes, alcohol, and food.

Once, when he couldn't find cash, he took the black-market shoes and sold them at a discount by the roadside. His dad got so mad when he found out that he swore he was going to chop off Mo Gong's hands. His uncles with the bushy eyebrows came to his rescue and saved him.

Another time, he almost killed a boy, who had been picking on

70

Mo Gong's small brother, and had tied his little penis to a frog. Mo Gong had picked up a knife and run after the offender. When he caught the kid, he sliced his shoulder open, filleting the flesh all the way down to the bone. Mo Gong said later that it was an insult to the manhood of all the Mo men, that his little brother could have died, and that the boy had to taste his own blood to know the pain.

When his parents were gone for days selling shoes in another county, his home became his friends' home. They drank up the last drop of cooking wine and gambled on the dining table. Each time when his parents came home, they would throw him out and swear he wasn't their son any more.

The reputations of Sen and Mo Gong were so bad that whenever there was a theft or fire they were always the first suspects. Their alibis usually lacked credibility and they often ended up being blamed for what they didn't do. When that was the case, they got very angry with the people who had framed them, and added their names to their long revenge list. Pretty soon half the town was on that list. They took their time getting their revenge – little things here and there, like a chicken missing or a plot of vegetables ruined. They never left any evidence behind. It was their way of saying, 'Fuck you,' and venting their feelings of being constantly maligned.

Siang became their friend by default. He was a good-looking fourteen-year-old from a wealthy family. His grandfather was an old revolutionary who had helped the Communist army occupy Putien. He now received a big salary for doing nothing, and used some of that money to build a huge, three-storeyed home. His mother was a nurse in a nearby hospital, and his father was a cadre in charge of a shoe factory.

Siang hated school and loved gambling. One year he lost so much money to Sen and Mo Gong that they were going to make him pay them back by stripping off his expensive clothes. He had begged for mercy, and agreed to pay back the debt by buying them cigarettes for the next year. They became really good friends when Siang got kicked out by his parents and Mo Gong took him in. They slept in the same bed for a week before Siang got enough money to buy a ticket to go to Fuzhou to his grandaunt, who was the president of the women's federation in the province of Fujian.

That left Yi, a short fifteen-year-old, who had become a carpenter at the age of twelve. He had goldfish eyes and bowed legs. His parents had died young and his grandpa had sent him away to be an apprentice at the age of ten. Yi said the first thing he learned from his carpenter master was how to slice his tobacco leaves and roll them into perfect rolls. His master urged him to smoke, saying it would give him the only excuse besides peeing to relax when working long hours.

Another early carpentry lesson taught him how to chat nonstop while working, because it made one forget about the boredom and entertained others at the same time. Among his many tedious monologues was the story of how one day he had been chopping at newly felled lumber but was doing it very unevenly. His master had looked him up and down, then asked, 'Do you feel those things swing down there when you chop?'

'What things?'

'Your balls.'

Yi said that it was as if he'd been struck by lightning; everything suddenly made sense. His balls. From then on whenever he chopped things he was always aware of his balls. If they swung evenly with each movement, good results were guaranteed. However unbelievable, this was an interesting story. He said his master's daughter started hanging around, and the master began dropping hints about him staying on after his apprenticeship ended. He hadn't objected to the idea. The rigid master was like the father he had never had, and the girl was blooming like a flower before his eager eyes. Day in and day out, he made sure his balls swung in good rhythm, and looked forward to seeing the swing of the girl's shapely behind.

Then Yi's master died suddenly and Yi was forced to leave his apprenticeship two years ahead of time. His grandpa brought him home, set up a shop for him at the back of the street; he had been in business ever since.

He smoked bitter tobacco, drank strong tea constantly, and could go on chatting for hours without boring himself. He made all sorts of furniture for neighbours. But he was, after all, still a young boy, and his heart was out there on the street. Sen and Mo Gong often went there to swipe tobacco leaves when cash was low and the urge to smoke was clawing at them. In return, they had to accompany the lonely carpenter while he worked, and endure listening to the same topics Yi had covered a hundred times before. But it wasn't a bad deal, really. When they were on the run from their parents or the law, Yi's humble workshop offered all they needed. It was out of the way, in a back alley, tobacco leaves hung drying from the ceiling, liquor was kept nearby in Yi's toolbox, and food came from Grandpa's kitchen. They could even sleep on a worn blanket on the soft sawdust. On occasion, the shop was used as a gambling pit. Yi spent more and more time being with the gang and became a part-time carpenter and a full-time street kid. Friendship endured.

Before I went back to school, I became an inseparable part of the now five-member gang. When school began, the group hung around the marketplace, harassed a few merchants, and bought candy and cigarettes. Then they climbed over the low wall at the back of my school and whistled to signal their arrival. As soon as the bell rang, I ran to the designated spot, where they lifted me up and threatened to toss me in the pond. Jumping back over the low wall, we lit cigarettes and made our plans for the day.

'Where are we going?' I asked, after sucking hard on my cigarette.

'To the middle school,' Siang said.

'What's the deal?'

They all smiled mysteriously at Sen. For the first time, I saw Sen's face turn red, and he giggled nervously.

'He likes a girl there. We gotta check it out,' Mo Gong said eagerly.

'Who is she?' I said.

'She's the daughter of Mr Huang, the PE teacher. She's got a pair of real roving eyes,' Sen said, still giggling.

'She looks at you?' I asked.

'The thing is, she always looks at our house when she passes by. The other day, she smiled a little at me,' Sen said.

73

'And he almost fainted.' Mo Gong laughed.

'Women. They can't make up their minds. I know a real lady from my days at my master's home . . .' It was Yi again, starting in on one of his old stories. We already knew what he was talking about; he had told us many times. The amazing thing about him was that he could tell the same story over and over and tell it exactly the same as the first time. The phrasing, pauses, and expression never changed.

We kicked the stones on the ground, broke the twigs that got in our way, and headed for the alma mater of my four friends, where they hadn't exactly excelled.

Sen was excited and nervous. He kept on smoking. We joked about his hair, which stood straight up. I scooped a handful of water from a nearby pond and sprinkled it on his head. He slapped my hands away, but happily finger-combed his hair, then peered at his own reflection in the pond.

'Not a bad-looking dude at all,' Sen said.

We all burst into raucous laughter.

When we leaned against the wall of the middle school, gazing from a distance at the dorm room of PE Teacher Huang, we saw a slender girl in her late teens come out carrying a bucket of water. She was a pretty thing, with beautiful eyes and shiny black hair that hung down to her hips. Her dress was printed with a simple design of little flowers. She reminded me of her good-looking father, who was once the champion javelin thrower in our province.

As she bent over to dump the bucket, she glanced in our direction and hesitated upon seeing five dark heads peeping over the wall. We ducked down, embarrassed. Slowly, she swung her slender body around and walked elegantly back into the dorm. We stayed there for a long time, our hearts beating fast, then quietly headed back.

'What do you think?' Sen asked, uncertain of our verdict.

'I didn't have any respect for your judgement of females until this moment,' I said.

Sen slapped me on the shoulder. 'Did you see that? I think she sensed I was there, that's why she stopped and looked.'

74

'I think she just smelled your dirty hair, that's all,' Siang joked.

On our way home, Sen did all the talking, excited as if he had just received a shot of adrenalin. 'She's a real pretty girl, and what a body! And that silky hair! If only I could touch it some day. Boy, I wouldn't mind calling Teacher Huang "Dad" for the rest of my life.'

'Maybe you should go back to school to be near her,' I suggested.

'That's a good idea,' Siang said.

'And attend only Teacher Huang's class,' Yi added. 'If he likes you enough, so will the daughter.'

Laughter again. The encounter had made us all feel good. The sunset seemed especially warm that day.

When the weather turned milder and the migrating geese honked noisily in the sky as they headed for the South China Sea to feed on young fish, we agreed to meet at the Dong Jing harbour in the evenings. The Dong Jing was a large river, along which boatmen shipped lumber downstream from the mountains. They rowed upriver carrying rice, salt, and fabric from the rich delta and plains. Each night at least ten flat-bottomed boats with woven bamboo coverings were moored there, patiently waiting to depart the next day after their owners had gone to town to get drunk and have a peaceful sleep before the week-long trip.

One moonlit night we found ourselves standing at the quiet harbour. Yi was an expert in the art of untying boats. He did something quick with his rough, calloused hands, and the thick knots easily unwound. We all jumped in and pushed the boat away from the shore with its two long bamboo poles.

It was so quiet and serene. I sat at the head of the boat listening to the gentle parting of the waters. Frogs and insects from the surrounding wheat and fava-bean fields sang in the background. While Yi manoeuvred the boat, we sat with our backs together for warmth. The moon in the clear sky seemed to be travelling with us.

On that perfect night, I told them my favourite love story, called 'Early Spring In February'.

'A handsome college student named Shi, from the city of Shanghai, left his rich, capitalist family and joined the Communist party. He took up a teaching job at a poor village school, in the beautiful countryside filled with wild flowers, fruit orchards, rivers, and endless green fields.

'He was modest and romantic. Every day, Shi read his own poetry to his starry-eyed pupils and taught them beautiful songs. His knowledge was boundless, and his voice was a mellow, throaty baritone. Early mornings, he could be spotted sitting before his easel in the peach garden when it was in full blossom, painting the fading spring. At night, the sound of his violin was sad and moving. Occasionally he was seen moodily taking a stroll along the river, where he would disappear for the entire day. No one knew where he went. Other teachers saw him give away his own food to poor pupils.

'One day, the school principal invited Shi to a family banquet to celebrate his rich landlord father's eightieth birthday. At the banquet, he met Jun, the principal's younger sister.

'Jun was a beautiful, shy girl who blushed in his presence. Her big eyes were so dark they were like pools of mystery, and her skin was as smooth as silk. She seemed like a dream in that fragrant garden where their eyes met for the first time on that magical night. Suddenly, the young teacher's loneliness vanished.

'They talked and talked like two old friends under the moon. She said she played the piano and liked Chopin and he said he liked Mozart and played the violin.

'"I know, and you're also a poet," Jun said.

'"How did you know?" Shi was surprised.

'"How could I help knowing, the whole village knows."

'She was a beam of light in the wilderness, a dock at which he could moor. Shi could have walked straight out of the romance novels Jun often read. He was handsome, noble, and refined, yet brooding and lonely, expressing his thoughts only in poetry and music. They fell madly in love that night . . .'

'Hold it, hold it,' Mo Gong interrupted. 'I gotta pee.'

'Shut up,' Sen said. 'We're just getting to the good part. What happened then?'

'I can't hold it no more.' Mo Gong stood by the edge of the boat, opened his fly, and a stream arched into the river.

'The story was so good we forgot to smoke. Here.' Siang whipped out a new pack of Flying Horse and lit one for me first. 'Okay, let's continue.'

'C'mon, Mo Gong, you're delaying us,' Yi said impatiently, holding on to the pole.

The boat had arrived at a wider section of the river, four miles away from Yellow Stone. The lights from the town flickered in the distance, and it seemed as if we were the only people alive between the silky water and the silvery, moonlit sky.

Yi laid down the dripping pole, crawled up to us, and sat next to me. The boat sat motionless, as if it, too, was eager for the story to continue.

'Every day Jun waited for Shi outside the school, picking wild flowers,' I continued. 'As soon as he appeared with his book, she'd run into his arms. They laughed and walked and talked. In the evenings, he played the violin and she accompanied him on her piano. Jun fell asleep with his poems in her hands. His music sounded more cheerful. Jun had never imagined love could be so sweet and wonderful. She would have done anything for him. She told him she would go anywhere he went and love him for ever. He cried in her arms like a baby.

'As time went by, Jun sometimes waited for Shi, disappointed, until dark. When she asked him about his absence, he turned silent and told her that it was nothing, but it began to bother her more and more as he turned gloomy and moody again. He would sit for hours just holding Jun, sighing heavily.

'"What's wrong?" Jun asked, fearful of losing her love.

'"Nothing," Shi said. "I just love you very much, and that's bothering me."

'Jun was surprised. "Why should that worry you?"

'Shi sealed her mouth with a long, passionate kiss and she melted away in the heat of his love.'

'Hey, you're getting too close to me.' Sen shoved Mo Gong away from his neck; Mo Gong was drooling, his head almost on Sen's shoulder.

77

'Want me to kiss you too? Here.' Sen planted a wet kiss on Mo Gong's forehead.

'Shit,' Mo protested in disgust. 'Go on, Da. What's next?'

'Yeah, what's next?' Yi echoed.

'Light me another Flying Horse,' I said.

'Oh, forgive me, Master. Please, leave no plot untold,' Siang joked and lit me a cigarette. 'Did they sleep together?'

'Don't be a dirty-minded rat.' Sen pinched his ear and kneed him.

'. . . Then one day, the young teacher came running to Jun and fell to his knees, crying, "I have to tell you this . . . I have to tell you."

'"What's the matter?" Jun was shocked at his outburst.

'"I am going to marry Lin Li. I'm sorry," Shi said in tears.

'"What?" Jun asked in a faint voice, her knees weak. "Who is Lin Li?"

'"She's the wife of my college classmate who joined the Communist party. He was just imprisoned and sentenced to death by the Nationalist army. I have been going to see his wife and three children at their home for the last few months. Remember all those disappearances?"

'Jun collapsed limply into her chair.

'"Are you all right?" Shi asked, falling to his knees beside her.

'She nodded sadly and looked at his handsome face. "Go on."

'"Life has been unimaginable in their household, and the wife has been sick. I have been giving my food and money to them. But yesterday, a comrade just informed me that my classmate had been secretly executed in prison. When I broke the news to his wife, she went crazy and fell into a seizure. Her situation is getting worse and worse. She remains delirious and keeps calling her husband's name. I have made up my mind to marry her this evening. I could not bear to see the family go down like that. Do you understand?"

'"No. Do you love her?"

'He shook his head. "You are my only love, Jun."

'Jun started weeping and ran out of the house, never looking back. That evening, Shi collected his belongings and left the school to marry the wife and take care of the children . . .'

My four friends were uncharacteristically quiet. They looked at the water, the moon reflected on the river. No one urged me to go on. It was as though they just wanted to linger in the aftertaste of such tragic love.

A few long seconds passed. 'Then what?' Mo Gong asked, casting a sorrowful look at me.

'The truth is,' I said, 'I was so disappointed myself at that point that I threw the book away and never bothered to finish it.'

'Well, that was something. I can't understand the young teacher. Do you think Jun jumped into one of the rivers?' Sen said dreamily.

'Maybe.'

It was midnight when I went home. Mum asked me where I had been and I told her I was with some friends.

'I know who you were with,' she said, 'and you smell like you have been smoking.'

'They're good boys at heart,' I defended them.

'Good guys or bad guys, you cannot smoke. Do you hear me?'

'But my brother smokes.'

'He's older and a farmer. You are a student. Act like one.'

'Does that mean I can't go out with my friends any more?' I asked.

She paused for a moment. 'It's up to you to choose who to make friends with. You are grown-up now, I can't watch you every second. But no matter who your friends are, do not forget who you are.'

From Mum, that meant yes. She was perceptive enough to see the change in my life. I was happier. But the biggest compliment of her tacit endorsement was her confidence in me to remain strong and good. I felt a rush of love and gratitude for her wisdom.

In school, I became sunnier and more confident. The results of last semester's countywide examination showed I was the best student in fourth grade, putting group one and La Shan's cronies to shame. In the hallways, the group one children still gave me dirty looks.

Once, when I passed the son of the party secretary, he said, 'Grades mean nothing. You are still a landlord's son.' Then he laughed, showing his teeth like a vicious animal.

My teacher, Mr Lan, took me aside and told me the same thing. 'Don't let your good grades get to you.'

It soon dawned on me that it was a sin to have scored so high and to have focused attention on myself. Now, in addition to the usual scorn, there was jealousy. I could do nothing right. But it no longer bothered me as much. When classes were over, I would see my friends again and would forget all about school. I no longer stayed up nights, plotting and scheming. Han, Quei, and Wang were still hateful but now they were only small annoyances, like little, buzzing flies.

Eight

In the early Seventies Ping-Pong became the rage of the country because Zhuan Zhe Don had won the World Cup championship for China. In PE class, instead of the regular running and jumping in the dirt field, we would sit in the classroom and listen to the live radio report of the World Cup match in progress. With each score gained by a Chinese player against a western player, we pounded our tables and cheered. When the games were over, we all sang, 'The eastern winds blow and the drums of war echo. In today's world, who is afraid of whom? We are not afraid of the Russian and American imperialists. It is they who are afraid of us.'

The success of this Ping-Pong diplomacy made us swell like hot-air balloons. We were finally winning something in the international arena.

The school had a carpenter build two Ping-Pong tables. A stone slab served as a third table. During break, hundreds of kids crowded around the three tables and took turns playing. We played a three-point game. Good players could stay in a game for a long time. Bad players were thrown out as quickly as they came. I became so involved that even after school I practised at home. Gradually, I turned into one of the better Ping-Pong players on campus.

One day I said to Sen and Mo Gong, who were waiting for me at the low wall, 'We should go play Ping-Pong today. I have three bats with rubber facings.'

'C'mon, I don't know how to play,' Sen said.

'That's because you're a stupid lefty,' Mo Gong joked. 'It sounds like fun. Let's go.' We flung ourselves back over the wall and headed for a table.

There was a small crowd already there, including my three enemies. Han seemed to be dominating the game.

'I don't think we should take over this game,' I said, sensing Quei's gaze.

'Why?' Sen asked.

'Because my enemies are there,' I replied. 'Let's go.'

'What?' Sen asked.

'Han and his guys.' I pointed my chin in their direction.

'I'm not going anywhere. I'd like to know these guys better,' Mo Gong said.

'Da, we're playing right here,' Sen said. 'Don't tell me you're afraid.'

As the two famous personalities slouched their way to the head of the table, the crowd parted. Mo Gong hopped on to the end of the table where Han was standing.

'Stop the game, pick up your ball, and get outta my sight. Let us older men try the game, punks,' Mo Gong mocked in an old man's voice. He pushed Han away from the table.

Han looked daggers at me. 'You son of a landlord, you'll be sorry you brought these hooligans. I'm gonna report this to the teacher right now!' He stepped aside, glaring at Sen and Mo Gong.

'Well, well, well, you little piece of shit. Who are you calling a hooligan, and what's wrong with the son of a landlord?' Mo Gong's eyes were getting red. He walked towards Han. 'You're just like your shitty dad. I haven't taken him off my list yet.' Then he pushed Han to the ground and kicked him a few times.

'Let's go. We'll take care of him later,' Sen said. He was right. From the corner of my eye, I could see the principal striding in our direction.

'Run, the Frog is here,' I urged. 'You'll be in trouble if you don't.'

'Shit, too late,' Sen said. 'Mo Gong, stay calm, and don't curse in front of the Frog, okay? Let me handle him. If we run, we'll look like thieves.'

The principal was in front of us in a minute, breathless. His thick glasses were fogged with sweat.

'What are you doing here?' he barked, looking blindly at Sen and Mo Gong.

'Nothing, we're just coming back to visit,' Sen said sincerely. 'Hey, take a look at the Ping-Pong table, Mo Gong. I haven't seen one this smooth for a long time.' He touched the top of the rough table.

'I heard you were beating Han up. Is that true, Mo Gong?'

'That's not true. Where is the little piece of . . .'

'Stop it,' Sen said. 'Listen, Principal. I know you're having a hard time running the school. If our visit is so unwelcome, we'll leave now.'

'Wait a second,' the Frog commanded. 'Han is coming. I want to hear from him.'

Han limped up to the Frog with tears in his eyes. 'Mo Gong pushed me to the ground and kicked me. They came with Da, that son of the landlord.'

'Now what do you say?' the Frog asked, casting a brief look at me that said, *I'll take care of you later*.

'Han is a big liar, Principal,' Sen said. 'You can't trust someone like that. In fact, his whole family are liars. Last time Han stole from his family, he told his no-good parents that I was the guilty one. I just happened to pass by his courtyard that day.'

'I'm not judging you, but the other students and I saw you guys roughing him up. I'm telling you, I could have you arrested for disturbing the peace at school. I'm sure the commune jail is no strange place to you two.' The Frog's puffy face was red. 'Now get out of here.'

I saw the blood shoot up into Sen's pale face when he heard the word 'jail'. He was grinding his teeth to try and control his anger. He saw Mo Gong getting ready to strike out at the Frog and quickly dragged him aside.

'Let's go now.' Sen stared with his deadly, unblinking eyes at the Frog and Han for a good five seconds, then turned to leave.

'Da, did you bring them here?' the Frog asked me. Sen and Mo Gong paused.

'I did.'

'No, he didn't,' Sen said. 'We wanted to come here on our own. He just gave directions. There ain't nothing wrong with giving directions, is there? Again, Principal, with all due respect, I wouldn't trust that Han boy. He's a liar.' With that warning, they departed and I followed them to the wall.

That night we gathered at Yi's workshop and puffed on dry tobacco leaves.

'It's time we loosened a few spokes on the Frog's new bicycle,' Mo Gong said.

'We shouldn't do that right now, but I wouldn't mind taking a walk across Han's family garden,' Sen said. 'Let's go.'

We were soon in front of the lush garden overgrown with leeks and delicate scallions and some other vegetables I couldn't make out in the darkness. We waited to make sure there was no one around, then jumped in. I lagged behind, fearful and nervous.

'What's the matter with you? He's made your life hell in school. Don't you remember?' Sen whispered in my ear. It worked. I felt the blood rush to my head and the old anger clawed inside me like a wild animal. I jumped in and danced wildly as if each plant I stepped on was Han's head. Soon the whole garden looked flat, as if a typhoon had just blown through it. We fled, went straight back to Yi's place, and looked for food in his grandpa's kitchen. Grandpa gave us some dried peanuts.

It was Sen's idea that we be seen by Grandpa, who then could stand in front of others tomorrow and say without guilt that the gang had been at his house, not at the Hans' plot.

In the morning, when Han's mother screamed like a hurt pig in the middle of the street, accusing the gang of the atrocity, Yi's grandpa was right there to defend us. He was a hospital worker, old and respected. He swore to heaven that it was just another false accusation, she was attacking the wrong kids. This time, the ardent defence of Yi's grandpa worked. People believed him. We stayed very quiet, peacefully smoking our cigarettes.

The next day, the principal met me at the entrance to the class. Behind him stood Han and his cronies.

'Da, my office, right now,' the Frog said angrily. He hadn't scared me before; he didn't scare me now. I stared at my enemies angrily until they silently looked away. I followed the Frog to his office.

'Where were we?' he asked, his usual opening line while he cleaned his desk.

'I forgot.'

He looked up, a little lost as usual. 'I heard you are hanging around with those hooligans nowadays.'

'They are friends from my neighbourhood,' I said firmly.

'They aren't good people to be with.'

'At least they don't beat me up and curse at me all the time, like my classmates Han, Quei, and Wang.'

He paused. Then he seemed to want to say something but didn't because he had forgotten what it was.

'If I catch you with them in our school again, you will be expelled for good this time. Hear me?'

I nodded. 'But if they come by themselves, I can't be blamed.'

'You are nitpicking. Be careful. You are forgetting who you are. You think a few good grades can make you better? Think again.' It was an unexpected outburst.

On my way back to class, I thought about the spokes on his bike that Sen and Mo Gong wanted to do away with. I really wanted to see him plunge on his flat face.

I was expecting insults and curses from Han and company when I entered the class late. They knew I had been questioned. In the old days, they would do a war dance around me, laughing like hyenas to embarrass me in front of the whole class. But today they avoided my gaze and sat quietly. I walked in with a straight back, head high. In my mind's eye, my friends at home were smiling at me.

One weekend we heard that there was a new movie being shown twenty miles away from Yellow Stone in the capital city of Putien. That was a whopping distance of hills and valleys, especially if you had to wheel yourself around. The young tractor driver of our commune had seen it on one of his trips carrying fuel to the big city. A small crowd gathered around as he told everyone about how good it was. When he came to the description of the leading lady, he stopped, looked into our faces as if to prepare us for a shocker, then slowly made a few curves in the air with his hands and whistled.

'Is she that beautiful?' someone whispered.

The driver nodded. 'Simply beyond words. Go see it.' We were sold.

Sen took out his old bike, splashed it down with water, and sent a little boy to call me at home, respectfully keeping a distance from my strict mum.

'Your friends sent the messenger to call you,' Mum said. He had apparently spilled our plans. 'Be careful when you are in Putien. There is a lot of traffic there.' To my surprise and delight, Mum gave me half a yuen for the trip.

Sen's bike was a museum piece. It rattled in places where it shouldn't have and was mute where it should have made noise. It was, nonetheless, mounted with a long back seat. There were five of us; we rode that bike the acrobatic way. One pedalled, two straddled the back seat, and one sat sideways on the handlebars, barely giving the pedaller room to see. The fifth passenger ran behind and helped push the heavy load uphill. Every two miles we changed seating arrangements so that both runner and pedaller would get a rest. It was pathetic to see the old bike grinding under three hundred pounds, slogging through the rough, muddy road with almost flat tyres.

It took us a good three hours to reach Putien. We were covered with sweat and a layer of sand when we dismounted at the bridge, which looked like the entrance to the ancient city, and walked the rest of the way. Had a cop seen us riding so precariously, he would have thrown us off the bike for riding so dangerously in heavy traffic. He might even have taken the bike away since Sen had never ever got a licence for it.

As we walked single file along the crowded street, I told them about the time my brother had lost me here when I was five. I had

86

had to hitchhike home. When my brother got back later, crying, he almost peed in his pants when he saw me. My friends hit my head and kicked my butt for being so naughty at such a young age, and we laughed loudly and happily.

Siang whipped out a new pack of cigarettes. Here, in this big city where nobody knew us, we each smoked a cigarette and walked around with the butts hanging from the corners of our mouths like grown-ups.

'Hurry,' I urged, 'it'll be hard to find tickets for such a hot movie.'

'Don't worry, we could always go to our old friend Three Foot Six, if you can't buy them at the ticket booth,' Siang said.

'We love the guy. He has everything we want,' Mo Gong said.

'Hey, how come I don't know him?' I said.

'We might have to go to him anyway,' Sen complained.

'I heard the lines yesterday were incredibly long for today's show and that they had even sold out all the standing-room tickets,' Siang said.

Soon we were in front of the county's largest movie theatre, pride and excitement gripping our hearts. We stared at the tall iron fences, the thick columns, and the fashionably dressed young people wearing their long, greasy hair in ducktail style and skintight, bell-bottom trousers. The girls wore colourful nylon skirts that flew above their creamy white knees as the sea wind whirled the dusty ground. Since most women in China usually wore standard blue pants just like the men, this was a rare sight.

'Mo Gong is a little lost for words here. I bet he likes those white thighs,' said Siang, the known cosmopolitan who had travelled far and often. He hit Mo Gong's head with the side of his hand.

'You're absolutely right, Siang. I'd love to lick every inch of those white legs for the rest of my long and boring life,' he said with his eyes glued to a particularly tall and leggy girl. 'Tell us who these angels are, Siang.'

Siang took a long draw on his cigarette, narrowed his eyes like an old sailor, and said, 'Those are the children of Chinese families who came back after they were kicked out from places like the Philippines, Malaysia, and Indonesia when those places turned

87

against the Chinese. Those foreign countries were all anti-China. Can you imagine?

'Now they live on a farm especially set aside for them by the government with a special supply store. They're rich people, with rich relatives back in their home countries who send them money monthly. A postman covering that area said that at the New Year he had to carry money to the farm in large canvas sacks.'

The five of us stood there admiring the youthful crowd as they rode around on fancy scooters, their girlfriends holding to their waists. It didn't seem too bad a fate.

'And there's a lot of free sex going on on the farm,' Siang commented casually.

'Free sex?' Mo Gong exclaimed.

'What's free sex?' I asked.

'You're too young to know that sort of stuff.' Siang hit my head with his hand. 'I don't think your mum entrusted us to teach you things like free sex.' They all laughed.

'Free sex means you don't have to pay,' Mo Gong said rather thoughtfully.

'Nah. Free sex is fucking your fiancée before a wedding without a marriage licence issued by the commune,' Sen said.

'Free sex is screwing someone without the danger of being called a pervert and being put in jail,' Yi said after a long silence.

'No, you're all wrong,' Siang said. 'Free sex means you can have sex with both people and farm animals.'

It was a terrible joke. The four of us flipped Siang to the ground and kicked him some before helping him back on his feet. Even after that, he still chuckled over his joke.

'I'm sure some of them are screwing the animals on the farm. Just think, there are more men than women. What are they going to do?' Mo Gong said.

'That's why they do it with different people, with no fixed partner. That's the real spirit of sharing.' Yi summed it up so well, we all applauded.

'Shit! Tickets,' Siang reminded us. We were at the deserted ticket booth. A large sign read, 'TICKETS SOLD OUT FOR THE NEXT THREE DAYS OF *THE SEA LADY*.'

'I told you they would be sold out. There's a lot of corruption going on inside the ticket booths, you know,' Siang said. 'Eighty per cent of the tickets were sent to the cadres, the county administration and other interested groups such as the electric companies, and meat or fruit stores and department stores. It's a hot movie with limited showings. They're only showing it for a few days, then it moves to another town. They take care of one another.

'As for us, we better get our fat asses out of here quickly, before the cops bother us. Right now, we're just a bunch of ticketless hoods from another town.'

We saw a blue uniform moving our way and rushed out.

'Good thing you know all this stuff, Siang,' I said gratefully.

'This ain't nothing. You should go to Fuzhou. That's a big city,' Siang said.

We all nodded in agreement, since none of us had ever been there.

'Let's go to Three Foot Six now, before it's too late for the three o'clock show,' I said.

Sen rode his bike by himself and we all ran after him, obeying the city's 'No Riding Double' law.

Breathless, we stood in front of a tiny store in a dead-end lane so narrow that two fat guys would have stuck if they'd walked abreast along it. Chickens ran around noisily, scratching at the cobbles.

And so I met the infamous Three Foot Six, the biggest city trader in the history of Putien. To say he didn't measure up to his larger-than-life reputation would have been an understatement. Only three feet, six inches tall, he was a dwarf with a huge watermelon head. It took me three long minutes to finally close my mouth, which had dropped open at his incredibly comic appearance. Yi stepped on my right foot to make me stop the stupid stare.

'So, what can I do for you young fellows?' A high-pitched voice came from behind the counter. The dwarf smiled professionally, knowing that no one visited his crummy store for nothing. People said that he could persuade even curious onlookers into becoming willing buyers.

'We want some tickets to *The Sea Lady*,' Siang said smoothly.

'Uh-huh, I just knew it. What a beautiful lady she is. I have seen the movie three times, and she would be worth seeing a fourth time, ha, ha, ha, maybe even a fifth time. Tell you the truth, I'd love to have her as my wife if I wasn't married to three women already, ha, ha, ha.' The little man rocked in his seat, laughing his pants off.

'My son swam in the same pool with her when they were making the movie near his training camp. You know, Sonny is a swimming champion of our country.' He pointed at a framed picture behind the counter of a little fellow in a dripping swimsuit holding a gold cup.

'Not your son again, mister,' Siang protested. 'I've heard of him each time I've been here. Last time you said he shook hands with our Premier Chow, and now you say he swam in the same pool with the most beautiful star.'

'It's true, it's true. He was in there, I swear.'

'Okay, okay. What's the price of the three o'clock show?'

'Shhh . . . you're talking too loud. You know the last time they did that here I had to call up my son at his training camp and have him call the party secretary of Putien, who in return called the bureau of commerce to release me from detention. It's tough out here. I swear I won't be in this business in my next life, that is if I am a little taller and have some muscles like you fellows. I could be a violinist or even a professor.'

'We really gotta have the tickets,' Siang interrupted again.

'I'm not quite sure I got any.'

'We're going if you don't,' Sen said curtly.

'Wait a second, wait a second, young man. What's the hurry? Show me you have money,' the dwarf said.

Siang pulled out three ten-yuen bills and laid them on the counter with a flourish.

'Young man with money, very admirable, very admirable. I happen to have just five tickets for you, and come in here, I'll show you other things that you might fancy, tapes of love songs from Hong Kong and a lot more. Real sexy stuff.'

'How much are the tickets?' Sen said.

'For you, two yuen each,' he said seriously, shrinking all the smiles out of his face.

My heart sank like a sack of wet sand. It was robbery. The original price was only ten fen.

'I hear silence? These are the only tickets left for the show in town. I wouldn't miss it for the world. Whadda beautiful face. I still dream of her every night when I'm in bed with one of my wives. You young men should go see what real beauty is before you marry someone ugly. Then you'll have the same problem I do, and have to keep marrying until you find a better one. And guess what? It never gets better, only worse. They all live under the same roof now and, boy, is it noisy there. I don't mind staying here in the shop all day long.' He paused. 'Yes or no?'

'One yuen each,' Siang bargained.

I felt Sen push Siang to stop him. He pointed to the clock. It read 2.45. In ten minutes the little man would be on his knees begging for us to take the tickets off his hands.

'No, I think we'll just wait for the next show,' Sen said.

'Listen, kids, one yuen each, for the sake of Buddha. I'd really love you to see it, how about that?'

'We could wait.' Sen started pushing us out the door as he saw the merchant soften.

'Wait, don't go. Don't make a poor old man get down on his knees to beg you.' As he said it, he slipped nimbly from the chair and stood, a sorry three feet six, at our feet. He held on to our legs and started weeping. 'Don't go, you can have them, just name a price.'

'Ten fen each,' Mo Gong said.

'You're killing me. Double that and I will call you all grandpa.' No sooner had he said that, he was on his knees calling us all grandpa to humble himself.

'Give it to him, guys.' I couldn't help feeling sorry for the little man, kneeling on the ground calling us his ancestors.

'He's a tricky guy, Da.' Sen shot me a cool look.

'Fifteen fens.'

'Done deal, Grandpas,' he said. He got back up on his seat, having wiped his teary face on our trousers.

91

We all fished out change. He took the money, smiled, and said, 'How about five more fens for calling you grandpa on my knees. Just let me keep the change.' Mo Gong grabbed the dwarf's fist and forced it open, taking back his five fen change.

By the time we got to the theatre, it was filled with smoke and the hallways were packed with people holding standing-room tickets. Kids hung from the windows trying to get a better view. On the platform stood a wide screen, with loudspeakers on either side. There were even children sitting behind the screen, looking up. They were going to watch the movie in reverse. We had to push and shove to get other viewers off our seats in the last row against the wall.

The place smelled like sweat and felt like an oven, but it was well worth all the trouble we'd been through to come here. The plot of the movie was run-of-the-mill Cultural Revolution stuff. The story took place in a seaside village. A landlord was plotting against the local Communist party, whose leader was the gorgeous goddess of curvy contours. In the end, the landlord was trashed and the good guys won. Throughout the movie, I could feel Mo Gong and Sen *ooh* and *ah* with each close-up of the star. Siang was so drawn into the plot and carried away by the beautiful goddess that he forgot to smoke and almost burned his fingers.

When we finally walked out into the afternoon light and joined the rest of the crowd in the cold street, Sen said pensively, 'It's kind of sad, you know. She makes us all look ugly.'

'You're ugly to begin with,' Mo Gong replied. 'Some day, guys, I'm gonna marry someone just like that.' He shook his head and stuck a cigarette into his mouth.

'In your wet dream,' Siang replied.

'You don't have to fucking put me down each time you get the chance, Siang. I know I don't have a revolutionary grandpa like you. You think you could marry someone like that, right?'

'Maybe.' Siang smiled naughtily, just to annoy Mo Gong.

'Go take a look at yourself in the Dong Jing River. You got an ugly nose, big mouth, and a pair of roving eyes. You look like an idiot ninety per cent of the time.'

'Calm down, you guys.'

'Yeah, calm down. I thought the movie was supposed to make us feel good. Why the fuck are we fighting?'

'You started the whole thing.'

'No, you did.'

As we were riding and running home, I saw Han riding on the back seat of his skinny father's new Phoenix bike. He tried to hide his face with a paper fan as his father overtook us on the bumpy road. I was sitting on the back seat, hugging Mo Gong's waist, and at the same time lighting a cigarette for Sen, who was pedalling. I hoped Han didn't see me do that. It was quite dark already. I really hoped he didn't recognize us at all, but it was hard to miss an acrobatic show like ours on the deserted road. The old fear appeared only briefly before it was replaced by the warm companionship of my friends, who by now had become more like my brothers. I wasn't going to let that fly spoil my mood this time, not on the afternoon when I had seen the most beautiful creature in the world with my own eyes.

We got home at nine in the evening, hungry and tired. Mum had cooked a pot of delicious noodles with vegetables and had kept it warm for me. With her approval, I took it to Yi's workshop and shared it with my buddies. First, there was surprise that my mum had allowed me to do this, then there was a fight among my hungry friends to scoop up portions into their bowls. We slurped those long noodles silently. When we put down our chopsticks, full and relaxed, a warm feeling of being together like a family swept over us. We celebrated the good time with loud and long burps, laughing until our stomachs hurt. Though we sat in a humble mud hut with a flickering kerosene light, it felt like we had the whole world within our hearts.

Nine

'Open your schoolbag,' Teacher Lan demanded.

'Why, Teacher? There are only books in it,' I protested, sensing the eyes of Han, Quei, Wang, and the rest of the class searing into my back like the hot summer sun.

'Someone saw you smoking outside school,' Teacher Lan said. 'I think you've got cigarettes in your bag.'

I held on to my bag and shot a long, cold stare at Han, who sat with his feet on his desk, smiling with acknowledgement. His cronies flanked him, grinning and showing their unbrushed teeth.

Teacher Lan snatched the bag from my hand. At the bottom lay an unopened pack of Flying Horse. I'd used the half yuen Mum had given me to buy them from Liang, the cigarette merchant, on my way to school. I had planned to share them with my friends over a good story at Yi's workshop.

'What is this?' Teacher Lan waved the pack in front of the whole class. 'I helped you come back to school and make all that progress and now you want to throw away everything you have achieved. You are very stupid. You do not realize how people around think of you. Some of them still want to throw you out of school. You just gave them good a reason, and to tell you the truth, I am beginning to see their point. Those hoodlums will drag you down to the bottom again, even lower. Do you realize that? To the bottom.' He threw the cigarettes on the floor, spat on them, and stomped them with his feet until they were totally crushed.

94

I had never seen the mellow, awkward Mr Lan so forceful or so angry before, and I was shocked. He knew everything about my friends and me. I felt torn with pain at having our wonderful friendship trashed in front of my classmates and enemies. My head was becoming numb and my temples throbbed, but this time instead of the old fear, I felt anger, anger at my enemies, who still picked on me at every opportunity, whose mission in life seemed to be my complete destruction.

They were ignorant of the beautiful, honest friendship those 'hoodlums' offered me and would never be able to fathom the depths of our devotion to each other. Nor could Teacher Lan. He did not know how hellish school had been for me for so many years. I wanted to yell back at him and make him understand, but he had gone back to his podium, opened his book. Class had begun.

As my fury receded into a trickle of dull pain, I tried to digest what Teacher Lan had tried to tell me. There were people out there who were still trying to get me. Why didn't they leave me alone and let me just be like the rest of the kids? Who were they?

I walked home under a cloud of gloom and went directly to the gang at Yi's workshop. They had been helping Yi slice some new lumber with huge saws that had long and ugly teeth. Sawdust covered their faces.

'We've gotta job for you, Mr Student.' Sen wiped the sweat from his forehead. 'Take over my saw and I'll slice some tobacco. By the way, you look like an idiot.'

'What's the matter?' Yi put down his saw. 'You're very quiet.'

'Where's my Flying Horse cigarettes?' Mo Gong flapped his arms up and down like wings.

'I'm sorry, my teacher trashed them,' I said darkly.

'What?'

'And he gave me a whole shitload of crap right in front of everyone.'

'About what?'

'About me hanging around with you guys.'

'The bad-influence shit, right?'

They understood even though I didn't nod.

'It was all my fault. I got you guys dragged into this,' I said.

'How's it your fault?'

'Because of my family and what had happened to me in the third grade.'

'Wait a second. Are you giving us the sorry-and-goodbye-forever speech?' Sen asked.

I felt badly that they could even think so. 'Not at all. I'm here, right? You're my brothers,' I said sternly.

'So we're not bad apples?' Mo Gong asked quietly.

'You don't think I'm just a no-good landlord's son?' I asked in return.

They looked at each and laughed as if it was a joke. Siang picked me up, planted me on his lap, and they all started tickling me until we were covered with sawdust.

'Hey, look what he's got here,' Siang said as he encountered something square in my coat pocket. He stuck his hand in and pulled out a pack of unopened Flying Horse.

'You snake, you lied about your teacher,' Siang said jokingly.

It didn't matter where the cigarettes came from. My friends scrambled for them.

'Hey, where didya get this, truth?' Sen asked.

'I bought it on credit from Liang.'

'Hey, I love that, little brother!' Sen put his arm around me and then around Mo Gong. 'We have to figure out how to deal with that rascal Han slowly. I'm sure it was him.'

'How?' I asked.

'We'll give a hint that something is coming his way, then we'll let him wait and sweat it out.'

I put down my schoolbag, picked up a saw, and got right down to business. It so happened I had a good eye for sawing real straight.

The cigarette incident didn't ripple beyond the classroom. Even though Han and my other enemies shouted, 'The smoker is here!' a few times when I entered the room, they didn't get the whole class to respond as they usually did. One day, the shortest fellow in class actually came up to me and said nervously, 'Da, I had nothing to do with the cigarette thing. I hope you and your friends understand and leave me alone.'

96

This took me totally by surprise. The little guy used to trail along behind my enemies. I sensed the fear in his voice as he tried to distance himself from his bosses. As he turned to run away, I grabbed him and brought his face close to mine. 'Tell your boss that the hooligans still remember him and his friends.'

The kid shrank back and ran off as if fleeing a ghost.

For the next few days I was given extra space as I passed down the narrow aisles, and silent stares came from my classmates. It was a stare usually given to an older guy with a rare disease, a drinking addiction, or a wife-beater. It was an innocent, mind-speaking stare, that said, 'You scare me, stay away.' I enjoyed it and was in no hurry to dispel the myth around me. Soon I started to walk with my jacket hanging open to my belly. I spoke less, and forced my eyes to move slowly from one spot to another. Occasionally I sucked in air loudly like I was suffering from a terrible yearning for some bitter tobacco. Though it wasn't his intention, Teacher Lan's public criticism did more for than against me. I was now the smoking buddy of the hooligans and, in comparison, my enemies looked like trapped rabbits.

One day after school, the little guy came running to me in the hallway and said, 'Look, your enemies didn't believe me when I sent them the message. They pushed me over to you to confirm it.'

I saw my three enemies standing ten yards away, looking at us.

'What do I need to do?'

'Give them a smile, that'll be the signal that I told the truth. Please do it, otherwise they'll beat me up and say I was lying,' he begged.

I spun the kid around to face the three of them, and slowly and unmistakably gave them the finger. Then I smiled.

The smirks on their faces disappeared.

'See, I wasn't lying, the hooligans really want your ass,' the little guy yelled, running in their direction. But my enemies were long gone.

They knew revenge was coming and they waited in agony. Every day they watched me come and go, and whispered to each other. I stayed in my corner and sometimes threw a quick look their way, accompanied by my middle finger. They'd look away immediately. I hated using the influence of my friends to make life better at school, but I couldn't help enjoying the mind games I tortured them with. And I didn't feel one ounce of remorse, not after what they had done to me. It was their faces I saw in most of my nightmares. I told myself that the real revenge was yet to come. It was only a matter of time.

One evening I bought a bag of freshly baked fava beans and went to join my friends at Yi's. As soon as I stepped in, I noticed Sen acting a little strange. He hummed a broken tune, grinned from ear to ear, and kept looking into a half-mirror that hung above Yi's coal stove, fussing with his unruly hair.

'What's with him?' I asked the rest of the gang. They were doing their usual stuff, slicing tobacco leaves, brewing tea, and getting ready for some juicy chatting. As I placed the beans on the counter, Mo Gong jumped down from his chair, grabbed a handful and almost burned his hands.

'They're hot!' He sampled the beans with relish.

'He saw his girl today,' Yi said, giving me a wicked wink, which I returned.

'And now he can't keep his mouth shut,' Siang said, also grabbing a handful of beans.

'What's the story, Sen? Details, details.' I was happy for him.

Sen turned, still wearing a silly grin. 'Well, I was riding on my old bike to the market this afternoon, right?'

'On the street?' I asked.

'No, on the narrow dirt road near Dong Jing River.'

'And?'

He kept beaming. 'And there was no one else around.'

'It sounds better each time,' Mo Gong said, chewing the beans. 'Keep going, Sen.'

'Outta nowhere, there she is.' Sen narrows his eyes as if he could still see her figure and lowered his voice. 'Hair down to the waist, loose and fluttering in the wind. Still wearing that dress with the little flowers, real tight up here.' He grabbed his own breasts. We all smiled and he waved at us, annoyed.

'I was getting nervous as I came closer to her, because the

narrow road wouldn't let the two of us pass without touching each other.' His grin got wider.

'Touching each other!' I exclaimed. 'Did you touch her?'

'Wait. I was afraid of losing my balance and falling off the bike into the ditch, so I got off and stood on the edge of the road to let her through.'

'There was you and her with the bike in between?' I asked.

'No, I was between the bike and her,' he corrected me.

'You old dog,' I said, slapping his shoulder.

'Of course, my heart was pounding and my face musta been like a real red lychee. I felt like I needed air . . .'

'Normal feelings during sexual encounters.' Yi threw in a few goodies from his old days at the master's house.

'Do this part slowly, Sen,' Siang urged. Mo Gong and I stopped chewing the beans and our jaws hung slack as we waited.

'She turned to face me and our chests brushed lightly. It was . . . oh, how should I say it . . . a lively moment. I can still smell her faint fragrance and feel the touch of her chest. Feel this, my heart still pounds at the thought of her sinful body.' Sen grabbed my hand and let me feel his heart. It was kicking like a baby's foot.

'That moment seemed so long and sweet. I thought I was dying and I felt completely happy with this shitty life I've lived.' He closed his eyes and shook his head earnestly. 'Then, as I was admiring her from behind, she turned her head and gave me the sexiest smile. I felt my head explode. It was a heatwave. Those eyes pierced my heart. She knew I was looking at her and she didn't dislike it. No, no, not at all. Her smile told me she really liked it, or she woulda started yelling and calling me a hooligan.'

'She shoulda done so, anyway,' Mo Gong joked. Sen hit him with a fava bean.

'Real poetry!' I said dreamily. 'I can't believe you touched her chest. Anyone else would have fainted and dropped into the ditch.'

'I almost did,' Sen said.

'I think she was flirting with you. That's a good sign. She likes you,' Yi said.

'I think I should do something about it or I'll go crazy,' Sen said, all pumped. Then he paused, suddenly deflated. 'But I have no money, no brains, no job, no future. Some day I'll probably end up marrying a virgin from the mountains who walks like a duck and sounds like a man.'

'You're definitely not much to look at,' Siang joked. 'Your chance of getting her is like a frog in a deep well, hungry for a passing swan in the sky.'

Sen didn't think it was funny this time. His face turned pale as he said to the good-looking Siang, 'Fuck off. You think you're pretty? Just check that garlic nose in the mirror, and those swollen lips.'

'Okay, okay. Let our friends be the judge,' Siang challenged. 'Loser buys cigarettes for the next three days, deal?' It was always about betting and winning.

'I'm ashamed of you guys. What's this? You want us to judge your Ugly Contest?' Mo Gong said, disgusted. 'Forget it.'

'That ain't very nice of you, Siang, to say all that,' Yi said. 'He has his dream and he's happy when he dreams. It doesn't matter who he ends up with, he still can dream about Ms Huang, even lying next to another woman in bed. A man always dreams.' Yi sounded like an old man again.

'Right, the same way you dream about marrying your "Miss Yellow Stone", Siang,' Sen said. 'You think your chance is that good? I saw her brother bring those tall, muscular basketball players to their house. You don't think they have a better chance at getting her than you?' Siang's girl happened to be his next-door neighbour, a dentist's daughter by the name of Ping, meaning *lotus blossom*. Ping's whole family were beautiful. She recently inherited the title, 'Miss Yellow Stone', from her sister, who had married a college graduate, an engineer.

'Okay, leave my Ping out of it,' Siang said. 'I wish to say no more on the subject.'

'You shoulda stopped a long time ago,' Mo Gong said.

'Why don't you write to her?' I asked Sen, remembering what my elder sister had told me about her high school life. 'Everyone in the school has a locker, where they get letters and postcards sent to them.'

'Ha, ha, ha. Right, me writing a letter.' Sen laughed sarcastically at himself. 'I couldn't even remember the last time I touched a pen. I can't write a love letter. I don't know all those beautiful words and sayings.'

'I think our intellectual could help,' Siang said, grabbing my neck and shaking it fondly.

'No, I wouldn't know how either,' I protested. 'Besides, this is your girlfriend. I have no personal feelings for her.'

'Hey, that sounds like a great idea, Siang,' Sen said, warming to the idea. 'Have Da jot down something sweet. What an idea!'

Sen turned to me, smiling. 'C'mon, don't play hard to get. I know you're well read and can write a mean piece of prose. Just think of the love stories you used to tell us.'

'You gotta help your elder brother here, Da,' Yi said. 'The same way I'd repair your chair if it were broken, 'cause I'm a carpenter.'

'Okay, I'd love to help,' I said. 'Tell me what you want to say.'

'You go write something, then I'll see if it fits me.'

'Make sure you tell her that Sen would jump into the Dong Jing if his love goes unnoticed,' Mo Gong said.

We all laughed.

The following afternoon, everyone lay on Mo Gong's bed and listened quietly as I read aloud the letter I had spent the night composing.

Dear dear Huang:

I do not know where to begin or how to end.

I am an ignorant boy lost deeply in the placid pond of your love.

I am a silly man, tortured day and night by the fire of love, which only burns hotter each day. I want to whisper in your ear those tender words, which sometimes I find myself scared to utter: that I do love you.

Only the Dong Jing River knows my thirst for you and only the Ching Mountain sees my drying tears. If you were the shepherd girl in a meadow of green grass, I would willingly sit beside you like a timid lamb. Your eyes, which carry warmth and love, lay bare my soul. I have no place to hide except to confess on my knees that I love you, I do love you.

If only you know that I would jump down cliffs thousands of feet high for you, and I would travel to the corner of the world to look for you if you were at the last post of human civilization.

In case you ask me why I think you should return my love, I want to say honestly from my heart that I am only a poor, poor man with a rich, rich heart that is full of love for you only. I know for a girl as pure as you there is no precious stone big enough to win even a faint smile from you. Only a heart full of love genuine enough could win your heart.

My only qualification is a dream that contains only you and a strong body. I promise you that I would take good care of you, and use my two capable hands and strong knees to crawl along the rugged path of life, forever serving you as your obedient slave . . .

Yours,

SEN, with mountains of love

Nobody stirred. It was as if they had all fallen asleep.

After several minutes, Mo Gong sat up and said earnestly, 'Da, can I give you a kiss? I've never heard something so moving. It gave me chills.'

He leaned over to grab me, but I dodged and he almost fell off the bed.

'Well, I wish it was longer,' Siang said. 'You've gotta write one like that for me one of these days.'

'I think Sen is getting a hard-on,' Yi joked. 'He's quiet.'

Sen lay undisturbed by the statement.

'What do you think, Sen?' I asked.

'It's so good that she wouldn't ever believe it was from me,' Sen said finally.

'That's easy,' I said, relieved. 'What you need to do is to copy it in your own writing and she'll believe it's from you.'

'Da's right. Naturally you're gonna be missing a letter here and there. What'd be more convincing than that?' Mo Gong said, knowing what his buddy was capable of doing with a pen.

The same night, after everyone had left, I sat alone with Sen at Yi's. Sen copied the letter with difficulty in the dim candlelight. I could see the beads of sweat forming on his forehead. There were a lot of words that he misspelled unintentionally, but the letter still read smoothly and was strangely touching for the misspellings.

'How'd you learn to write such a mean letter at this young age? You have to have a pretty corrupt mind,' Sen said putting his pen down and stretching.

'It was taken from a few love letters that I read in novels. I just changed the name of the river and the mountain and that's it.'

'Thanks, Da. Out it goes in tomorrow's mail,' Sen said.

'Best of luck.'

'You know, Da?'

'What?'

'Someday she'll find out and will probably fall in love with you and marry you.'

'If that happens, she won't marry me,' I answered. 'She'll kill me.'

For the next few days, Sen was especially interested in the old mailman who rode his bicycle around town every morning. He heard nothing. He began to suspect that the letter had got lost or that the return address to Yi's workshop was such an obscure alley that the mailman didn't know it existed. We all were getting anxious. It seemed like a united effort by all of us. When Siang joked that Teacher Huang might have wiped his butt with the letter, we threw him to the floor and kicked him until he was reduced to tears.

One Sunday we finally took to the road in search of Sen's girl again. We smoked all the way to the high school, where we thought she might possibly be practising basketball with the rest of the school team. What a sight! As we leaned over the low wall, we saw a dozen tall, slender girls running around the dirt basketball court, stretching their arms and kicking their legs to the rhythm of a coach's whistle. Ms Huang was somewhere in the middle. Her gestures were especially supple, and her long hair was bound into a huge bun. For the first time we could see her long, elegant neck.

'Sen, I think you came at the right time. Check her legs out.' Mo Gong was drooling.

'What do you plan to do with her? Just stare?'

'Isn't that good enough?'

'I guess so, for the time being.'

Now she was bending forward stretching her back, her bottom to us. We couldn't conceal our excitement. What a lucky man that coach must have been. The back-stretching exercise lasted for a long time. Our five heads moved in unison to the movements of the warm-up.

'She looks really beautiful today,' Sen said absentmindedly. 'Think she got my letter?'

'Maybe,' I replied.

'There's no way of finding out,' Sen said.

'Perhaps we could try smoking, to give her a signal. She saw the smoke last time, that's why she stopped and gazed lovingly at you,' Mo Gong said.

'Hey, that's not a bad idea at all.'

I fished out a pack of Flying Horse, distributed it among us, and lit them all with a single match without burning my fingers.

Smoke rose up above our heads, thick and blue.

The girls were busy with their work-out. Ms Huang didn't turn her head our way, not once. We puffed harder and spat the smoke out at the same time.

No response.

'What are you boys doing here?' A deep male voice boomed from behind our backs, startling us all. As we turned, I saw the handsome head of the famous PE Teacher Huang, who, with a stroke of luck, could be our best friend's father-in-law. He stood there tall and trim, wearing a white sweatsuit, and eyed us reproachfully. Silently, we bunched together like a litter of frightened mice who had forgotten where their nests had been, then ran off for cover in all directions.

'Stop there. You, the tall one,' Teacher Huang shouted, pointing at Sen. 'Come back here.'

Sen kept running like the rest of us.

'I'm not going to bite you. Stop.'

We stopped, believing the authoritative voice of the man who had once held the gold cup for the proud province of Fujian.

'Come over here, you, the tall one. I recognize you,' he said again.

Sen bravely walked back to face the man like a prisoner about to receive the death penalty.

When they were facing each other, Sen stood a head shorter. I saw Teacher Huang put his hand in his pocket and take out an envelope, then bend over, and whisper in Sen's ear.

Sen nodded a few times, then took the envelope from him. They shook hands. He walked back, paler than I'd ever seen him.

Teacher Huang smiled briefly at us, frowned into the setting sun, and left.

We circled Sen like a hero surviving a bloody war, itching for a detailed report on the whispered message.

'What was all that about?'

'A gentleman's handshake on giving you money to go away?'

'He wants you to marry his daughter?'

'What did he say, something nice?'

We all speculated.

Sen kept walking and lit a cigarette. 'The letter was returned unopened,' he said. 'He said he would beat the crap outta me if I ever tried it again.'

'Aren't you mad?'

'Nah, at least he didn't treat me like shit. He was a gentleman.' And that was all Sen said for the rest of the day.

Ten

In the middle of the semester, a young teacher named Sing organized the yearly elementary school Ping-Pong match for the purpose of qualifying for the commune and eventually the county championship event. He was a decent guy with a head of salt-and-pepper hair. I had always admired him for his many talents – calligraphy, basketball, writing, and he could play all kinds of musical instruments.

Each time he passed me, he always greeted me readily. In fact, he was the only teacher who joked with me. One afternoon he came to my class and sat next to me with his arm over my shoulder. 'How would you like to participate in the school championship match? I know you're pretty good.'

'I'm not sure my political background would allow me to do so,' I said uncertainly.

'I'll take care of it. You just make sure to be there for the game.'

'Okay.' My heart leapt with joy.

As far as Ping-Pong was concerned, there was only one other boy who played as well as I. If I wasn't there to challenge him, he would take the title, hands down.

That evening, I borrowed my brother's bat and played three games in the match at the school cafeteria, a temporary game room. I spun and struck. Within two hours, I had defeated all the other players. The next night, with Sen, Siang, Mo Gong and Yi watching from the windows, I beat my enemy, Han, and another opponent to become the champion for our commune. When the results were announced the next day at the morning exercise break, the whole school turned and looked at me. After so many years, I felt once again as though I belonged there. Proudly, I waved my hands and bowed my head to their cheers.

The gratitude I felt for Teacher Sing was beyond words.

Representing our elementary school as the champion in Yellow Stone commune placed me as first seed to attend the county event. To me the county game was my Olympics. I felt proud and humbled at the same time.

Teacher Sing personally wrote a petition for me to take off one month from school for training at the high school, together with other players on our team. Friends watched with envy as, accompanied by my four friends, I carried my luggage and registered at the desk in front of the Yellow Stone High School.

Mo Gong took my luggage to my assigned bunk bed. Sen said that they would come to visit me every day and see me during my training breaks.

Mum wasn't too happy about it because of the absence from school, but I promised her that I would make up for that when I came back. She knew it was good for me to be representing our commune. It was an honour not many children of my background could enjoy.

The commune sent a chef to the high school kitchen just to cook for the two dozen young athletes. He was a beefy guy with a bright smile. He prepared three good meals a day and a snack at night if we had an evening session. There was always meat, fish, and all kinds of bread. Fresh fruit was available by the bucketful, and fruit drinks flowed freely. It was food heaven. At home, we always had dried yams every day and rarely had meat, so I ate as much as I could without appearing too greedy. It was like New Year's every day. I wished this training thing would go on for ever.

Occasionally, a representative from the commune would swing by and watch us train. They gave us political lectures on the importance of the games. Had those meetings been held after lunch, we all would have fallen asleep.

Sen and Mo Gong visited often, and I always gave them fruit to eat or to take home to Yi and Siang. They kept telling the other onlookers that I was their best friend. Once they got into a skirmish because a boy outside the window was bad-mouthing me and calling me a landlord's son. Mo Gong hit him on the nose, making it bleed profusely.

The head coach announced a two-day break before we got together again for final training and our trip to Putien. To my pals' delight, I packed up my things and headed home. I gave them some bread and boiled eggs from training camp, which they finished in five seconds.

'Before you go to the competition, we'd like to hold a swearing ceremony among us five at Mo Gong's tomorrow,' Sen said. 'What do you think?'

'You mean sort of like in ancient times, when the outlaws cut their fingers and let the blood drip into their wine and drank it together to become sworn brothers?' I asked excitedly.

'That's it,' Sen said. 'We've been talking about it since you left. Da, you like the idea of having us sworn like brothers?'

'And say something like, can't be born on the same day, but would like to die at the same moment.' Mo Gong quoted a phrase from a well-known classic about a bunch of outlaws hiding deep in the mountains, who became sworn brothers and fought the establishment.

'I'm in,' I said. 'What do we need to do?'

'Prepare a banquet with some hard liquor.'

'Here, I got five yuen from the training allowance.'

'That's great.'

The next day I went to Mo Gong's house, a two-storey place that was totally empty since his parents had taken off again to sell shoes in another county. Siang had bought two lively young ducks from the market with my five yuen and three pounds of pork from home. Yi came up with some vegetables and Sen ventured back home and had us sit under his kitchen window while he passed out some much-needed lard. Yi got the noodles and we all pitched in to buy the liquor and cigarettes.

During his apprenticeship days, Yi had learned to cook. He was the only one who knew anything about it. I had my usual job of washing the vegetables, picking over scallions, and cutting them to match the specification of the chef. Mo Gong chased the ducks in the backyard, causing the dirt and dust to fly, and Siang sharpened a knife, ready to behead them.

'Da, I want you to write some rules for us to go by,' Sen said, squatting next to me.

'Let me think about it,' I said.

When the food was finally brought to the table, along with the chopsticks, spoons, and plates, we couldn't help shaking our heads in surprise. The two ducks, well simmered with garlic, ginger, wine, and Yi's secret soy sauce recipe, lay lamely on a large plate with their skinny heads on one side. Next to them sat a deep pot with steaming pork shoulders, succulent and juicy. A king's feast was about to begin, and our stomachs growled in anticipation.

It seemed more like a normal, happy family meal than a swearing-in ceremony for a bunch of self-acclaimed outlaws. What civilization had done to us since the time of the kings and dynasties!

We sat in order of seniority – Sen, Mo Gong, Yi, Siang, and me – clockwise around a round wooden table. Sen opened the first bottle of liquor, a locally brewed rice wine that gave out a pungent fragrance of grain, and poured us each a tall glassful. Wearing a serious look in those famous cold eyes, Sen declaimed, 'Fate has brought us together. From now on we are brothers, not by blood, but by spirit.'

'What happened to our swearing and all?' Mo Gong asked.

'That was the ancient thing. There's no need for slitting open our fingers,' Sen said. 'But I asked Da to write out a few rules that we all should live by faithfully.'

'What happens if one of us doesn't follow the rules?'

'Here.' Sen pounded his big fist on the table. 'I'll take care of it.'

'What if it's you?'

'The second in command would take over and have me punished the same way. Okay, what's the rules, Da?' Sen asked.

I took out a piece of paper and read solemnly. 'No betrayal. No better friends outside than us. We suffer together, enjoy together. No jealousy. And we are all equal.'

'Does everyone agree?' Sen glanced at each of us intently.

We nodded.

'You all meant it, didn't you?' Sen shouted like an older brother.

We nodded again.

'This is serious. Anyone who can't live up to these rules, leave this place now,' he shouted. 'I don't want traitors in here.'

The drama seemed to work. Everyone was quiet and thoughtful. For the first time, we all realized that it wasn't just food, drinks, smoking, and having fun together. It was more than that now. We were bound by rules. The moment filled me with strength, courage, and emotion. I felt I had grown a few inches.

'Now, bottoms up,' Sen said, casting a long look at me in particular. 'Da, you gotta do it.'

'But I've never had anything this strong before,' I protested. 'Can I just have a few sips first?'

'This isn't strong, see.' Sen poured the whole thing down his throat. His face suddenly twisted into a fierce grimace. Then he turned red down to his neck. He opened his mouth as wide as he possibly could, waggled his tongue, fanning his mouth wildly gasping for air. After a long pause, when the liquor apparently had settled, Sen said, 'See, I did it.' His voice was raspy like sandpaper. We covered our mouths, trying not to laugh.

Then everyone did the same thing, clockwise.

When my turn came, I pinched my nose, closed my eyes, and downed the contents of the tall glass. Like I predicted, it burned all the way to wherever it went inside my body. I could picture the flow of liquor, a stream of hot liquid steel, burning every inch of me. The miracle of pure alcohol. I instantly felt dizzy.

'How does it feel? Here, have some soup,' Sen said, holding the spoon to my mouth. Yi and Mo Gong supported me, and Siang stuck a piece of duck inside my mouth to dispel the bad taste.

'Like fire.' I coughed a few times, swallowed the soup, and chewed on the duck. My head was throbbing and everything was dancing around me. The whole house seemed to be moving in circles.

'Now, brothers,' Sen said, 'it's time to eat.'

They dug into the duck. I went for a cigarette.

'Don't smoke now, it'll be like oil on fire, on top of liquor,' I heard the wise voice of Yi say. But I lit one nonetheless. It felt heavenly.

For the rest of the banquet, I sat there dazed, watching the others laugh, chat, joke, drink, and smoke. They saved some food for me before we all went to sleep for the rest of the day.

When I awoke in darkness, my head ached as if a brick had hit it, throbbing with waves of pain each time I turned it. I struck a match and lit a candle and saw my newly sworn brothers snoring like a litter of puppies, huddled in one another's warmth. Sen was drooling on Yi's face and Siang was holding an empty bottle, his legs over Mo Gong's shoulder. The food was almost untouched. I figured they hadn't lasted much longer than I had. I felt hungry and bet my friends would feel the same way. So I warmed up each dish and cleaned up the place, while putting on a kettle of fresh green tea to brew. Then I woke them up; they blinked like it was murder to be woken at this hour.

'Let's eat. Aren't you hungry?'

They nodded, scratching their heads and yawning.

'First, hot tea to wake you all up, brothers!' I smiled as I served the steaming tea.

'Ah! I feel a heck of a lot better now with the tea, Da,' Sen said.

'Thanks. I'm sorry the liquor knocked you out like that. I didn't know it was strong enough to catch fire off the match. We all got knocked out.'

'It was so strong my mouth still feels like rubber, and the food tastes like an old rag,' Siang said.

We couldn't help laughing at ourselves. But laughter wasn't the best thing at this moment. Each movement multiplied the pain attacking our heads and necks.

'I think they put fire powder in the liquor. It was a fake, Sen.' More laughter. More pain.

Two days later, I rode along with the rest of the Ping-Pong team in the back of the commune's tractor, as it drove through the narrow street of Yellow Stone with a red flag flying on top. Children ran after us and the whole street stopped to watch. I waved only twice, once when the tractor passed our house and I saw my parents were watching, and a second time to my brothers, who were sitting smoking high on a hill at the southern tip of town. Then the tractor picked up speed on the dirt road and we headed off to Putien.

I turned out to be a failure at the match. After beating four greenhorns in two gruelling days, I lost to a boy two years younger than I in a semifinal. He wasn't a much better player, but his dad and three coaches plus a team of twittering girlfriends were there with water, juice, and hot towels. His uniform was well-made, and a bright colour, fitting like a professional's, while mine was an old, ill-fitting faded pullover that smelled like old sweat even when I wasn't sweating.

They actually laughed when I hit the ball the first time, thinking that my stance was a little provincial, but I gave my partner one heck of a ride. They cheered when he scored. Soon I was losing concentration. I wished that my fast-talking coach was at least there to cheer me on against those fair-skinned city people, but he was busy coaching a more important game, the semifinal for our high school team. I lost in the fifth game, though it was a near thing. My coach later said he should have been with me, the other player had lost by a large margin. What he said made me feel somewhat better, but I wasn't really champion material. The champion title eventually went to a boy who had recently dropped out of a provincial team, a mighty force whom I watched with great admiration. His speed, style, and everything about him convinced me that I should pack my belongings, head back to that outlandish seaside farming town of ours, and never return.

In school, my popularity didn't exactly soar, but I could sense that people began to look at me differently. The morning I was back, Teacher Sing announced my 'victory'. I was the first elementary representative in our commune ever to be in a semifinal, a fact that even I hadn't known. The whole school, all but the principal, cheered.

By this time my dad had become quite an acupuncturist. Before Grandpa died, he had had a minor stroke, and Dad, unable to afford an acupuncturist for him, would study books on the ancient

112

art, staying up late every night, sometimes even taking the old classics on Chinese herbal medicine to bed with him. After Grandpa died, Dad began offering free services to some close friends and neighbours. Soon his reputation spread. He began to see patients in our home, and sometimes even made house calls.

Ar Duang was a local merchant's wife. She had skin as rough as a turtle's and spoke with a strong Fuzhou accent. Every morning at seven she would knock at our front door and bring us a bucket of fresh fruit, anything her husband was selling that day in the market. Her son had recently had a stroke and his right arm and leg were paralysed. Dad was treating him. Mum would fight with Ar Duang each time she arrived with the fresh produce. We couldn't accept it, Mum said, but she never won, for Ar Duang was a tough woman with a raspy voice who had seen the world and saw fit to pay back my dad in her own way. She would spin my tiny mum around, making her walk to the kitchen with the basket, then sit down for a cup of hot tea with Dad. I liked watching the blue of her cigarette smoke spiralling in the sun up to the ceiling. She would cross her legs like a man and tell Dad how many times she had had to wake up and clean or feed her son, because her daughter-in-law wouldn't do it.

'My daughter-in-law used up all his goodies and now she doesn't want to clean the shit,' she would complain. 'What do you say, Dr Chen? You give my son a little heavier doses of those needles for the next few days and see if he responds better.' She negotiated like a merchant, crossing and recrossing her legs.

'I can't do that. It's like MSG. You can only use it with the right portion or you will spoil everything.'

'MSG.' She would nod with understanding.

The conversation was always the same, even though the fruit she brought was different every day.

Another daily fixture every morning in Dad's living room was a thin, neatly dressed countrywoman named Tien. She wore an old-fashioned blouse buttoned down the side. She came from the village of Heng Tang, where her elderly mother was paralysed from the waist down. Dad wanted her to report her mother's condition to him whenever she stopped in Yellow Stone. Once a week, he would borrow a bike from Ar Duang and have me carry him on the back seat to visit Tien's mother.

Dad said that a generous patient would pay me for the sweaty ride, but at the least, I would earn some free food. And so, every week I would pedal, breathless under the scorching sun, along the narrow road to the village of Heng Tang, which lay hidden among persimmon trees about eight miles from Yellow Stone. Dad would sit in the back seat telling me what pressure points he would use for the next treatment. When the road became too hilly, Dad would jump down and push the bike with me. The patient's family usually treated me like my dad's driver. They graciously sat me in their living room and gave me a bowl of noodles or rice with meat piled on top. Sometimes, they would give me cigarettes and pour tea for me while I waited.

The patients' families welcomed Dad as though he were a saviour sent to them by the grace of Buddha. But his presence was always a double-edged sword to the patients themselves. They wanted to get better, but dreaded the prick of the needles. Sometimes Dad would ask me to observe a patient's reaction closely. He would insert needles and spin them to stimulate the dead nerves. At first, there would be nothing. The family watching would sigh and worry that the legs or the arms would never be active again. Then suddenly one day, the patient would scream, feeling the pain, and everyone would smile with relief.

Dad lived for moments like that. He would laugh and talk all the way home as I pedalled along the narrow road.

Under Dad's care, a few patients regained their basic ability to go to the bathroom and eat on their own. As his renown spread, a truck often drove him to treat patients in remote towns. Dad was shy about charging a fee, which would have made him an illegal practitioner. But people brought grain, rice, bananas, fish, shrimp, and all manner of food to repay him for his services. One of the patients even secured a temporary job at the county's canned-food factory for one of my sisters.

Dad was a happier person. Even though he still had to work at a few more labour camps, he was treated differently. At one camp near the Ching Mountain, Mon Hai, a burly man with an unsightly birthmark over his right eye, was the supervising cadre. One evening he sent for Dad to be brought to his cabin. Much to my father's surprise the cadre offered him a cigarette. Dad bowed humbly. Normally, the campers summoned to Mon Hai's cabin were there to be lectured or humiliated until midnight.

'I need a favour from you,' Mon Hai said in an unusually low voice, after first closing his door and window.

'Anything, sir, I am here to be reformed.'

'No, no, no, please sit down. I wanted you here for a different matter – shall I say, a private matter.' The Communist smiled, revealing his gold-capped front teeth. 'My dad fell ill last night and had a stroke. He is still in a coma and the doctor says he is paralysed.'

'I am sorry to hear that.'

'You know what the doctor also said?' Mon Hai lit a cigarette for my father.

'What did he say?'

'That you are the only one in this area who could cure him.'

'No, no, I'm an amateur. It is purely a hobby, that's all. I did try treatments on my own now-dead father, but I would not call myself a doctor or anything like that. You should really seek other help,' he mumbled nervously.

'Are you saying no to me?'

'I'm not, cadre. You don't understand,' Dad said.

'Then what is it?' Mon Hai asked. 'Money? That's no problem. My brother is the head of a fertilizer factory and he has loads of money.'

'No, it is not money.' Dad shook his head.

'I know what it is. You are afraid.'

Dad remained silent.

'It's totally understandable. I would be also if I were you, but please don't be. Just try to treat me as if I'm one of your regular patients.'

Yeah, right. Dad could still feel the pain inflicted on his back where Mon Hai had kicked him for slowing down at another camp site. Mon Hai's father sounded as if he was in a critical condition, and if anything happened to him, Dad would be blamed.

115

'I really wouldn't feel comfortable, cadre.'

'Look at me, doctor, I also have a heart.' He pulled open his shirt for emphasis. 'I apologize for what I have done to you.'

'No, no. There is no need for that.'

'I shouldn't have kicked you.' His eyes turned misty. 'I'm sorry. I will make it up to you.'

Dad was quiet, watching this bear of a man tearing his guts out. 'Even if I agree to take a look, I wouldn't be able to do so. We are not allowed to leave the camp site.'

'I'll take care of that.'

Dad was told to stay in his cabin the next morning while the rest of the campers rolled out of their beds and headed for the chilly mountains to dig some more hills and fill some more valleys. At nine o'clock, a biker came by and picked Dad up, carrying him to Mon Hai's house a few miles away.

It turned out to be a light stroke. Mon Hai's old man was only sixty-five and in good health. It took Dad about two months to bring him back to where he could walk with only a slight limp.

At the reform camp, Dad hardly had to touch his farming tools. He had been ordered to stay behind and write confessions, but in fact all he did was read his medical books and be taken to see the patient every day. He was allowed to come home for dinner after dark three times a week. The rest of the time he spent at the cadre's cabin, where Mon Hai would do his drinking and pour out his admiration for Dad. It was there that Dad learned that the good food, liquor, and cigarettes that Mon Hai shared with him all came from the campers, who bribed Mon Hai for lighter work and a guarantee that they would avoid punishment. In one of his drunken states, Mon Hai even revealed that he had occasionally slept with the young wife of a newly branded counter-revolutionary, a camper under his supervision. He further admitted that he slept with the wife at her request because she wanted to ensure that the poor young man would live to see his infant son.

Dad itched to inflict some pain on that son of a whore, and offered Mon Hai the use of his needles to cure his drinking addiction, but he refused.

116

One day Mon Hai was suddenly rushed back from the work site where he spent an hour a week on inspection. Two strong young men took turns carrying him on their backs.

'Chen, come here,' they said to my father. 'Mon Hai was hurt.' A rock had rolled down the side of the hill and landed on his waist, bruising him badly before bouncing off into a ditch.

'Doctor, I think I could use some of those needles you got there,' Mon said, looking up in pain from his bed.

'I think so, too,' Dad replied.

During the following weeks, Dad gave Mon Hai double the number of treatments necessary. He chose longer, thicker needles, and spun them harder, telling Mon that he would improve faster that way. Mon Hai would shake with fear as he watched Dad slowly prepare the needles, wiping them on an alcohol pad. He would squirm in anticipation of the pain until the needles were actually inserted under the skin, then his hysterical and terrifying screams could be heard for miles around.

Before each session Mon Hai begged for more, and during every session he cursed and rolled in agony. After each of my father's visits, he would shed tears of gratitude. His pain soon disappeared, and Gang Chen openly became known as 'the Doc' around camp.

Dad was discharged from labour camp early that year, and received a glorious report on how his anti-Communist way of thinking had improved. The report was signed in big letters by the now-healthy Mon Hai, who ironically was selected by the people of Yellow Stone as an outstanding member of the Communist party. His picture appeared on a wall outside the commune headquarters, only to be washed off a week later by a cold winter rain.

Eleven

Zhang Tie Shan, an army recruit from north China, wrote on his college exam paper a big zero, accompanied by the following words: 'To make revolution, one need not answer above questions.'

Instantly, he became a hero throughout China, epitomizing the true spirit of the Cultural Revolution. School was chaos. Everyone ran around mindlessly, doing nothing. Everyone wore red armbands bearing the words 'Little Guard'. Teachers could do almost nothing to remedy the situation for fear of being branded a stinking intellectual or a counter-revolutionary.

Our fifth-grade classes were made up of three categories: labour, politics, and self-study. We dug up the playground and turned it into vegetable plots so that young kids could labour under the scorching sun and have empty but healthy minds. We had to bring all the needed tools to water, weed, and harvest the vegetables, then sell them back to the teachers at a discount, using the money to buy more seeds and plant more vegetables.

In the political science classes, teachers read the newspaper to the students. When we were left to study on our own, the chairs became hurdles. We jumped them and counted the minutes until it was time to go home.

Every day after class, Dad read me classics that we had buried under the pigsty, and I learned to play the bamboo flute in the morning. Dad said a real scholar should know poetry, chess, calligraphy, and music. The flute was the cheapest thing to study. Dad bought me one from the local market. At sunrise every morning, I got up, pulled the skinny bamboo flute from under my pillow and tiptoed to the backyard and down the steps that led to the Dong Jing River. I'd wash my face with the refreshing water and hold in my shit because it gave me more power as I blew the flute. Each day, I broke the silence of the morning in Yellow Stone, standing by the river and playing innocent folk melodies. The sound bounced off the water, crossed the vast green fields, and ended in a lingering echo as it reached the mountains on the horizon. The occasional mooing from the buffaloes told me that at least someone was listening.

One day, Dad came back from a month's stay at a labour camp and rushed to the backyard where I was practising.

'Son, you play beautifully now,' he said, surprised. He gathered me into his arms and roughed me up excitedly. 'I hardly believed my ears as I walked along the fields. I could hear you a mile away from here.'

'Dad, do you really like it?' I asked.

'Like it? I love it. I think with a little tuning here and there, you're ready to perform in an amateur troupe somewhere and eventually graduate to a professional one.'

'Do you want me to be a professional?'

'Well, school is doing nothing now, not with that Zhang-something guy in fashion. It's wonderful that you have a skill. You have an edge over others.'

From then on I practised even harder – much to the annoyance of my family – and I began to hang around the rehearsal hall of our commune's performing group. In the evenings, I would invite my friends to come with me to the rehearsals at the commune. They went and clung to the windows for a glimpse of the young and pretty actresses and laughed their heads off when those pretty things teased each other and giggled in singsong voices. Yi always sat at the foot of the wall and smoked in silence.

There was an outstanding, arrogant flautist in the troupe from Putien City, who was paid to be the music director of the orchestra. He was a woodwind expert, and could even play the

French horn. Every morning he demanded at least five precious eggs. For lunch, half a chicken. And for dinner, lots of pork and another five eggs. He said playing the French horn and the flute used up all his energy, and he needed the nutrients. Hungry kids actually trooped by to sniff his French horn, which smelled like eggs.

I copied his techniques and replayed the music by ear. At Yi's, my friends would listen to my flute and smoke in silence. Do that one or this one again, they would say as they tried to hum along inexpertly. Yi loved a particular piece sung by a very attractive actress in the commune troupe, a young woman who had been selected from a faraway village. He requested it again and again until he could hum the tune when he was alone.

'You really like the actress, don't you, Yi?' Sen asked him one day when Yi was in the midst of his melody.

'Don't be silly,' Yi said, embarrassed. He kept his eyes on a doorframe he was planing.

'Something's going on here,' Sen whispered to me, but he let the subject drop.

One Sunday afternoon when we were smoking and drinking tea at Yi's, we heard a knock on the door. No one knocked on the door. Either you came in or you didn't.

Yi opened it.

At the doorway stood the actress with a red scarf around her neck and mouth, protecting her from the cold. We were rendered mute at the sight of this goddess. She looked more alluring up close. Her breasts were full and firm, her eyes big and full of life.

'Aren't you gonna ask me to come in?' she asked.

Yi stood aside, bowed humbly, and with a red face answered, 'Please, come in.'

'Hello, I've seen your friends before. Nice to meet you.' She was tall, curvy, poised, and filled with confidence. She smiled and her two sweet dimples deepened.

Who was she? Our hearts pounded. We were dying to know.

'Guys, let me introduce you to this lady,' said Yi, recovering a little from his redness. 'Fei is my master carpenter's daughter.'

The master's daughter! No wonder our poor little Yi couldn't stop talking about her. We had thought she was a thin, flat little country girl who smiled with yellow teeth. We had to pinch ourselves to make sure we weren't dreaming.

'I think we're going now,' Siang said, poking Mo Gong to move.

'Hey, you don't have to go on my account. I'm just visiting Yi. In fact, I'd like to invite you all to one of our shows when we're ready.' She radiated with life and energy. Our hearts ached.

'Here, I got these for you, brother Yi.' She opened a bag of broad, yellow tobacco leaves. 'I figured you could use them.'

'Those are the ones from the master's garden!' Yi's eyes lit up as he pulled a chair over for her. 'Since when did you become an actress?'

'I always liked to act, sing, and dance, but Dad would never allow it when he was alive. The whole feudalism thing. Now, I can do it.'

'I'm happy for you. I'm sorry I left your people and came back after master passed on suddenly,' Yi said.

'No, I'm sorry you had to leave.' Fei was blushing now, but she smiled to cover it. She looked at Yi with a touch of sisterly love.

Both became silent for a moment.

'Could you stay for dinner with Grandpa?' Yi asked. 'He'd love to see you when he's back.'

'No, I have to run. Everything at the commune is scheduled. We live by the clock. Tonight is the dress rehearsal and I can't be late, but I'll visit you again, brother.' She smiled at us warmly and took off the way she had come, the red scarf around her neck flying in the wind. Yi's eyes followed her until she disappeared at the end of the narrow street. For the first time, the little hut felt empty.

'I think we're talking at least engagement, Yi.' Sen broke the silence. 'Cigarettes?' He threw each of us a Flying Horse.

'Don't be silly,' Yi said, shaking his head.

'What's the matter?' Mo Gong said. 'I'd marry the girl tomorrow. She's the most' – he searched for words – 'delicious girl I've ever seen.'

'She's not the same girl any more,' Yi replied coolly.

'What do you mean?' Sen asked.

121

'She has a bright future as an actress. Maybe soon she'll be a professional at our county's performing troupe. The sons of party leaders will be flocking around her. I'm only a no-good carpenter.' He stretched his hands out and laughed. 'Feel them. She'd run away at my touch. In fact, I'd run away at my own touch, my hands are so fucking rough.'

'But she was promised to you by your dead master, her very own father,' I said.

'That was then, and now is now.' Yi was talking like an old man again. 'I respected her father, so I'll never embarrass her. It's sad enough that her dad passed away. I should help her, not trouble her.'

Two weeks later, Fei came again and dropped off five tickets to the theatre near the commune. Yi dressed up nicely in a new coat, asked us not to joke too much when we saw her. We sat through the show like five sullen adults and talked in an awkward, serious manner about the performance. Fei was a heart-stealer. She would soon be a big star. We could tell from the audience's reaction.

After the show, we waited outside as Yi went to say good-night to Fei. They took a long time.

When we got home, Yi brought out two bottles of liquor and said, 'I feel like drinking.' It wasn't a noisy celebration. We drank quietly, savouring the burning sensation and dull throbbing at the temples. Everyone felt good, but we refused to admit out loud that our hearts had been touched by an angel. Silently, we wished her success.

As my interest in music grew, I became fascinated with the violin. The first time I heard one, I was picking grains of rice from the muddy rice fields under a summer sun. The commune had set up a crackling loudspeaker at the edge of the fields and played a simple violin solo through it. The music was supposed to cheer the farmers up, and I fell head over heels in love with it. It was sensuous and tender, and caressed my soul in a way that no instrument had done before. I stood there holding the dripping rice, lost in the beauty of the music.

'Go to work,' a farmer's voice behind me urged. She was the

opposite of what a violin was. I bent down again and went on working, the melody resonating deep in my soul.

I wanted to learn that instrument, but how? For the next few days, I locked myself in my room and daydreamed. I thought of writing to a national newspaper, asking for a donation for a poor boy who didn't even know what a violin looked like. Maybe my letter would be published and someone would send me a violin.

'How's it going with the letter, dreamer?' Sen asked, seeing me with my head in my hands.

'Not good,' I said.

'Why don't you ask Yi to make one for you? Just go find a maple tree. I'll help file and chip it,' Sen said earnestly.

'Sen, that's a joke. I can't make an instrument. I make doors and chairs and tables. It's a western instrument. Americans play it,' Yi said.

I agonized for days over a piece of blank paper. It was harder than a love letter. I gave up the idea.

Dad started a campaign to find a used violin for me. Word spread among his friends and patients. One day, an old man with a long beard dropped off a bag and told Dad that it contained a peanut-shaped wooden box with a long neck.

'That sounds like a violin to me. Where did you get it?' Dad asked him.

'My son brought it back from the Navy. It used to have a case but his brother uses it as a pillow.'

Dad thanked him and offered to pay for it. The old man pointed at his leg and shook his head. 'I have to pay you, doc. You cured my pain down there.'

I was thrilled. The only problem was that there were no strings on the thing. Dad asked another friend to send some from Fuzhou. I waited day and night while Yi and I made a square box for the instrument. After a month, the strings finally came: thus the first violin was born in the town of Yellow Stone, many years before its destined time. Neighbours and friends marvelled at the strange instrument, shaking their heads. No one knew anything about it, much less how to play it.

Once again, Dad came through like a champ. This time he

123

contacted a young man named Soong, originally from the city of Putien. He was the son of a Christian dentist who had died in jail. The family had been labelled as counter-revolutionaries because of their dogged belief in God and had been sent to live in exile in a tiny village near Yellow Stone.

Dad had heard of him on one of his house visits to a patient who was a neighbour of Soong's and who had complained often about the strange, foreign music the young man played at night.

Having met with Soong, Dad reported that the young man had readily agreed to teach me the basics if I was willing to walk there every day during the summer vacation.

The fifth grade finished without the expected finals and report cards. Everyone graduated. But whether I was going to high school remained a mystery. Politics was in; grades were out. My fate stood undecided, wavering in the wind like a blade of grass along the Dong Jing River.

A violin, a straw hat, a pair of shorts, a cut-off shirt, and dirty bare feet. I was dressed for my first violin lesson in the village of Heng Tang. It would be an hour-long journey if I ran a little and didn't stop to play with the geese that swam by the Dong Jing.

The narrow dirt road shimmered under the summer sun, and my toughened feet curled on contact with the burning earth. I tiptoed in the patchy grass on the roadside and dipped my feet once in a while into the river's cool water. As they headed for the market, occasional bikers whistled by me, carrying tall piles of vegetables on their back seats. An old goose farmer waved to me as he smoked his bamboo pipe and dangled his feet over the river bank. He cast a bag of tiny, dried fish into the water, and hundreds of white geese glided in, chasing after the food with a vengeance.

As I passed a deserted temple, overgrown with weeds and wild sunflowers, my superstitious nature got the better of me. I stopped and looked over my shoulder. There wasn't a soul within half a mile except for a stray dog sniffing gingerly at a pile of manure along the roadside. I took out a Flying Horse cigarette, lit it, puffed on it a few times, then held it between my hands and pretended it was incense. I got on my knees, facing the torn-down entrance of the temple, closed my eyes, and rapidly murmured the words of prayer I'd learned from Mum. I begged for a bright future as a musician. I paused and puffed on the cigarette to keep it going, then begged for good health for the entire family.

I checked behind me again. It would have been quite embarrassing to be caught hitting one's head against the baking ground, here out in the middle of nowhere. Assured that no one was around, I gave the Buddha inside three deep kowtows.

Heng Tang was nestled at the foot of Hu Gong Mountain. When the sky was overcast, the village floated like a mirage among the clouds. When it rained, it totally disappeared. During the summer, it was hidden under the thick foliage of persimmon trees, but in spring the village blossomed like a wild garden.

I finally arrived at Mr Soong's dental office, located in an old temple at the edge of the village.

'Da, right?' Soong greeted me warmly, taking off his surgical mask. He had just finished with a teary-eyed young boy who was being comforted by his mum.

'Mr Soong. How did you know it was me?'

'The violin.' He smiled and revealed the whitest teeth I had ever seen. I supposed it came with the business. He shook my hand and invited me into his office. 'I like the wooden box. You made it?'

'A good friend made it,' I said, a little embarrassed about its primitive appearance.

'It looks sturdy.' He smiled with his teeth. I smiled back, hiding mine, regretting not brushing my teeth again before coming. I studied him as he washed his hands and hung up his white coat. He was in his twenties, fair-skinned and good-looking, with long hair that touched his collar. He wore a pair of tight, bell-bottom trousers and a silk shirt. A city dude to the bone.

'A barefooted violinist?' he said, smiling at me. 'Let's see what you've got there.'

I took out the violin and he plucked a few notes on it, adjusted the pegs, redid the bridge, tightened the bow, then cradled it between his neck and shoulder. He closed his eyes and a soothing melody flowed out of my instrument. His fingers ran quickly along the strings, up and down, and the bow jumped, making curt sounds. I was amazed at his skill and was falling in love with the music when he stopped suddenly. 'You got a great violin here.' He put it down carefully. 'Smoke?'

I shook my head.

'Want to be an artist?'

I nodded, not knowing where he was heading.

'Then take one.' He threw me a filtered cigarette and lit it for me with a lighter. I puffed on it and inhaled deeply. 'I'm no teacher. Don't call me *teacher* or anything, but I could use a friend like you.' He looked out of his small window, then at a pile of dentures lying on his messy desk. 'It's boring here. In fact, if you want to be a dentist, I can teach you that as well. I have plenty of time on my hands and all these teeth need to be filed to fit into patients' mouths.'

'I'll do the violin first,' I replied, 'but I can help with your work during my break.'

'No need, I was joking.'

It didn't take me long to like him.

The next few days I spent walking around his office, holding my violin between my shoulder and neck and practising bowing. It was a painful experience that made my neck swell and left my shoulder raw, but he kept saying I was making progress. He showed me pictures of stone busts of Beethoven and Mozart and told me stories about them, amazing stories.

When I hunched over a little, he asked me, 'Would you do that in front of an audience of a thousand people as you are giving your solo performance on the stage of a grand concert hall?' Of course not. I straightened up and never dipped my head again.

During my breaks, I would file the dentures with him and he would tell me about his family. They were all pious Christians, which made them a minority anywhere in Buddhist-dominated China. His father had been a famous dentist, who fought against the Communists for his Christian belief, was jailed, and died in prison four years later. His brothers and sisters, all talented musicians, were forced out of their mansion in the city of Putien and sent to the country just as he had been. His mother had come with him to Heng Tang. Their former mansion was divided up and used as the Red Guards' headquarters. They now lived in a two-room dirt hut with a leaky straw roof. It had originally been an animal pen and still smelled like one.

Soong had learned dentistry from his dad, and by the age of eighteen was an accomplished one. Communist leaders loved him. He was personally responsible for all the gold dentures in their mouths. An employee of the commune, he worked five days a week, four hours a day. The rest of the time he was a daydreaming artist.

His neighbours complained about the eerie western music he played on the violin and 'the bellows', an upright organ that hissed when he stepped on its pedals. Rocks and rotten fruit were thrown at his window, but it didn't stop him. He put a sound dampener on his violin and played on.

I practised constantly and was making fast progress, which Mum and Dad noticed with considerable pride. To thank Soong, Mum would sometimes ask me to bring fruit and meat to him, and Dad sent him cartons of cigarettes and liquor, gifts given him by his acupuncture patients. Soong would cook the food I brought and ask me to stay for dinner, then send me home on his bike in the evening. Sometimes, when his mother was visiting his brothers, I'd bring a lot of food and stay over for the weekend. There would be no violin lessons or any other music during those times. We would go hunting.

Summer attracted large flocks of the mountain birds called *woo yaa* to the hilly village. They were big birds with black-and-white feathers that made nests among the thick persimmon trees. Soong and I sneaked into the mountain at night. He carried a hunting gun and I carried a flashlight and a large cotton bag. As we went along the meandering road, he would stop and ask me to focus the light at a bird a few feet away. Then he would aim and fire. *Boom!* The bird would fall with a thud. They weighed over a half-pound each, and within two hours I would be begging him to stop as the bag got too heavy for me to carry. The last leg of our nightly hunting expedition involved his jumping into a vegetable garden and stealing all the necessary ingredients for the night's feast. Once at home, I would show him the liquor I brought, and we would drink it in his kitchen as we skinned the birds.

'Keep the heads on. They taste great sautéed with garlic, ginger, and wine,' he would say. I avoided them because I didn't fancy eating anything that stared back at you.

Soong the dentist became Soong the chef. He peeled off his shirt, and the skinned birds, their heads making them look still alive, became a huge, steaming dish laced with green vegetables. We would eat and talk until sunrise.

Near the end of the summer, Soong said, 'Da, there isn't much I can teach you any more. From here on, you have to practise and just figure it out for yourself. Besides, school is starting soon, right?'

'I'm not sure I'm going to high school.'

'What do you mean? Of course you're going. You're so young.'

'I haven't got my notice yet. Others already have.' I hung my head.

'Come on, young fellow. Don't feel bad, you could always come to learn dentistry with me. Kids are learning nothing in school now anyway.' He smiled. 'But I want you to come and visit me on weekends and I'll take you to Putien to meet some of the coolest young musicians in the city.'

'I promise.'

Finally I was issued a notice stating that after careful consideration by the commune education board, I would not be given the opportunity to pursue my schooling any further. Neither was I allowed to do so at other schools in another commune.

No reason given. No reason needed.

A patient of Dad's secretly told us that the board's reason was simple. My ancestors and family had had enough education; it was time we made do without more.

I felt sad and isolated again. Everyone in my school went on to high school, even the worst of the students. I couldn't go because my dad had gone to college, as had my grandpa. What kind of reasoning was that? Why did I have to carry the burden of my parents' generation?

I walked around gloomily and was vague about it when friends asked what class I was in. My close friends were behind me

128

totally. Yi offered to teach me carpentry, and Mo Gong said he would let his parents teach me the shoemaking business. Sen even suggested that we make wooden hives and raise some bees, collect the honey and sell it. High school was the last thing on their minds. They loved to have me around, not in school.

My eldest sister, Si, who by this time had grown to be a lovely lady with an eloquent mouth, took me to meet the high school administrators, trying to persuade them to take me in, the commune's decision notwithstanding. The junior high school was under a different jurisdiction and had in the past reversed some of the commune's rulings.

I would bring with me all the tools of my résumé: a Ping-Pong bat, my flute, violin, school grades, and scrolls of calligraphy. I often had to perform on the flute and especially on the violin on the spot to anyone who would listen. They had never seen the instrument before. They would applaud my performance, and I would feel used like a toy puppy, but the answer was always the same: great candidate, but *landlord* was a tough label to fight. I could have been on the school Ping-Pong team the next day, and they would have loved to have had me be the first violinist in the school orchestra, but sorry. The school authorities were friends of the commune education board. It would take much more than a good, even talented, student to move the mountains of bureaucracy.

Dad talked to my cousin Yan about sending me off to her remote school district on the island of Milon. She said she could try, but she was in an unfavourable position with the school authorities at the moment and in the long run it wouldn't be good for me.

Mum prayed day and night, promising three chickens and four piglets to Buddha if any high school accepted me. I promised a thousand kowtows on my own. And then, good news came in an unusual way. Dad's regular guest, the sugarcane farmer, casually mentioned that he had delivered some high-quality fresh canes to the high school last night because the all-mighty principal's ageing father had just had a stroke. The only thing he could eat was juice squeezed from the fresh sugarcane. The principal was upset and restless and didn't know what to do.

Dad ran into my room and interrupted my violin practice, a thing he had never done before, and said, 'Son, I think you will be going to school soon.'

'Why? That's wonderful!' I was so excited that I almost dropped my violin.

Dad told me about the principal's father and predicted that he would be consulted the next day at the latest. Dad's confidence was always his winning card. I believed him.

All day long, Mum was smiling and giggling and repeating, 'Buddha did it again.'

That evening at dinner, a young high school teacher came hurriedly to our house and wanted to meet Dad privately. Dad took him into our back room. Five minutes later, Dad emerged and said he was going to see the principal's father right away because the patient was still in a critical condition.

We smiled with perfect understanding. Just as he stepped out of the door, he excused himself from the young man for a moment and walked back to us. He bent over and gently whispered in my ear, 'I will hold my needles until the principal says yes.'

I nodded, feeling a rush of tears fill my eyes.

He came back late. The news was good. I would be in the fourth group in Grade One of junior high a month from now. The delay was due to the specific order from the commune that I was not to be admitted under any condition. They would sneak me in after all the hubbub died down. I thanked Dad and then crawled quietly to the attic, got on my knees, and kowtowed a whopping thousand and five times. Five extra were done to make up for any possible miscalculation in the hasty up-and-down motions.

I dragged my aching body to bed that night, and I lay there with my eyes open, too thrilled to feel sleepy. A high school badge, calculus, English, the school team, and the orchestra. And no more snakes like Quei, Wang, and Han.

Junior high, the only one for several counties, was ten times the size of my elementary school. The possibilities beckoned to me. Suddenly the nightmare of elementary school was over.

Twelve

'You're the guy who plays the violin, I heard.'

'Yeah, what do you want?' I looked up from a stack of new textbooks to see a well-dressed fellow sauntering up to me. His clothes were neatly layered from the inside out. He wore shoes and socks with brightly coloured patterns, a rarity among Yellow Stone boys. He was flanked by a couple of shorter fellows with toothy grins.

'Nothing, nothing, just a casual visit.' He stuck out his hand. As the sleeve rode up, a gold watch glistened in the morning sun that filtered through the window of our classroom. 'Name is I-Fei. Do you care for a cigarette during the break?'

'Sure, I-Fei.'

'You could call him "Watch" if you like to.' One of his followers, a shorter guy commented, laughing.

I-Fei hit the guy's head with his elbow and kicked his behind.

'I'm sorry, I'm sorry.' The kid said while making a funny face at me.

Another one of those, I thought to myself.

During the whole hour of English, nothing sank in. I had missed an entire month of class. The grammar and phonetics sounded wacko. My attention kept turning to the fellow who had just introduced himself to me, I-Fei. I kept forgetting his name. He spent the first fifteen minutes of the hour spitting on his watch and polishing it carefully. He kept winding and rewinding it again

131

and again. Then he positioned the face of the watch to reflect the morning sun right into another boy's eyes.

The English teacher didn't like what he saw. He asked I-Fei to stand up and read some simple sentences. I-Fei stumbled along, making the English language sound like some sort of Chinese local dialect. The whole class roared with laughter, especially the tall girl with a plump bosom who was sitting in a back seat. She laughed so hard she had to cover her face with her hands. I could see that I-Fei was a popular man on campus. The teacher failed to embarrass him, the attention evidently only made him feel glorified.

I-Fei whistled at me when the class was over and tilted his head, asking me to follow him, then effortlessly threw himself out of the paneless window. His two followers jumped through after him like two monkeys. Why couldn't they use the door? I thought, while closing my books, and leaving them in my desk drawer. I-Fei was winking at me from outside, so I climbed out of the window as well.

It was a smoking picnic. A line of young junior high boys sat along the wall, puffing away like small smokestacks. The ones without cigarettes were chasing others who had them, so that they could get a puff to quench their addiction during the short break. I-Fei pulled out a full pack of my favourite brand, Flying Horse, and let me pick one out for myself.

'Take a bunch, Da.'

I looked at him and shook my head.

'Friends share everything.' He stared at me, testing.

'They sure do.' I grabbed a few, thinking of my own friends awaiting me at Yi's. One of I-Fei's followers jumped in and grabbed one from the pack. He slapped the guy's wrist and kicked him again. 'Get lost, you beggar,' he shouted.

Slowly I pulled out an unopened pack of Flying Horse from my inside pocket and said, 'Allow me to return the favour, my friend. If you want friendship, smoke one of mine.'

I-Fei's face broke into a smile and he slapped my shoulder. He pulled one from my pack and lit it with a red lighter, after first lighting mine.

He became my best friend in class. His pomposity came from his family's background. His father was the mayor of Han Jian, the second largest town in Putien. His mother was the president of the women's federation at a government dried goods manufacturing factory. Both were seasoned Communist cadres. His parents had become caught up with their lives and had deposited him at his aunt's, thus making him a big fish in a small pond. He lived on a fabulous monthly stipend and rode a brand-new bicycle to school once in a while, just to show it off to the girls. The teachers tolerated him because his mother controlled the supply of sugar and cooking oil in the county. She was all sugar and oil. Poorly paid, some teachers often could be seen begging I-Fei for oil and sugar coupons, which would allow them to buy those rare commodities that were unobtainable on their pathetic rations.

On his first day at Yellow Stone High School, the principal was seen lighting a cigarette for I-Fei in his office, welcoming the VIP student on board. It still remained his favourite joke about the school. According to him, all the other teachers should be manicuring his – I-Fei's – nails.

He searched out interesting fellows in school and made alliances with them. Even the cool guys in senior high greeted him like an old pal. He dragged me around wherever he went and introduced me as his buddy. We were the same height and build; soon we were wearing the same hairstyle. I even asked Mum for socks to wear, a giant step for someone who had only operated in bare feet before.

Mum kept saying I should be a straight A student and try to impress the teachers, but high school was one big mess. I had visited our English teacher once after class to discuss how to make up the lost lessons. He was about sixty-five and a heavy smoker. I told him I was interested in the subject. He took out an ugly, burned pipe, stuffed it with a pinch of tobacco and lit it. *Puff, puff.* The tobacco sizzled. He suddenly started a coughing spasm. Choking, his face turned red and his chest whistled like leaky bellows. I thought he was going to drop to the floor, but he held on to the desk.

'What's your name?' He had a raspy voice. His eyes stared at me like dead oysters.

'Chen Da,' I said. 'Should I call the school nurse for you?'

He shook his head. *Puff, puff.* 'Chronic. This is no good.' He looked at the pipe.

You bet it's no good. It'll kill you, maybe it already has, I thought. I became aware of the pack of Flying Horse I carried in my back pocket. Got to quit.

'What class are you in?'

'The fourth, first grade.' He had seen me three times.

'You want to make up the lessons?'

'Yes, please.'

'I have a sick wife. Sicker than I am.'

Can't be lung problems, I thought.

'Lung cancer.'

'Sorry to hear that.'

'There's more.' *Puff, puff.* I could hear the bitter smoke infiltrating his lungs with bubbling pus. Not a pretty sound, all that wheezing.

'My son is in jail.' His oyster eyes fixed on mine. 'Stealing.'

'Sorry.'

'And my daughter.'

I had had enough. I would have left, had it not been for those oyster eyes begging for an audience.

'She's still in elementary school.'

'That sounds good.'

His oyster eyes widened. 'She's sixteen.'

I was out of there in a second. The teacher needed more help than I did.

In physics class, I-Fei casually walked out, had a smoke, and came back. The teacher stared at him, but said nothing.

'They allow you to do that here?' I asked him after school.

'They can't stop you. You could tell them science corrupts you and makes you bourgeois and they can't say anything. If they do, they better be careful what they say.'

'You mean the students could control the teachers?'

'I guess you could say so. The other day my friends in senior high booted the teacher out of his classroom. In the end, the teacher had to apologize to the students.'

No wonder the teachers hadn't been showing any interest in my problems.

By midterm, I was on the school Ping-Pong team and also in the school band. Three days a week I practised Ping-Pong after school, and the rest of the week, I played the flute and stumbled along on my violin, preparing for the rehearsal of a grand, seven-act play.

Schoolmates were amazed by my violin. They called it 'the shoulder thing'. There were always eager faces pasted at the window-panes of the rehearsal hall. Now they had one more thing to look at besides the alluring faces of the school's stars.

Soon I was a recognizable face in a school of two thousand students. I-Fei referred to me as 'that violin fellow' to all his friends. But one day he mentioned that we weren't spending time together any more and life had got pretty boring for him.

'Why don't you try out as an actor? You're a good-looking guy,' I said to I-Fei.

'I can't act. It's embarrassing.'

'I have another idea,' I said. 'I was going through the school storage room and I noticed that there's a good button accordion lying around collecting dust. Maybe you could learn how to push a few of those buttons, and then you'd be in. They'd love to have more western instruments in the band. How do you think I got in?'

He looked at his feet and kicked the dirt. 'I don't know anything about music.' An embarrassing confession.

'We'll get someone to teach you. I bet by the time rehearsal is over you'll be able to play along in the background.'

He was excited. 'But who is going to teach me?'

'I have an idea.'

I convinced Mr Ma, the art teacher in charge of the school production, and fetched the dusty accordion for I-Fei that afternoon. I-Fei spent the whole evening polishing it until it shone like a sword.

The following day, he rode his bike with the accordion strapped on to the back seat, impatiently circling the school, waiting for me to be finished with rehearsal. As soon as I was done, we headed for Heng Tang, riding double.

Soong was happy to see us. His mum was away again.

'Another crash course,' he said. 'I do happen to know a thing or two about the instrument, not as well as I know the violin though.'

He showed I-Fei the basics. Soon I-Fei was cranking awkwardly along the loose buttons.

On our way home after the first lesson, I-Fei acted like a gambler who had just won big. 'I really like Teacher Soong.'

'He's a good guy.'

'I'm going to learn real fast like him. There must be something I can do to pay him back.'

'Find him a wife?'

'Just oil or sugar. I am sure he could use them as well.' Both were precious.

'Is there anything else?'

'I don't think so. I'll see.'

Two weeks later, I-Fei joined the band. He sat behind me in the twenty-piece group, unsure of the keys or the scores, but smart enough to start playing late and end early, never getting caught hitting the wrong buttons. From a distance, his gestures looked fluent and up to speed. Near him, all I could hear was a puffing sound from a leaky box, not unlike the lungs of the English teacher. Each day before the rehearsal session, I taught him the scores of the day. He would hum them over and over again, beating them to death. It was as if he had found his calling.

I was proud of him and very happy to have him around. He felt good being included in the in crowd.

'Did you hear that?' I-Fei asked me angrily one day as we walked into the rehearsal room.

'What?' I asked.

'There was a guy out there, bad-mouthing you, calling you a landlord's son, and this and that.' I-Fei's face was burning.

'Who was it?'

136

'A skinny little rat from group one called Han or something. Aren't you going to do anything about it?' He put his hands on his waist.

'Listen, he was my old enemy from elementary school.'

'And you let him run through you like that?'

'I'll take care of him later.'

'Not later.' He stared at me. 'Now.'

'I don't want to make a scene here.'

'I'll make a scene. Let's go.'

'Not now. You don't understand.'

'I do understand. They used to pick on you, but not in here.'

He marched me out of the room and we went towards a small crowd.

'You stay cool, okay,' I-Fei said in a hushed voice, 'and do as I say.'

'What are you going to do?' The fear of getting kicked out of school washed over me.

He didn't answer. I saw him walk straight to Han, who stopped laughing and turned to face I-Fei.

'You've been cursing me behind my back, you son of a whore,' I-Fei shouted, spitting at Han and waving his fists.

'I wasn't talking about you,' Han said. 'I was talking about him.' He pointed at me.

'That's not true, I heard you do it.' He moved in closer, his eyes were popping. He started to push Han. Han pushed back.

'Come on, Da,' I-Fei yelled. 'Now the rat confessed he has been cursing both of us. How dare you!'

My blood rushed to my head. The old pain began to come back. I was shaking and trembling.

'Come on, Da!'

Suddenly I turned fearless and hit Han right in the temple with my fist. Han stumbled back a few steps. I-Fei ducked down and swung his right foot against Han's unsteady legs. Han fell on to the dirt ground. A cheer went up among the crowd.

My legs flew and I started kicking him in his chest and groin. He screamed. I-Fei pinned his head down. Then I jumped on him and hit him till I was in tears and my arms were exhausted. We let go

137

of him. Han crawled to his feet like a dog hit by a truck and limped away, mud, sweat, and tears covering his face.

'Why are you crying?' I-Fei asked, puzzled.

'Happy.' I wiped my face. 'Thanks.'

'He would never dare look you in the face from now on.'

That evening, Mr Ma took us into his office and severely criticized us. I said it was my fault, I-Fei said it was his. Mr Ma said if it were not for the upcoming dress rehearsal of the revolutionary drama, we would all be fired from the production. We tried to suppress our laughter as we left the office.

Our show was ready by the New Year. For that period, we had already got fifteen bookings, mainly from the small villages under the Yellow Stone commune. Our play was about how a female high school student, at first a bookworm, was helped by the Red Guards to join the revolutionary camp. She became a Red Guard and denounced her past affiliation with a counter-revolutionary who was trying to corrupt her young mind with intellectual studies. The total cast was about fifty people, including teachers. It was not much of a play, but to a village where there might be a movie once a year, any form of entertainment was reason to celebrate, especially when it coincided with the New Year.

A few days before the New Year, we were invited to perform in the village of Ding Zhuang, where my distant cousin Wen Qui lived, and where I had hidden myself earlier. Now it was time for a happy reunion.

In the morning, the village sent tractors to pick us up. We sang all the way there, crowded into the back. When we arrived, small children chased us with interest. 'The music men are here!' they shouted.

The band's job when we got to each destination was to hang all the curtains, layers of them, and set up all the props. Ding Zhuang had an outdoor dirt platform facing a large square. A few bamboo poles were erected at the four corners. I-Fei and I climbed up the poles and tied the curtains to them while others carried the heavy props to the back of the stage and passed the curtains to us. Teachers shouted at us as we rocked on the tips of the poles for fun. Then we helped the electricians set up the spotlights.

Out in the dirt yard, villagers had long since claimed their spots with their own chairs, camping out since the day before. These kids hadn't had such fun for a long time. At the village headquarters, where all of us would be staying for the night, a large kitchen was preparing a banquet for us.

'Three big fat pigs and lots of other food,' the chief of the village said proudly. 'You will have plenty to eat.' He passed out cigarettes on a tray to everyone, including the students. Mr Ma stared at us like a disapproving parent and snatched them all back.

That afternoon, I visited my cousin Wen Qui, bringing along my violin.

'Welcome, welcome. I didn't expect to see you.' Wen looked a few years older and now had an unruly moustache. 'All I knew was that you were in high school.' He was beaming with joy. His wife patted my shoulders lovingly.

'I am in high school and I'm playing the violin now.'

'Just like your dad. That's very good. Here, play something for us.'

I played a simple melody and they listened quietly.

'I can see you are surviving well, on the school propaganda team and all. It makes me think of the old days, when you were hiding here,' my cousin said sentimentally.

His wife's eyes were misty, but she smiled and held my hands in hers.

'How is school?'

'Well, no one is serious about school nowadays. That's why I'm doing this.' I plucked a few notes and put the violin away.

'But it's difficult to make a living doing that, unless you're very talented.'

I was quiet.

'It's fun, singing and dancing and a lot of good food – and probably lots of smoking. I've done all that before.' Wen Qui looked at his wife, who smiled back. 'But you should try to study as much as possible in school.'

'What's the use?'

'What's the use? Knowledge. Nobody can take that away from you. Times will change, then you'll be sorry,' he said.

I stayed quiet. I came here expecting to talk about my exciting winter schedule with my favourite couple, discussing my music and friends. He had just dumped a bucket of cold water on my head.

'He mentions this because we care for you,' his wife added gently. 'You're a really smart kid. Don't waste your talent.'

'It's wonderful to have a hobby, but go back and study hard. You will thank me when you grow up.'

In the audience that evening, I didn't see Wen or his wife. Like he said, he had done it all and seen it all in his youth. I believed him, and I loved them both.

That night after the banquet, I-Fei and I took a walk along a dark dirt road.

'What are you going to do when you grow up?' I asked.

'Not sure yet,' I-Fei said. 'I could work for my mum and be an oil and sugar man. But Dad wants me to be a driver.'

'Why?'

'You make the most money, only second to being a butcher.' Under-the-table money.

'How about going to college?'

'I don't want to be a stinking intellectual. I'm from a revolutionary family. What do you want to be?'

'A violin soloist, performing before thousands of fans in a great concert hall. I want to travel by plane, wear good suits and ties, and have female fans fainting at my feet.'

I-Fei couldn't stop laughing. I hit his back with my fist and he stopped. But I agreed with him, it was a ridiculous dream.

'That I couldn't help you with,' he said earnestly. 'If you want to be a teacher or something, my dad might be able to help get you a job.'

'I don't need your help. I'll study hard and make it on my own.'

'Study? Are you crazy?'

I nodded.

He offered me a cigarette. For the first time, I refused.

'What's the matter with you?'

'Nothing. Just don't feel like one.'

He lit one for himself. I took it out of his mouth and threw it away. He tried to hit me but I was already a few steps beyond him. We ran back to the headquarters. All the way, I felt the eyes of Wen and his wife staring at me, smiling and hoping.

Thirteen

On the ninth day of the ninth month in 1976, Chairman Mao died like an ordinary man. Superstitious farmers said nine was the number of an emperor, and heaven had intended that he die like an emperor. It could have been a coincidence, but the sun, covered by clouds, didn't shine over Yellow Stone for ten days following his death. Rumour had it that it was mourning the loss of a great leader, but Dad thought the sky was upset because Mao hadn't died earlier. But a leader, no matter how rotten, was almost a supernatural figure. Confucianism had taught people to be obedient to the emperor unconditionally. Mao's rule had re-inforced such a tradition. For days after his death, people gathered in knots, in the fields, under the trees, whispering quietly and mysteriously as though a disaster were about to befall the whole nation.

Mum and Dad told me to be especially careful about what I said. We, the enemy of Mao, should not appear to be gleeful about the news. The leaders of the commune would thrash every one of us before the system could change. We could be easy targets for their wrath in the mourning. There might be martial law, even civil war, Dad cautioned.

Leaders and cadres of Yellow Stone commune held long meetings, during which some were said to have cried until they collapsed. There was a sense that they had lived their golden days and that what might be ahead was totally unknown.

Everyone in the street wore a black band on his right arm. Day and night, the gloomy and weeping sounds of Mao's funeral music haunted every dusty corner of Yellow Stone, transmitted through temporary loudspeakers. It never stopped.

Superstitious farmers stirred up all kinds of eerie stories that I had never heard before. They said Mao was a devilish son from heaven who got away and wreaked havoc on this earth and now would be punished for the next nine lives. No wonder he had no offspring. People even claimed to have heard laughter at night from the old site of Buddhist temples, temples that had been toppled down by Mao's revolutionaries. For the first time in my life, I heard people talk about ghosts as though they were a part of our lives, only living when we were all sleeping. Only the insomniacs got to hear and see what the ghosts had to say.

But Buddha wasn't the only one laughing. I saw the uncontrollable joy in Mum's and Dad's eyes. Long after we kids went to sleep, they could be heard whispering and laughing in the dark. Once, I overheard them talking about our lost land and houses behind the closed door of their bedroom. When they sensed my hesitant footsteps outside, Dad slowly opened the door and winked at me, asking me to go away.

Mao's funeral was held nationwide. People of Yellow Stone gathered in long columns in a public square, thousands of them, wearing only black and white.

As though the rift between the Red families and the landlords' families were widened by the death of Mao, I was told by the school authorities not to attend the ceremony. Landlords' families were not invited. I was saddened, humiliated, confused. I thought I was slowly blending into the system after changing schools. Now they told me I couldn't go and mourn the most forbidding leader, the only leader, I knew. In my heart, there was no other leader who mattered as much to me, regardless of how good or bad he was. I had been told not to analyse him because he was wiser, no, the wisest. I was to follow him and love him with all my heart. As a young boy, I had once shouted the slogan 'Long Live Chairman Mao!' so many times that by the next day I had lost my voice. Even though my parents' generation hated him, I had embraced him in my own way. I didn't know any better. A cult mentality had already been forged on me, and it hurt me deeply to be separated from such an event. I wanted to say goodbye to him, the dead Chairman Mao, but I didn't even have a black armband.

I stayed at home while the crowd marched in the street, heading for the square. Dad said there was nothing to it and that even if he had been paid to attend such an event, he wouldn't go. Such a bore, he said. The fat guy should have been dead a long time ago. Mum quickly asked him to stop. He smirked to himself. Then he brewed himself a large pot of red tea, made himself a fat tobacco roll, and stretched out in his comfortable rocking chair with an old medical book, his favourite spare-time activity. He was a happy man.

Ten minutes before the funeral, one of Dad's patients stopped by our house on his way to the ceremony and Dad treated him to some tea.

'I'm really not up to standing for such a long time in the square,' he said. 'My feet will be killing me.' He looked at me, a picture of gloom and sadness, and said, 'Young man, you can have my black band and go stand in my spot.'

I bounced out of my seat, grabbed his band, and ran as quickly as I could to the square, which was guarded by armed militiamen wearing serious looks. Sneaking into the entrance with my head down, I felt like a thief as I tried to avoid familiar faces.

I waded through columns of people, surprised that some of them were actually smoking and joking with each other while waiting for the massive funeral to begin. When I finally located the man's villagers and joined them at the edge of the dirt square, a couple of farmers were sitting on the grass, taking a nap. There were crying children and toothless old people among them. I was quietly moved by their devotion until a man napping next to me said that his brigade would count their participation as a day's work in the field and pay by the head, including children.

Dad was right. The ceremony was long and boring. The life story of Mao, the long list of his titles, dirgelike music, and silence. They said at that moment the whole country was silent, even the most important machines were turned off. The trains stopped. In my mind, the whole country was silent and sad, except my dad. I could imagine him blowing on the steam of his hot tea before he sipped and spitting loose tobacco leaves out of his mouth after each drag, while he dangled his feet from his chair. I smiled, unable to stop thinking about him.

One day, some time later, on my way home from school, I saw a large crowd gathered at the market square. A young man with a large brush was splashing characters on a white wall that read, DOWN WITH THE GANG OF FOUR!

Who were the Gang of Four?

I stood closer at the edge of the crowd, watching. The young man wrote the names one after another, to the total surprise of all.

JIANG CHIN, FORMERLY KNOWN AS MADAM MAO, YIAO, ZHANG, AND WANG.

It couldn't be. How could Mao's wife be down while Mao's bones were still warm? Mao's wife had been running the country since Mao had been sick. Someone was taking over the government, I thought with alarm. Maybe there would be a war, like Dad said. I rushed home and breathlessly told Dad the news.

'Are you sure?' he asked. 'They could throw you in jail if you spread untrue rumours.'

I told him I didn't make it up. He grabbed Mum and closed the door behind them. I could hear them whispering and laughing again.

That evening the bikers, who spent their days carrying passengers back and forth between the city of Putien and Yellow Stone for thirty fens each trip, confirmed the breaking news. They said people were painting the names of the Gang of Four on the cement streets in Putien and then crossing them out. Some even made effigies and burned them. At nine o'clock that night, through a crackling radio system, there was a special announcement from the central government confirming the downfall of the Gang, which had consisted of some leading figures in Mao's cabinet.

Soon, we heard that the party chief of Putien County had been arrested and put in jail and that another group of leaders was taking over. Two days later, the other cadres disappeared into the mountains. During the next several months, massive executions of former leaders followed. Among those executed was the arrogant Putien police chief. They shot him in the head and gave his son a life sentence for corruption, rape, and embezzlement.

On my way back from school one day, I saw a large crowd standing outside the house belonging to the party chief of Yellow Stone commune. You could hear a boy sobbing amid the chatter. I stopped, jumped on a vegetable peddler's stool, and strained to see what was happening. Two cops were brushing glue on the front door of the house and pasting white paper over it. They were sealing the house, as they had done to those of the landlords and counter-revolutionaries just a few years ago. And the chief's son was wiping his eyes with his sleeves, standing obediently by a bicycle packed with his belongings.

I asked an old man standing next to me what was going on. He said that they had gone to arrest the chief today, only to find that he had escaped early this morning, leaving his son behind. And now they were sealing his house and sending his son away to his grandpa, who lived in the mountains.

Well, I thought to myself, the chief, the formidable chief, was now a criminal fugitive and he had abandoned his son. I still remembered the boy who had spat at me in the school hallway and plotted with my teacher, La Shan, to kick me out of school in third grade. I don't think he ever thought this would happen to him. I thought about La Shan, secretly hoping that he might end up being hunted like the party chief, with whom he had tried so hard to ingratiate himself.

Dad wasn't surprised to hear the news. He said that soon we would be able to do what others could do – like going to school and finding a job. I nodded in disbelief as Dad kept saying, 'Son, you could be the lucky one.'

At night I dreamed about becoming a real artist, performing before thousands of people in a cavernous concert hall. During the day, I rehearsed with my schoolmates for another lengthy show that would celebrate the downfall of the Gang of Four.

This time, Mr Ma, the school drama teacher, even cast I-Fei and me in the play. I was to take the part of the former cultural minister, Yiao, and I-Fei was to play Madam Mao, two of the Gang of Four. We all wore masks with an opening at the mouth. We went to school in the morning and took to the road in the afternoon to do the show for villagers miles away, often coming back at midnight. We were carried around in narrow boats along the rivers to get to the villages near water, and the mountainous communes would send their noisy tractors to haul us back and forth. For each show, I would pad my stomach to appear fat, and I wore a pair of shiny leather shoes two sizes too big. My part was not much of a speaking role. It was I-Fei's role that brought laughter from the audience each time he appeared. He wore a long wig, a tight red dress, high heels, and did an amazing catlike walk, twisting his tiny waist and narrow hips. He would curl his little finger as he held a cigarette and push his boobs up once in a while, whenever the sponges inside his dress dropped too low. He spoke in a high-pitched, rather raspy voice. Older schoolmates grabbed his bottom behind the curtain – he looked like a really attractive, mature woman.

He enjoyed the role so much that he began to walk and talk like Madam Mao. When I asked him how he was able to do such a good female imitation, he said that as a young boy he used to dress up in his mother's clothes and shoes and copy her walk. Locked in the house for hours, he would do this while she was away doing her revolutionary work as the president of the women's federation.

In school, I was getting by with the help of others. I had become everything I was not in elementary school, popular with friends, with nobody picking on me. But teachers looked at me as if I didn't belong there. I was behind in all the subjects. They didn't try to help me. They generally left me alone, and I was forgotten. They thought I was the rotten type that they had to cut off, so they never inquired about my homework and never asked me questions in class. They knew I hadn't prepared for it. I was always with I-Fei, leaving early to rehearsals or coming back late from them. It was a wonderful feeling for a while, because now I had finally become what I had wished to be and could not be in elementary school. There were no enemies chasing me at every corner, concocting dirty tricks behind my back every day. I was respected and had a lot of friends, significant friends. I was my own master. I did not have to fear, worry, or fight. I felt safe and anchored.

But soon I was feeling empty about school. I used to love studying, and had known the joy of being at the top of the class. I knew about basking in affirming smiles from the teachers, people my family had taught me to respect. Though I was having a good time, I felt as if I were violating something special.

In class, serious teachers began to talk about the possibility of restoring our country's college system. During the Cultural Revolution, all colleges were either closed, or they enrolled only a small number of students from politically correct families through a corrupt system of selection. The teachers would end their speeches by saying that even the musicians had to pass other tests to go to art school. They would cast a look my way.

The more they talked about college, the more I was determined that I wanted to be an artist, because I was doing so badly in school. I was sure I was beyond hope, academically speaking. I had to do something with my life.

One day that winter, Mo Gong ran breathlessly to our home and told me that our county's performing troupe was holding public auditions for actors and instrument players. I was so excited that the next day I-Fei and I rode his bike and headed for Putien, so that I could sign up for the audition. During the next few days, Dad dug out some old music scores, traditional classics that had been banned for the last twenty years, and said, 'The Red Guards' music is over. Pick one of these for your audition.' He understood my feelings and appreciated my passion for art. After all, it was he who had inspired me.

His friends had only to make the slightest demand, and he would nudge me into playing a few songs on my violin, which his friends mysteriously called 'the western instrument'. He would introduce the violin, explaining the relationship between the four strings, and show off the amazing range of such a tiny instrument by plucking the strings with his fingers. Sometimes he would ask me to tag along on his occasional gigs playing classic Chinese folk music for weddings, which probably made me the first to render the thousand-year-old melodies on such an instrument. At those gigs, such traditional instruments as gongs, drums and flutes usually drowned out my tiny violin.

Soong had warned me of the temptation to play everything on the violin. Being a purist, he had asked me how I could play that stupid, traditional music on something on which so many magnificent masterpieces had been played. He said it would ruin my style, but I had ignored him. I wanted to make Dad happy. He was proud because I was the only one of his five kids who played an instrument as he had done when he was young. We shared an intimate bond.

Since the classic romantic plays were coming back into fashion as Dad had foretold, I concentrated on my flute, not the western instrument, for the audition. For three days, I practised only three short classical pieces while Dad listened and coached. It was his territory and he was a master. He knew every fluttering of the finger and softening of breath to capture the true spirit of the piece. He would demonstrate and I would work on it until the melody came naturally to me. I would never have imagined myself imitating his rougher, stronger, less refined, less flowery style. It reminded me of ancient times when the emperors were entertained in the luxurious courts by flutes made of jade and when people fought on horseback with long swords. I wished I could play one tenth as well as he did.

On the day of my audition, my sister Si carried me on the bike to Putien at sunrise, where we waited in a long line of self-acclaimed artists, eating our packed breakfast of cold and dried yams. My teeth kept clicking as the line began to move. I had to run to the smelly bathroom every five minutes for a two-second pee. Si saw how nervous I was and said that I was still very young and that if I failed this time, I could always try again. I thought about my friends and about I-Fei. If they had been here, they would have lit a good cigarette for me, kicked me in the butt, and tried to make me smile. I yearned for a cigarette but the thought of having a coughing fit during the performance stopped the terrible urge.

149

To seek peace, I closed my eyes and said aloud in my head a few words to all the gods that I had kowtowed and prayed to thousands of times before. Now I regretted taking money from my brother and sisters for kowtowing for them. The gods would probably teach me a lesson today, one that I would never forget. I prayed again that they delay punishing me for such greed until later.

When I heard my number called, my sister patted my back and I walked slowly into the hall. It was an old, small theatre. As I walked, my footsteps echoed. Before me sat six of the most prominent musical figures in our county.

Teacher Dong, a big fish stranded in a small town, was the only college graduate with a music major from Fuzhou Music Conservatory. He wore his glasses on the tip of his nose and looked at me without an ounce of interest in his drooping eyes. Ding, the famous Putien opera singer, was filing her nails. Flautist Min, the first flute of the county, known for his long breath and unusually large testicles, was slumped low in his armchair. Drummer Jia was reading an old newspaper, and director Liao, a bearded man, smoked a pipe, fighting the numbing boredom without much success.

I felt small and unworthy.

'What will you do?' Flautist Min asked. 'Not another flautist again?'

I hoped he was joking.

I nodded and announced the title of my piece.

'A Trip to Gu Su,' I mumbled. My teeth were still chattering. There were hundreds of people pressing their noses against the windows, watching the contestants. It was hard to conjure up the environment of a scenic lake with sweeping willows on a moonlit night, a mental picture my dad told me I should have when playing this piece. It was a romantic, melodious solo, depicting a lonesome young man strolling beside a lake, seeking love on a beautiful night.

All I could think of was my sister's worried look as I left her, the fetid public bathroom, the faces at the window, and the sagging eyes of the music teacher. I closed my own eyes and forced the first sound out of my old flute. The flute sounded as if it was crackling and getting dry, so I started again. It was a steep uphill ride. I felt I couldn't breathe at all. After only a few long bars, I felt my lungs wheezing. My heart pounded like a rat in an iron cage.

From the corner of my eye, I saw an uncomfortable twitching of Flautist Min's nose. He must be so disgusted. I was sure I had ruined it with the first note. Gradually, I forced my eyes to close and tried to think of the peaceful Dong Jing River, by which I had practised every morning, the green fields that stretched beyond it, and the colours of the mountain at sunrise. Soon the desire to win started to churn within me. I remembered every twist and turn Dad had taught me during the last three days. When the final note had faded away, I opened my eyes to see that all the judges were making busy notes.

Flautist Min was the first to look up. He smiled at me and said, 'Well done. It didn't start out right but you handled the piece unusually well.'

I blushed, not knowing what to say. 'Who teaches you?' he asked.

I thought for a second. 'My dad,' I answered.

'What is his name?'

'Ar Gang.'

'I have heard of him. An acupuncturist?'

'Yeah.'

'Come here. Let me have a word with you.'

I heard another name being called, and a girl walked in, a ballerina with her feet turned out like a duck's. I walked over to Min's chair. 'One of my distant cousins was getting treatments from your dad,' he told me. 'I heard he was doing a wonderful job. I didn't know he was also a flautist. Here, let me tell you the truth about this audition. We have enough flautists already. Do you play any other instrument?'

'The violin.'

'No good. We are going back to the old things now – you know, the sort of stuff banned by the Gang of Four. If you are serious about our troupe, try out as an actor.'

'Do you think I'd qualify?'

151

He stood back and sized me up. 'At most, you would be a semi-lead.'

'What's that?'

'That means you're not good-looking enough to be a full lead. Have you acted before?'

'Not really.'

'Go home and make up your mind about your career. This is not just for amusement. You need to think and talk to your parents, put your heart into it. If you are still interested, I'll be happy to talk to you. But no instruments. We only need good actors who have the classic looks to perform all those classic plays. Got that? By the way, I might drop by to see your dad next time I'm there. Arthritis.'

I thanked him and left the hall.

My sister was smiling at me, waiting. She said I did a good job. I told her about the conversation I had had with the flautist.

'Do you want to be an actor?' she asked on our way home, pedalling her bike hard against the afternoon sea breeze.

I was quiet for a while. 'I'm not sure.'

'You want to play the violin before thousands of people?'

I nodded.

'You don't have to be an actor if it's not something you want.'

I was quiet during the ride back. I wasn't going to be an artist, nor a carpenter, nor a shoemaker. Definitely not a farmer. For a while I was lost. Time had changed everything for me and I was always behind, it seemed, like chasing my own shadow. What had once been right wasn't right any more. I wished I knew the future, while hoping that the past would not be repeated.

That night, Dad said it would probably be a good time to start being serious about school. He had just heard from my aunt in Shanghai that her son was already preparing for the college entrance examinations that were open to all test-takers, regardless of age, race, or family background. People would be admitted solely on the basis of their scores. He added that I was the only one in our family who was still in school and therefore able to benefit from such great news.

I went to sleep with a heavy heart. I kept thinking about the indifferent way the teachers treated me. I had been acting like a bad student. No, I *was* a bad student. Now I was miles behind everyone. It was unfair. When I was a good student, winning honour for the elementary school with perfect marks, they hadn't needed high marks. Now when they did want them, I was at the bottom. I wished I had excelled at the day's audition and could become an artist, then I wouldn't have to worry about my life. Despite my youth, I would have been able to support my family. I wasn't sure I could practise my flute any more. Maybe I should do something else. But what?

Next day, I put away my music, wrapped up the small Beethoven bust that I had kept at my bedside, and stored it under my bed. I loosened the strings on my violin, and locked its wooden box. Then I searched for all the textbooks that I had long since stopped bringing to school. They were new, untouched, and covered with dust. I cleaned them and laid them neatly on the desk beside my bed. Slowly, I leafed through the physics book. It was filled with strange symbols and new formulas, expressed in oddly shaped letters and filled with words I couldn't understand. It didn't look like I could just close my eyes and sink my teeth into the subject. The only formula I recognized was H_2O. I shut the books with dismay and hopelessness. Time had deserted me, or, rather, I had deserted myself. The knife of regret cut deeply into my soul.

Finally, I opened my English book. On the first page I had drawn the face of my wheezing English teacher, with his dead eyes and stooped back. The sketch had really captured his spirit. I gave a small laugh and turned the page. It listed the twenty-six letters of the English alphabet. I stood up, closed my bedroom door to make sure no one would hear me, and twisted my tongue and lips trying to pronounce each letter. I could only get as far as *F*. Next to the letter *G* I had drawn a chicken, because the Chinese word for chicken came closest to the sound of the English *G*. The letter *H* became *love paint*. For the rest, the symbols I had drawn and characters I had written next to them didn't help. It was another dead subject for me. I slammed the book closed and stared at my violin for a long time, until I drifted into a little nap.

'Hey, what's this?' I-Fei asked jokingly the following morning before class. 'Is this a schoolbag, or are my eyes seeing things?'

'We have to do some studying,' I said seriously.

'We have no time for this, Da. Remember, we're having a major rehearsal this afternoon. You're looking a little down after the audition.'

'I don't know. Maybe we shouldn't be skipping class for the rehearsals any more.'

'And then what?' He pulled out a filtered cigarette from his pocket and lit it. 'Grab one for yourself.' He threw me the whole pack.

'Sit in class and try to learn something. The whole country is talking about college. My cousin in Shanghai is attending a crash course to prepare for the entrance exams.'

'And *you're* thinking of college?' He looked at me, surprised.

'What do you mean by that?'

'I mean, when was the last time you did your homework?'

'There's always time.'

'No time can make up for that. We're two years behind everything. And this is a lousy school to begin with. The teachers are suckers. Good thing I don't have to depend on them.'

'Right, you can always go and become a driver.'

'I'll make you a driver, too. I really could try my dad on that one,' he said, smiling. 'Here, smoke.'

I pushed his hand away.

The bell rang. The first class was English.

'Let's go in, I-Fei.'

'You go ahead, let me finish smoking,' he said coolly, a little grumpy at my new attitude.

I threw myself inside through our usual route, the window, and landed right in my seat. The teacher was leaning against the desk, trying to catch his breath. His glasses slipped to the tip of his nose and his beady eyes were looking around but not seeing anything. Boys and girls were still talking noisily. The teacher commanded no respect. He did not and could not care. He weighed two pieces of chalk in his hands. One he held like a cigarette, the other was to throw at the most badly behaved student in class. You could count on being hit right on the tip of your nose.

'To what do I owe this honour, Mr Da?' the teacher asked.

I ducked down. I hadn't been to his class for a long time.

'No rehearsal today?' The teacher threw the chalk at me. It landed on my head.

The class laughed.

I stayed down, quiet.

'If you had let me know earlier, I could have prepared something special for you, like an ABC lesson.' He laughed along with the rest of the class and as usual, ended up coughing until his face turned blue. He leaned on the desk until the spasm passed.

I felt embarrassed and ashamed, but I was angry, too.

Cough some more, you fool, I thought.

Outside the window, I-Fei was making a face at me, gesturing for me to join him.

'Yeah, why don't you just let yourself out and have a smoke with your pal down there?' The teacher caught his breath then threw another piece of chalk at I-Fei, which hit his forehead.

Laughter again.

I could feel my face turn red, then white. I decided to leave the room and never return. As I crossed the threshold, I heard him say, 'Now we can start our lesson.'

I-Fei had already lit a cigarette for me. Quietly, I took a long drag as soon as I was out of the teacher's sight.

'What did I tell you?' I-Fei said. 'There's no place for us there. We might as well be the kind of students that we have always been.'

'I wasn't always like this,' I said, puffing.

'I know,' I-Fei said. 'You should have learned then what you know now.'

'You know everything.'

'You're my best friend. People told me things after we beat up that Han guy.'

'I used to be a very good student.'

'But you were a miserable wimp,' he said.

'That wasn't my fault,' I said harshly.

I-Fei changed the subject. 'Suppose you *were* a good student. Do you think the college would take you?'

'Do you mean with my family background?'

He nodded.

'But my aunt said it was regardless of one's family background.'

'And you believe that?'

'Why shouldn't I?'

'Because my dad said it was just a pretence. There will be different standards for admission. This society isn't going to change that fast. No offence to you people.' He shook his head and threw a stone at a passing bird as we left school for the day.

From then on, miserably, I carried my schoolbag, heavy with untouched books, heading for classes I didn't understand. I would ask this student and that student, humbly trying to catch up on my own. But the more I learned, the more I realized how much I had missed and the more depressed I got. I was too ashamed to talk about it to my parents or to any teachers, most of whom had given up on me by now.

But my parents had noticed that I had been spending more time in my room, using a kerosene light at night, looking at my textbooks, and occasionally gingerly trying out some English pronunciations. I often heard Sen and Mo Gong whistling outside my window to get my attention, but I tried to control myself.

One night, the whistling lasted longer and I knew they couldn't wait any more.

'You fucking become a bookworm nowadays,' Mo Gong said. 'You can't simply close the window and not answer us.'

'What's going on, brother?'

'Well, Yi is leaving.'

'Where's he going?'

'His grandpa is retiring from the factory and Yi is taking over his job as an office worker.'

We walked to Yi's workshop, where there was a table of food waiting for us. Sen, Siang, and Yi rushed over, picked me up, and threw me on to the sawdust.

'The place is clean,' I exclaimed to Yi, dusting my coat. 'You're really getting the hell out of here?'

'Yeah. I was hoping you would get into the county performing troupe so that we could be working in Putien together.'

'You have to go alone for now,' I said.

'Let's celebrate our first breakthrough among the brothers,' Sen said. 'Yi, don't you ever forget us. I'm still the eldest.'

'He's going to marry a fair-skinned Putien city girl and she's going to say she'll leave if you keep those dirty friends,' Siang joked.

'Talk about marrying,' Sen said. 'Da, you should write a letter for Yi to his old master's daughter, Ping. Remember her? And tell her the news.'

'Maybe in English,' Mo Gong said. 'I heard you making those funny sounds.'

'Shut up, you,' I said good-naturedly.

'Don't be shy. We want you to do good. I would want you, if anyone, to make us proud by being a college student,' Sen said. 'The rest of us are history. You're our only hope.'

'I guess I could jot down something. Hope it doesn't backfire like last time,' I said.

'There's no need for the letter,' Yi said. 'Let's eat.'

Grandpa had prepared the food for us. He was glad that his company had allowed Yi to take over his job, that his grandson would be doing exactly the same thing he had done his whole life. It was easier than carpentry. All he need do was keep a neat, clean inventory of the contents of the warehouse he was watching. So long, sawdust, goodbye ball-swinging!

'But why?' Sen said.

'She came here yesterday,' Yi confessed.

'What did you do to her?' Sen said eagerly.

'Yi, you dog!'

'She said she was quitting the commune's performing troupe and returning home to the village to get married.'

'What!'

'Yeah, she was promised by her mother to the Communist chief of her village. She came here to give us candies and cigarettes to celebrate.' Yi opened a box filled with her gifts. We chewed on the candies and smoked the cigarettes thoughtfully.

'Do you think she wants the party chief to be her husband?' I asked.

'I doubt it. I knew the guy when I was working there.' Yi took a drag after a sip of tea. 'He's about forty, with a pitted face. His wife committed suicide for an unknown reason. She hanged herself. They had three kids. He once wanted to sleep with a young teacher in the village. When she refused him, she was fired.'

'Sounds like a criminal.'

'Close. He was a local warlord. I wouldn't be surprised if he had forced sex on my master's wife first and then made her promise her daughter to him.'

'That sounds like foul play to me.'

'She was crying yesterday and didn't tell me anything, but I guessed.'

'Shouldn't you do something about it?'

'I don't know.' Yi turned moody.

'I bet you could start a rumour that would somehow ruin the engagement,' I said, thinking of how my dad had helped my cousin Yan to get rid of an unwanted suitor.

'He would ruin you all,' Yi said. 'He has no enemies, because he has done all kinds of things to get rid of them. He is the Communist warlord in that corner of the country. Unless something changes, he is going to be there for ever.'

The party ended with us wrestling each other on the soft sawdust. I promised to go with Yi to his factory next day and help him carry the luggage. We chatted about the future until midnight. I told them I wanted to go to college. They laughed and said if I could master the art of that four-stringed thing, the name of which they still didn't quite know how to say, then I should have no problem. They were my true friends. There was a generous spirit among them, not jealousy. As I walked home alone in the darkness, I saw a star shine brilliantly over the top of our ancient pine tree to the east of Yellow Stone. I was like that, only a twinkle in the dark.

Fourteen

The western tip of Yellow Stone was all river and ancient lychee trees that dipped low in the water. In summer, straw-hatted boatmen poled along slowly between the green branches that were in their way. The lychees, ripe and juicy, burned red like the cheeks of a gaudily painted woman, and made the branches droop even lower. Only cicadas disturbed the tranquillity.

When I was young, I would take off my shorts and jump into the river, swim underwater until I reached the lychee trees, then shoot up like a little fish, grab the red fruit, and fall back into the river. The napping old man guarding the lychee trees would wake up and blindly throw stones at me. I could hold my breath underwater until I reached the boats docked on the opposite side of the river, where I would emerge, naked, with the fruit in one hand and my shorts in the other, and run into the fields.

In the crook of the river, where the houses thinned and the trees thickened, nestled a three-storey white house with a red-tiled roof. A tall wall fenced it off. It was a small world within itself. The entrance stayed closed at all times. Only the tops of papaya trees could be seen from the outside. The little white house belonged to twin sisters, the Weis, who were Baptists and had never married. In the town where Buddha called the shots, the little white house by the river was a symbol of something alien yet sacred.

I remembered that years ago I had tried to poke a hole through the tall wall to see what lay inside that mysterious compound. The low growl of an angry dog had sent me running like a plucked rooster. I never got to see the rare roses they said the twins grew, or the tempting papayas hanging from the trees. People said the twins read the Bible in the sun and prayed under the moonlight. They lived a quiet life, and paid for a maid to do the shopping and cleaning for them. Occasionally, they had visitors on weekends. Townspeople whispered that they were secretly involved in some sort of ceremony. Their father was one of the first Chinese Baptist ministers in Putien, and the twins had grown up in a Baptist church run by American missionaries. The Americans taught them English, and they went on to become English professors at a teachers' college in Fuzhou. When the colleges closed down, they retired into the country, where their father had held the first Sunday service in the history of Yellow Stone. During the Cultural Revolution, they had been shaved bald and paraded down the street as special American agents, who had brought the seed of western religion to corrupt local minds. But when the Cultural Revolution ended, the government declared the Weis religious leaders, and made them the head of a bogus government religious agency meant to give foreign countries the impression that China had some degree of religious freedom.

The white-haired twin sisters enjoyed a special status among the townspeople. They were the closest thing to real Westerners. Those few who had been inside the home had had a glimpse of a mysterious life behind those closed doors.

The old vegetable man claimed to have heard the twin sisters talking in 'the language of the red hair', probably English, one day when he was making a delivery. It was gentle, like singing, he said. The old cleaning lady insisted that the twins only used forks and knives. It puzzled the local people. It was such a terribly unlucky thing to do, using a knife at the dining table. Maybe it was the different god they believed in who helped them ward off the consequences of all the wrong things they did.

The blind fortune-teller, Mr Mai, claimed to have felt the presence of Jesus Christ's seal on one of the twin's palms when they delivered some food to his house during a time of hardship. Then there was the inevitable subject of Buddha. The cleaning

160

lady, slightly blind and very deaf, had swept every corner of the house and sniffed every inch of space and she said that there was absolutely no sign of Buddha, no incense or shrine. But the sisters did a fair amount of singing, she noted. One played the organ, while the other sang foreign tunes at sunset every day. Their trembling, high-pitched voices flowed beyond the tall wall and lingered among the dense lychee trees. People would stop and listen. As time went by, the quaint western music somehow blended into the quietness of the town and became part of the sunset tradition at Yellow Stone. But one day the singing stopped. There was a rumour that one of the twins was under the weather. The respected country doctor was seen rushing through the entrance, and for the next few days their church friends filed in and out of the place, solemn-faced. The western end of the town became quieter without their singing and a hushed gloom hovered over the thick treetops.

One day, after dark, we heard a gentle knocking at the door.

Dad opened it. Outside stood the white-haired Professor Wei, one of the twin sisters. Upon recognizing her, Dad took a step back.

'May I come in, please?' Her voice was so gentle and sincere.

'Of course, of course.' Dad opened the door wide and let her in.

She bowed and smiled sweetly at us. We put down our chopsticks, and bowed back to her. She was a petite lady in her late sixties. Upright and dignified, she seemed taller than her mere five feet. Her white hair was braided and twisted into a bun, neat and elegant.

'How may I help you, Professor?' Dad asked politely. He gestured for us kids to leave the room. We hurried out, then stuck our ears against the closed door.

'Please forgive me for intruding at such a late hour.' She took out a handkerchief and continued: 'My poor dear sister has had a minor stroke, and now her mouth is twisted to one side. I have heard of your reputation. Can you please help her?'

'I am flattered.' Dad rubbed his hands like a joyful kid. 'I'll be more than happy to see what I could do.' Dad was in his best mood when he was called upon to help others.

'Mother,' he called out to my mum, as if he knew that we were behind the closed door listening to every single word. 'Get me the blue jacket and a flashlight. I need to go out.'

Mum hurried in with his jacket, the one with all his acupuncture needles. I passed him the flashlight he kept under his pillow.

'God bless you. You are a kind man, like they said. I don't know how to thank you, Dr Chen.'

'Please don't call me "doctor", just Ar Gang.' Dad was beaming. He didn't know what to do with the 'God bless you' part.

'We can wait until tomorrow morning. I just needed to let my poor sister know. If you agreed to treat her, then she will sleep peacefully tonight.'

'She needs to be seen as soon as possible,' Dad said.

'Oh, how can I thank you all!' She turned and bowed to each of us again.

We all bowed back.

After Dad left, I told the others that he had made a mistake.

'What mistake?' Mum asked.

'Well, when Professor Wei said "God bless you", Dad should have said something polite back. I'm sure she was expecting it.'

'And what should he have said?' Mum asked.

'Buddha bless you!'

They all laughed.

We were all proud of Dad. This case would put him at another level. I was sure he had chills crawling up his spine at being called a doctor by her. This was a landmark, a milestone in Dad's career. It would be whispered about for a long time to come.

The other twin had had a light stroke. Dad soon began to see some progress. He reported that she was able to utter her first clear sounds after two weeks of intensive and painful treatment. She was resilient and co-operative.

I questioned Dad each time he came back from his visits, asking him about the papayas, the twins' knives and forks, and the wild roses in the garden. Dad said it was all true. The papaya trees were from the Philippine mountains, the Weis' father had brought them back from his mission work there. Their fruit tasted delicious. Yes, they used knives and forks, and Dad said they insisted that he eat

162

some papaya with them. The wild roses crept across the rambling garden. Professor Wei told him it was an English-style garden, and they had brought back a hundred types of flowers to plant alongside what already grew there.

But it was about the English langauge that I asked most often. Did they use the language at home? Dad said it was rather hard for the patient to speak the local lisping dialect in her present condition, so yes, they frequently spoke in English. He said they had a big library filled to the ceiling with books.

To thank Dad, the twins insisted on paying him for his work, but Dad wouldn't hear of it. They asked him whether there was anything they could do for us in return. Dad said that the twins begged him to think of a way, otherwise they would feel bad.

One night I said to Dad, 'Maybe they could teach me English in their spare time.'

He looked up from his medical book and stared thoughtfully at me for a second. 'That's a wonderful idea. But your level might be a little too low for them. They taught in college, remember?'

'Maybe they won't mind,' I begged.

'I could try. Son, how did you come up with such an idea?'

'Well, they have been trying to find a way to thank you.'

'Yeah, but tell me why you thought of it.' He put aside his book.

'They talk about college in school. I have no future. I'm not doing well, and I'm a couple of years behind. Other subjects are easier to make up, and I'm working on it, but no one can help me with English.'

'What about the English teachers?'

'They made fun of me when I went back to their classes. Besides, their pronunciation is terrible. Each time my teacher reads English, he sounds like he's choking on a fishbone. He spits and gets red-faced. I don't think Englishmen talk like that.'

Dad laughed. 'Now, son, if you do get to study with Professor Wei, I want you to make at least as much effort as you did with the flute,' he said seriously.

I nodded.

That night, before falling asleep, I blew out the light, knelt down on the pillow, and kowtowed to Buddha to beg for help. For the first time, I didn't know what to ask for. I buried my face in the soft pillow until I began to stifle myself. I murmured in my head the word 'college', but I could feel my face blush with shame for even thinking about it. College was for the superior few who not only had extreme intelligence but diligence, too. What was I?

That night I dreamed about being sent to a remote farm where I was forced to dig a rocky hill until I collapsed. I woke up in the middle of the night in a cold sweat.

Fifteen

As the summer vacation drew near, Dad came back one day with the good news that Professor Wei would be willing to help tutor me in English, but she would be away in Fuzhou for a couple of months, accompanying her sister who would be in rehabilitation under the care of some famous doctors. She would see me when she returned.

I was happy and nervous at the same time. It gave me the whole summer to prepare, so maybe I wouldn't look too stupid. I drew up a study plan, leaving very little time for music or anything else.

I didn't care how badly I did in the finals. I just walked out of the English test, to I-Fei's surprise. He already had a good student waiting outside the window to guide us through the exams: the price, just two packs of Flying Horse.

'What's the matter with you?' I-Fei asked, running after me. 'Don't you want to pass?'

'Yeah.'

'So? I got a helper out there. He knows everything. You know he found the crumpled carbon copy of the test in the teacher's garbage can. It's a sure thing.'

'I don't want to copy any more. It means nothing.'

'You'll get zero.'

'But I'll do better next semester.'

'How?'

'I'm taking lessons from Professor Wei next semester.'

'You can't even say the ABC well, how can you take lessons from an English professor? That's a joke. Have a smoke.' He threw me the whole pack of cigarettes, after lighting one for himself. I threw the pack back.

'I'm not a good student because I haven't been studying. I skipped classes with you. I've been doing those stupid rehearsals and drama productions. I'm sure I could do well with the Weis' help.'

'Gee, are you blaming me for all this now?'

'I'm not blaming you. I'm blaming myself.'

'Blaming yourself is blaming me because we did things together. Maybe I shouldn't be hanging around you any more, let you be a good student again.' He picked up his cigarettes and left.

'Hey, you stupid dog,' I yelled at him. 'Come back here.'

I ran after him. 'You're still my best friend in school.'

'Best friend?' He stopped and looked back at me for a few seconds. 'You're different. I don't like the change. You don't want to smoke, you don't want to skip classes. Don't this and don't that. I have to go home early every day and stare at my mosquito net. It's getting so boring here in this tiny town.'

'I have to change, I'm sorry. I can't afford to goof off like you. Your mum and dad can give you a future, mine can't. Give me another smoke.'

He fished one out for me. I lit it with his lighter. 'I'm hoping we could study together like we did with your accordion. You did a great job.'

We sat down again. 'It was all because of your help.'

'Well let's do it again, this time with our work in school.'

He shook his head, blowing smoke rings.

'I'm not interested in studies. If I were, Dad could get ten teachers to coach me every day. Some of them would even wash my feet. I hate studying.'

'But why?'

'There are no girls in the books.'

'There will be girls, lots of pretty girls, after you are in college. They love college men. My cousin waited until she was almost thirty, only to marry a shorty with a funny face. Why? Because he was a college man.'

'You're too dreamy. Normally only one out of a hundred gets to go to college, but with the new system reopening after being closed for the last ten years, there are ten years' worth of accumulated high school graduates out there. Your chances are more like one in a thousand. You have no chance.' He threw the cigarette away.

'You think not, huh?'

'No.'

'Maybe you're underestimating me,' I said.

'Don't overestimate yourself.'

'We'll see, I-Fei. Maybe you're right, but I'm going to give it my best shot for the next couple of years, no matter what you say.'

We walked in silence until the fork, where we parted to take our separate roads home. Before he left, I patted him on the shoulder and wrestled him from behind like we always did when one of us was getting mad at the other. It didn't work this time. He pushed me away and made an ugly face before he left. I stood watching him until he disappeared along the dusty road.

A few days later, I-Fei rode his bike to my home and stopped briefly to tell me that he was leaving Yellow Stone for good and was transferring to another high school. Or maybe he would become a driver soon. He was extremely mysterious and his eyes kept looking beyond me. I asked him to stay a while and chat about the old days, but he said it was a long way to travel to his mum's. So off he went, without regret. I was deeply hurt. He had been a loyal friend and great to be with. School would not be the same without him.

June was a tough month for the farmers of Yellow Stone. Stretches of rice fields had just turned golden. The hot sun burned them, grilling and baking the rice until it ripened, and the husks filled with millions of little white pillows. It would soon be harvest time, but typhoons lurked along the Pacific Coast only miles away, like evil monsters. They brought torrents of rain, and could devastate the rice fields in a matter of hours. Each day, the farmers waited in agony for the rice to ripen a little more. They were at the mercy of the temperamental coastal climate. The wait was like pulling teeth out of a dragon's mouth. When the weather forecast was bad, farmers worked incessantly to harvest the rice before they lost it all to nature.

One day, when the remote Ch'ing Mountain was wrapped in layers of lingering clouds, that looked like a woman's hair flying loose in the wind, the commune sent an announcement over the loudspeaker systems to warn the farmers of an impending typhoon. Suddenly all was chaos. The brigade leader banged on every member's door, urging the villagers to head for the fields and harvest the rice. All of it, even that which was still green, was to be cut rather than be ruined in the flood.

My eldest sister was away in Han Jian, working at her temporary job in the canned-food factory – a violation of the commune's no-working-out-of-town-in-harvest-time rule. Dad asked me if I could step in and do her work, so the next day, while it was still dark, Mum awakened me at dawn. My brother, Jin, and my two sisters, Huang and Ke, were already at the dining table stuffing themselves with fried rice by the bowlful and washing it down with the soup Mum had been preparing since midnight. My brother, now a veteran farmer at the age of nineteen, could eat as many as three large bowlfuls before going to work. Everyone worked fourteen-hour days, and Jin couldn't stand being hungry in the fields. After burping a few times, he lit a cigarette and put on his straw hat, ready to go.

I had stuffed as much food into my mouth at four in the morning as I could. Mum had warned me that I wouldn't eat again until one in the afternoon. With my eyes half-closed, I smelled the freshly simmered rice as though it was still a sweet dream.

'Follow me, little brother.' After I, too, had burped with satisfaction, Jin gave me a sickle and out I went, barefoot, into the dark fields.

The edge of the sky was whitish, as if someone had barely lifted the lid off the earth. We walked in silence among the weeds and grasses still wet with dew. I dragged my feet, fighting the fatigue of being woken at such an ungodly hour, a time when I should have been having the sweetest dreams. I stumbled blindly after my brother, the leader of the group, who whistled, hummed and smoked as casually as if it were just another day.

'Here we are. We have about five *mus* (about one acre) of rice to cut before the sun sets.' He pointed at the endless stretch of rice fields looming in the whitish dark. 'The four of us will go in rows. I'll take the widest, then Ke and Huang will take the rows beside me. You, little brother, go slow and rest when you need to. Try to see if you could do that slice.' He indicated the edge of a huge plot and smiled at me.

'No problem. Give me more,' I said.

Jin showed me how to cut the tall rice stalks at their base and stack them behind me. He warned me not to cut my fingers in the dark. I stepped into the muddy wet field, making a squishing noise. Some frogs and wild rats ran at the sound. Mosquitoes and insects hummed constantly around my nose, eyes, and ears, and I had to keep batting them away. I could feel the little worms and eels slithering away from under my toes. I closed my eyes and tried to think of something pleasant. The violin.

I grabbed big handfuls of stalks and cut them fiercely. My sisters stopped to check on me once in a while and were pleased with what I was doing. Soon the sun rose above the horizon and the endless fields gave off steam as the morning light embraced them. The rest of the land was still asleep.

The knee-high rice plants with needle-sharp leaves got in the way of my face and neck as I bent down. The fuzzy blades needed only to brush my skin to leave behind a red kiss. Soon the summer sun turned from gentle to glaring. Sweat beaded my forehead and trickled down my eyebrows. My skin began to itch as though it were being attacked by thousands of slimy, crawling creatures, angry that I had invaded their world with my sickle. I unbuttoned my drenched shirt and peeled it off, wiping my cut, sweaty face with it before tossing it behind me. I clenched my jaw to keep from yelling out loud at the pain of my burning skin. I didn't want my sisters and brother to think that their little brother wasn't farmer material. As I stretched my sore back, feeling like the old hunched merchant next door who didn't know what the sky looked like any more, I saw that they were already thirty yards ahead of me, tirelessly bending over the rice that only seemed to end where the sky launched a rainbow.

My sisters and brother had grown up farming. I had seen them carry on their shoulders over a hundred pounds of animal manure, to be used for fertilizer in the fields. Their skinny legs had trembled beneath the weight, but they dared not slow down for fear of criticism by the commune leaders, who were especially harsh to them. They had all endured, their teeth gritted. Brother Jin had once had a rusty nail go through his right foot. It took two months to heal. Huang had once become so dehydrated under the baking sun that she had passed out. And they all complained of constant back pain, but they had to push themselves on, for the commune would not allow any leaves of absence. Their food ration would have been withheld until those absences were made up. They had all grown tall, thin and tanned like coconuts.

As I stood there watching them, I felt respect and fear. A future as a farmer stretched out before me like the brutal fields. There would be endless toiling under a brutal sun, all for a meagre existence that consisted of rice porridge and pickled vegetables. There would be hunger for at least three months a year, during which even the mouldy yams became treasures on the dining table.

'Have a rest, brother,' I heard Jin shout at me. His voice sounded tiny in that enormous field. 'You don't have to hurry.'

'Put your shirt back on or the sun will kill you,' Ke said, standing up to take a look at me.

'I'm fine, you guys.' But my mind was saying, *let me go home*. I was sick of it already. I dropped my sickle and drummed my back with my fists, imitating my dad when he had had a hard day. I sighed at the narrow stretch of rice still before me, standing proud and nodding lazily in the occasional breeze. Slowly, I bent my cracking back to pick up the sickle again, this time resting my elbows on my knees like a pregnant woman, and hacking the plants stem by stem. I wished the sun would go down faster, so that we could all go home and rest, but it stayed eternally motionless, a taunting fireball in the cloudless sky. Then I wished the rice would all fall on its back by itself.

I thought about the great future Mao had promised China, the machines and the modernization. Where was all that when I needed it? I had seen beautiful propaganda pictures of good old Russians using fancy combines to harvest their wheat and rice. Dad was right again. He said that we were farming the land the same way we had done thousands of years ago, the only difference being that we got paid less.

My friends' faces lined up at the gate of my mind. I thought of how lucky bowlegged Yi was, sitting in his office somewhere, crossing out each item on the inventory sheet and having juicy meat for lunch. He would no doubt be brewing his bitter tea there. Then there was Siang, probably smoking his Flying Horses at his penthouse home, where there was always a breeze even in the motionless summer noon, when the whole universe seemed to be frozen by the white heat. That lucky dog. I wished a long life to his old revolutionary grandpa, who had made it all possible. Then images flooded my mind of Sen being chased by his mum with a huge stick, while he ran like a dog, one hand holding his pants, the other carrying the bowl of lard he had just stolen. Mo Gong was probably ogling beautiful girls passing by his dad's shoe stand. He leered at anything that moved. His famous saying was there was always something to look at on a girl's body, it didn't always have to be a pretty face.

My thoughts were interrupted by the appearance of a huge mother of a green frog. She stared at me, flickering her long tongue. Her head looked like a turtle's, and her skin was like that of a grass snake. Her eyes were popping, kind and curious, rolling within teary sockets. A white pouch of skin hung under her neck, and her thighs looked meaty enough to decorate tonight's dining table. We stared at each other for a good long minute before I threw the sickle at her. The silly thing jumped like a world champion and landed on my chest. Her wet webs and sticky skin sent chills down my spine, but I grabbed it and wrapped it up in my discarded shirt. It weighed at least half a pound. I could already smell the fragrance of its juicy thighs getting sautéed with fine soy sauce, fresh garlic and plenty of ginger to kill the fishiness. I would give my brother half the meat to go along with the bottle of liquor he had every night before sleep. He needed it to calm his bones, Mum said.

The sun hung high above my head, and my back felt hot. Even the wet mud in the field was lukewarm, and the proud rice stems began to droop beneath the blaze, tired and sleepy. The day was only half done, but I was totally exhausted. My back hurt, my legs trembled, my face was covered with cuts, and my hands were a mass of raw blisters. I was so miserable I even didn't feel the walls of my stomach rub against each other. There was a burning in my throat that would take a whole fire brigade to snuff out. I felt angry, belittled, and pathetic. I could not beg to get out of my duty. It was just not done in the Chen family. We all worked hard together and played together. Mum and Dad would never approve of my giving up in the middle of my task. I hung on a few more yards, then the blisters burst. The raw flesh looked red and stung like needles. I heard my sister call my name.

'Little brother, come eat.'

I saw my mum stumbling along the edge of the field, carrying our lunch on a long bamboo pole. Her face was red beneath her straw hat. I was so grateful to see her.

'Come wash your hands and eat, young farmer.' Mum smiled at me as I dragged my feet towards her. The beautiful smile on her face was the highest praise she could give us. My sisters and brother gathered around Mum, who was pouring water from a bucket and passing out wet towels.

'You're not doing too bad at all. With your help, we will finish before dark.' My brother beamed, slapping my back.

I screamed before I could stop myself.

'What's the matter? Did you burn your back?' Huang asked.

I was silent.

'I told you to leave your shirt on,' she said.

'It was wet.'

They looked at me.

'Let me see your hands,' Jin said. I held them out. The blisters continued to ooze. 'Pack up and go home after lunch, okay? I'm sorry, it must hurt like hell.'

172

Mum and my sisters were upset. My mother hurriedly cleaned my bloody hands with a wet towel.

'I'm sorry, guys. But I can finish my share.'

'No, go home and take care of your hands.'

I was ashamed, feeling like a defector.

'It happened to me too, when I started out.' Jin extended his hands. 'Now look at them. They feel like iron. Go home and try to be a good student. Maybe some day you'll go to college and won't have to do hard work like this any more. You can still shoot for it. The rest of us are too old for that.' He looked at my sisters.

On our way home, I trailed behind Mum in silence, holding both my hands gingerly stretched out.

'Do you still want to be a farmer?' Mum asked.

I shook my head.

'Then study hard. You can choose your future, your sisters and brother can't. You're lucky. If they had blisters like yours, they would still have to be there till the last stem was harvested. It's their life.'

Mum's words stayed with me for a long time.

The smell of soil and a vague scent permeated the endless, brutal fields. I wouldn't miss it if I were never to return. The beauty of nature and the muddy fragrance at harvest used to fill me with emotion. Now it looked like a graveyard, filled with hungry ghosts that grabbed at my arms and legs. I didn't want to have my youth and future buried here.

As I followed Mum home, I felt a strong desire to start lessons with Professor Wei, to go back to school. There was a future somewhere for me other than hoes and sickles. There should be no hardship at school that I couldn't overcome. I was never more determined than at that moment. I felt fortunate. As Mum and Jin had said, I still had a chance. The pain in my back and hands throbbed, but all I felt was gratitude for my family and a desire to succeed at school.

After I failed at filling the spot for Si, Dad thought of another option. I was sent off to work Si's job at the canned-food factory for the rest of the summer while she returned home for the harvest.

173

I happily rode a borrowed old bike, carrying a small saddlebag of rice and a larger one of sweet potatoes. A few changes of clothes were packed in another bag that I carried on my back. The road to Han Jian was narrow, and ran along the curvy Pacific Coast. White waves chased up the beach like a large serpent's tongue, stretching out and curling back rhythmically. You could occasionally see sails, glistening in the sun. The fresh breeze carried a salty tang. I loved the deserted, lonely sea.

The old bike rattled along the rough surface, which had been left bumpy by torrents of rain, then baked dry by the sun. The footprints of various shoes and bare feet that had struggled through the rain remained imprinted like miniature models of high mountains and deep valleys. I stopped at midpoint in Bridge Town, which lay between Han Jian and Yellow Stone, two hours' travel time each way. It was a small, lonesome village, perched at the tip of the bay overlooking the sea.

On the narrow cobbled street, clustered with a dozen little white houses, a few women moved slowly, baskets on their heads, looking suspiciously at me. Some toddlers were playing in the dirt and empty shells, while a couple of old ladies dozed beside them. I looked around, but didn't see a man in sight. No wonder people called this fishing village 'Widow's Town'. The men spent weeks and months on their fishing trips. Some came back; others never did.

I got off the bike and pushed it along the short street. I passed the barbershop. Not surprisingly, inside there was a lady zapping away at another lady. A cat sat on an empty chair meant for customers. I passed the fish store next. It was empty, manned by a lady smoking a water pipe that bubbled like a brook. A large wooden sign at the door read FRESH CRABS, OYSTERS, CLAMS, MORE WILL COME AFTER THE TIDE IS OUT.

The lady with the pipe smiled at me, her hair bound up in clouds of smoke.

It was a funny town, with narrow gaps between each house that offered slices of the sea in the background. At the end of the street, my front wheels brushed by and scared a few roosters that gargled at me before running off to perch on a dead tree. Those were the only living male creatures I encountered. Bridge Town ended at an ancient archway. Beyond it was a stone bridge that stretched over the now-muddy Dong Jing River. The virgin Dong Jing had lost its chastity somewhere along the way and changed its colour after being seduced by the sea. It flirted, tangoed, and winked at the powerful waves before finally burying its head in the strong embrace of the Pacific, not knowing its fate. The bridge was about eighty years old. As a child Grandpa used to catch a ferry to cross the Dong Jing at this point, collecting rents and lease payments for the farmland we had owned along the delta area.

At the head of the bridge stood two lines of stone sculptures of heavenly guardians, wearing ancient war robes and holding fighting swords. They stood fifteen feet tall, gazing at the sea, aloof and mute. One of the stone men had lost his head during the air bombings by the Japanese in World War Two. The guy next to the headless fellow was leaning against his neighbour, toppled by the Red Guards during the height of the Cultural Revolution because they symbolized blind, superstitious worship. They had wanted to throw them all into the sea, but that day a jumpy Red Guard was squashed to death when the stone man fell on his neighbour. The rest of the Red Guards fled the site, not wanting to come near the giants again. Silently, they had beaten the Japanese and the Red Guards. There were our gods of the sea and land.

I parked my bike against the foot of one stone man and sat on his toe, fishing out a piece of rice cake from my bag. I was right at the spot Grandpa had told me about, the third man from the left, looking to the east. It was the best place from which to see one of the twenty-four supreme sights of Putien, known as 'The Morning Sun at Sea'. Local folklore had it that on one particular clear morning in May, the sun, in the form of a fireball, jumped a few times on the horizon before its ascent. At present, that part of the sea appeared to be red.

Ancient scholars had made trips to all corners of Putien, writing poetry about their favourite spots, leaving the following generation to wonder what had been in their crazy minds at that moment. Grandpa confessed that he had come here each year with his friends, following the seasons. None of the places matched up to the poetry meant to portray them. Surely none of his companions had seen the sun jump, he would say with a chuckle. He said he only came to this spot for the fresh oysters dipped in vinegar, and the clams served on seaweed.

As I looked at the sea, I thought about the fabled mirage and the many sunken boats that had belonged to the men of Bridge Town. Seagulls echoed the lonely tune of the village. Two rice cakes later – I guessed it to be around three in the afternoon, for the sun had cast a shadow over the shoulder of the stone man and the sea breeze had begun to gather speed – I picked up my old bike and tailed a biker with a tall pile of dry hay on his back seat, who sheltered me from the wind.

Han Jian was a seaport town with two long intertwining streets. The tail of the town was on the hill, while its head dipped into the water. From a distance, it looked like two snakes reaching down to drink from the sea. It wasn't the county capital like Putien, but the atmosphere was relaxing and commercial. Wealthy retirees from Hong Kong and South Asian countries roamed the streets, fanning away the summer heat with large coconut-leaf fans. The men wore colourful polyester shirts, unbuttoned, revealing their drooping nipples, and swapped stories across the narrow crowded streets, speaking in their accented Putien dialect. Some said speaking Cantonese had ruined their accents, but Dad said they had stayed too long in the wealthy capital of Hong Kong so that they talked as though they had silver coins in their mouths.

As I pedalled among the pedestrians, bikers, hawkers, kids, and trucks loaded with fruits and food heading for the seaport, excitement began to build. I was going to live near this town for the whole summer, free from the watchful eyes of my family and able to do what my heart wished. I stopped by a cigarette kiosk and bought a pack of Flying Horse, which I would smoke later in the leisurely manner of a man with a salary.

Si met me at the gate to her factory on the edge of town. I hadn't seen her for two months. She was wearing an attractive short hairstyle.

'The city look,' I said, smiling at her.

'You like it?' Si asked.

I nodded, patting my own hair before entering the grand entrance of the factory.

Guards with rifles slung over their shoulders patrolled the gates. They checked my sister's badge and we were let in.

'Why the rifles?' I asked.

'People steal things all the time. The general manager was a military man.'

A group of young people on bikes flew by us, yelling and screaming my sister's name.

'Who are they?'

'Friends, getting off work.'

When we reached her division, water treatment, her manager and her best friend greeted me with enthusiasm. The manager was a stocky man with a missing arm. The story was that it had been sawed off and dropped into a burning stove while he helplessly watched it burn. Her best friend was a fat boy of twenty, with hair on his face like a wolf. He smiled at me and both his eyes became two lines beneath his thick eyebrows. He pinched my ears and slapped my back.

'Why are they so nice to you?' I asked Si after we left the office.

'Fatty is a buddy, loyal but stubborn. And I had just bought two cartons of Flying Horse for the boss. That will be good for a month or so, then you'll need to buy him another carton. It's a corrupt place. Bribery is the only way to make your job safe. Everyone does it, from the general manager to the division head and team leader.'

She showed me where I would be staying, a tiny bed in a tiny, windowless cubicle behind a boiler room. There were no toilets and the light in the hallway had a nasty habit of blinking and resting whenever it wanted to. The dark smoke-coloured ceiling was covered with webs. I didn't have to stretch my imagination far to think of rats, roaches, and nasty hungry cats lurking behind those old barrels and bits of abandoned machinery.

Si told me that occasionally there was another girl who stayed overnight in the room opposite ours. The *occasionally* prompted me to walk the surroundings outside the wobbly house. The ground was overgrown with tall grass and mangy weeds, the kind that hid all sorts of unspeakable evils and ruined the beauty of the neighbourhood. I could just imagine myself alone, huddled beneath a flimsy blanket as wind and lightning clashed outside on dark nights.

Si knew I wasn't the bravest when it came to being alone in the dark. When I was younger, Grandma had to stay with me until I fell asleep in my cot in order to keep the headless blue ghosts away from me. There wasn't a single ghost story I hadn't heard or read. The sad part was I believed them all. Darkness invited all these characters back into my mind, until I was cowering under the sheet, sweating and trembling.

Si said that she had been lucky to find a free place to live, and that I could bunk with Fatty if I needed to. She had to hurry to catch a truck from the factory that was heading for Yellow Stone on its delivery route. The price for the ride had been a pack of Flying Horse to the driver. As I saw her off, I couldn't help admiring her social skills. She seemed prettier and much more capable away from Yellow Stone. People listened to her and liked her. I couldn't believe that she used up more Flying Horse than I did. It was a Flying Horse society here. Long live Flying Horse!

The next day I reported to the drab water-treatment office. The manager wasn't there. Fatty was playing cards with a couple of girls. He stood up and brought me over to join their poker game.

'I'm here to work, Fatty,' I protested.

'This is work, you farm boy,' Fatty said, smiling. 'We wait here, watch the water tower outside, and take the measurement of the water every hour, rain or shine. That's it.'

'Nothing else?'

'Nope. You just need to come here and sign your name. Once a week you work overnight and sleep here. The factory gives you free food for the night.'

'Gee, this is heaven,' I said.

They all laughed.

I soon came to know that the office was staffed with people from important families. Fatty's dad was an old revolutionary who had fought in the mountains of Fujian. His mum was his third wife and his father was often mistaken for his grandpa. The short girl, Ying, was married to an army veteran who was now the deputy party chief of Han Jiang. The comely girl, Ning, had a habit of sitting by the door of the office every morning waiting for the mail to come, then disappearing and reappearing red-faced whenever she got an airmail letter from her lover in Hong Kong.

They sat around gossiping about their men, knitting sweaters. They hummed lullabies out of tune, while I rotted with boredom in the corner, staring at the traffic outside the window. I volunteered to run up the water tower and check for them even when it wasn't my turn.

'I'm so bored,' Ning said one day, arching her slender back. 'Hey, I heard you play the flute. Is that true?'

'Not too well,' I said.

'If you play for us for twenty minutes, we'll let you go out and play for the whole morning.'

'Wouldn't I get into trouble for doing that?'

'What trouble? For entertaining us?'

'Isn't there some sort of rule against it?'

'We make the rules here. If anyone doesn't like it, we'll turn off their water.'

So from then on I played my flute, doing the songs they picked. Then I got to go around town with Fatty on his bike, and see movies. Even the manager would slouch in his chair behind the empty desk, sip his tea, and tap his finger on the table to the beat of the music.

One day he took me aside and told me that my sister had been gone too long, and he didn't think he could cover for us much longer. The factory would never allow a fourteen-and-a-half-year-old to work here, and he could get into trouble.

After I went back to my cubicle, I checked my calendar, depressed. It had been a month, and it was Flying Horse time.

I went to town, bought him another carton, and dropped it off at his residence, saying that he had forgotten it in the office. It worked. The next day he took me aside again and said that he would be willing to have me for as long as Si needed to work back in our commune.

I had somehow got used to my living arrangement. Each night I walked the long, dark, narrow road to the boiler room and down the squeaky hall before it turned completely dark. I brought a pee-pot with me and placed it under the bed. I had hidden a small knife beneath my pillow that I grabbed whenever there was a disturbance in the house. One night, I heard a crash at around four in the morning, and I spent the rest of the night holding the knife in my hand, curled up under the blanket like a shrimp getting fried. The next morning, I saw that a huge piece of ceiling tile had dropped on top of the old boiler. The rats must have been having a party up there.

During all those lonely nights, I never heard any sound or movement from my invisible neighbour. I was hoping she would show up some day and make the place a little noisier. Anything was more welcome than being alone, but then that night finally arrived. It was drizzling, and the sea breeze was picking up. The clouds, thick and dark, were gathering on the western horizon. I had my dinner early and went back to bed, reading an old warlord story. The thought of an impending storm kept me up past midnight. As I was slipping into a dream, through my thin wall I heard laughter roaring from the hallway. The wall consisted simply of boards pasted with old newspapers to cover the cracks, so soundproofing was worse than zero. The walls trembled. There was a man and a woman. The man mumbled something incoherent, his tongue thick, and the girl was giggling and cursing teasingly. Unsteady footsteps made the hallway shake.

I nimbly crawled out of the bed and removed a piece of tape from an existing hole, what I called my watch hole, glimpsing the back of a heavy man with an arm around the girl. His other hand was on her chest. He was a big, bearish guy and she was a shadowy, petite figure under the dim, fifteen-watt lighting. They stumbled into the wall and stopped at the door as the girl fumbled for the key. The man did something quick and the girl laughed and slapped his wrist, like a mum admonishing her naughty son. They disappeared behind the door and the light went off. It must be her husband, I thought, and thanked Buddha for saving me from a miserable night alone in the storm.

Soon enough, there was noise. Unbearable noise, like water falling from a tall mountain. There was a loud moan from a desperate, helpless-sounding man and a loud cry of pain from the girl. The man was doing something rhythmic and the girl yelled to his beat. There was heavy breathing and the bed squeaked. Something was knocked off the table, dropping to the ground. It went on for four or five unbearable minutes before the man let out a cry. It sounded like he was beating the girl. Suddenly it ended. I could hear the raindrops drumming on the roof. My heart was racing and my ears echoed with their cries. I squatted at the foot of the wall, puzzled, worried, and curious. I wondered whether I should storm out with some sort of weapon and help her.

'Now get out of here,' I heard the girl say.

'No, please. I'm not going.'

'Get out, you drunk.'

I heard the crash of a bottle, and then heard the man stumbling into the hallway. I glued my eye to the hole. He limped and rubbed his face with his hand. I didn't see his face, just his back, and the slight limp. The girl slammed the door and I heard her breath catching unevenly.

Something had gone wrong, but it wasn't my business to interfere. I rolled into my bed and tried to think of what those desperate moans and cries had been about. I wished my brothers in Yellow Stone were here to explain. The storm began to pick up and the wind made my walls rattle. At such times I would usually curl up and paste my back to the wall, covered by the sheet from head to toe, but I was too occupied with the mystery to be scared that night. I stayed up long afterwards, waiting for the man to storm back and for the girl to scream again, but there was only the rain and the sound of the girl's snoring, light and even.

Like the face of a child, the next day the sun crawled along the window bar shamelessly, as if there had never been a drop of rain last night. I checked the alarm clock. It read seven. I jumped out of bed and flattened my nose to the crack in the wall, watching for my neighbour. Not a sound. I opened the door and looked up and down the hallway. No traces of a broken bottle. I sauntered down, hands in pockets, whistling, and slowed down as I passed the girl's room. It was quiet, like before. Then I opened the window at the head of the hallway and the sun flooded the floor. Only in the light did I see the evidence of glistening bits of broken glass, glass that hadn't been there yesterday. So it hadn't been a nightmare last night. There had been a girl, a man, and a bottle. As I looked closer, there were traces of a broom having touched the surface of the dusty floor. She had tried to clean up the evidence. She had probably left before I woke up.

When I went to work, I couldn't help telling everyone about what happened in my boiler room last night. My listeners – Ying, Ning, and Fatty – laughed at me hysterically.

Fatty smiled his silly smile, making his eyes disappear into the folds of his face. The two girls blushed and looked at each other with a secret understanding before turning away to whisper to each other.

'What's the matter? Don't you think it was scary?' I asked Fatty.

He shook his head and said, 'Outside, not here.' He looked at the girls and his face, too, reddened.

I followed him out of the office.

He sat down on the cement steps that led to the water tower and gestured for me to sit beside him.

'You want a smoke for this one?' He pulled out a Flying Horse for himself and one for me. We lit the cigarettes with a single match.

'What is it, something funny?' I asked.

He nodded. 'It's embarrassing in front of the girls.'

'Come on, tell me. What's so embarrassing about it?'

He drew a few long, deep puffs and said, 'Do you know what a man and a woman do when they are alone at night?'

I wasn't getting it. I smoked and shook my head.

'Don't tell me you haven't seen a male ox humping a female, with that long dick slipping in and out.'

I could feel my mouth drop open at the realization. 'But she was crying!' I said.

'They do' – he nodded – 'with pleasure.'

I felt a stir somewhere inside me. 'So they were doing the cow thing?' I was overwhelmed by the discovery. I had actually overheard the whole episode of the cow thing performed by humans. It wasn't very neighbourly. The little boy in the room next door had almost come running with a knife to defend her. I felt ashamed and stirred in an odd way.

Fatty nodded, smiling with relief at my understanding.

'Does it always involve a bottle?'

'Oh, that part I don't know.'

'The girl called him a drunk.'

'They must have had a good time.'

'How do you mean?'

'Liquor and women, they go hand in hand like a banana soaked with honey.' He smacked his mouth deliciously. Fatty sounded like an expert. I wondered why we hadn't had this conversation earlier.

'Have you done it before?'

His fat face broke into a smile. 'You may think so.'

'Well! With whom and how?'

He shook his head, looking at the tip of his cigarette.

'You're not sharing it with me?'

'It was a long time ago and I don't want to corrupt your little mind.'

I begged and begged.

'It's bad for you to know, and besides, you heard enough from your neighbour. Next time get a telescope or poke a hole into her room and watch.'

'You shut up. I would never do that.'

'Hey, did you see the man's face?'

'No, but I remember the limp.'

'The limp?'

'Yeah, why?'

'Show me how he limped.'

I stood up and limped around, dragging my right foot just a little, like a broom sweeping the floor.

'Was he big or small?'

'Big in the middle, small at both ends, like an olive.'

'Tall?'

'Yeah.'

183

'And a little drunk?'

'He talked with coins in his mouth, slurring.'

'It can't be.'

'What can't be.'

'Nothing.'

'Nothing? I answered all your questions. You're not answering mine? Thanks for nothing.'

He just shook his head.

For the rest of the day, I couldn't face the two women in my office. I pretended to read the newspaper, covering my face. A couple of times, they looked at me and smiled their knowing smiles. I looked away as soon as our eyes met.

In the factory cafeteria, I stayed away from the table where the two girls sat with the other factory girls at lunch, buried my face in my bowl, and gulped my food. As I left, I heard laughter coming from behind me. They must have been laughing at me, for I heard Ning's voice. She was telling everyone about my naive encounter. I fled the scene like a convicted felon.

That night I returned to my boiler room with a strange feeling. I stared at the girl's door for a long time. Her cries, the sinful, now pleasurable cries echoed in my mind. I tried to imagine what she looked like and wished I knew more about her. The idea of poking a hole through her wall crossed my mind. The mystery was only a thin wall away. What kind of a gypsy life did she live? Was she beautiful or not? Was she married or single? Was that man her lover or her husband?

I'd never get any answers. There was no one to ask. I poked some more holes in my wall and patiently waited for the next sighting. Her door became the shrine of my imagination and I would have my eye glued to the peephole at the first sign of any movement in the house.

One afternoon as we were playing poker in our office, we heard people yelling and shouting like at a ballgame. We all put our cards down and went outside to see what was happening.

'Shit, it's that bastard again.'

I saw our one-armed division manager being chased around the water tower by a big man with a red face. He was screaming and foaming like a drunk, and brandishing a bottle. And he limped.

'Who is that?' I asked urgently.

'The bodyguard of the factory's party chief.'

'Why is he chasing our manager?'

'He's drunk. Our manager was probably drinking with him.'

'Why isn't anyone stopping him?'

'He'll attack anyone in his way. He's an animal. Within the factory, he fears no one.'

'Where did he come from?'

'The party chief came from the army and brought the bodyguard with him. He drinks every waking hour and you don't want to get in his way,' Fatty said.

The poor manager was still being chased up and down the road and the bodyguard was getting tired. As he slowed down and limped across our office, his pot-belly, fat ass, and small head paraded right before my eyes. When he walked by me, he turned his broad back on us and the images of the man in my boiler room holding the girl's breast suddenly jumped to life. I almost let out a cry before I covered my mouth with my hands. It was the same man. I had no doubts. I had seen him limp in and out of our boiler room. He couldn't fake a limp like that. It left me thoroughly disgusted. How could any girl sleep with a dog like that? His eyes, red and dirty like muddy water, had no light in them. His mouth flapped with white spittle. What a slob. I couldn't imagine seeing him naked on top of the small frame of my invisible neighbour. The enormous belly must weigh seventy pounds and his nipples were so fat they looked like the breasts of a pregnant swine. His fat ass alone could have fed a party of four.

Finally the chase was over. The bodyguard collapsed in the middle of the road, the same way many previous chases must have ended. His face hit the dirt and his mountain of a body lay like a dead buffalo. Flies hovered over him, licking the sticky sweat from his neck folds. No one wanted to touch him. Our manager left the scene breathlessly, after sticking out his tongue at the limp carcass and waving to us.

Ten minutes later a decrepit electrician pulled out a water hose and sprayed the bodyguard. He awoke instantly, and shook his head wildly like a dog shaking off water. He hauled himself up and crawled to his feet, limping along the wall, leaving his wet footprints behind.

'Get out of here before you get hit by a truck, you lousy bastard,' yelled the old electrician. Because he was the founder of the factory and a revolutionary himself, he was the only one in the factory who dared to do that.

The bodyguard limped away, minus one shoe, into the shadows of the factory's chimneys. Everyone watching him went back to work, the electrician rolled the hose up again till the next time. Everything went back to normal.

That night, I came back to my room mourning the sad discovery. I stared at the door, feeling sorry for my neighbour. She had been raped, pleasurably. I was the witness. Not quite an eyewitness, but I had had an earful. Her door became the shrine of a heroine. I wanted to lay wild flowers at its foot in sympathy.

The boiler room was never the same after that night. When darkness fell, there was always the possibility of drama and mystery, but such a scene never happened again, nor did the girl ever return.

Sixteen

Han Jian Canned Food Factory produced 80 per cent of the canned mushrooms lining the shelves of supermarkets in the U.S. and the rest of the corrupt western world. It was a cash cow. The value of the U.S. dollars it brought in had made Mr Tui, the manager, the most important member of the Communist party in Fujian province every year, since the mushroom account had landed on this lowly food manufacturer a few years ago.

Mr Tui, who also doubled as party secretary of the canned-food factory, rode around in a Fifties model Russian car with tinted windows. His bodyguard could be seen every morning running after the car, trying to put on his shirt as he was left behind by his angry boss, who invariably found him still recovering from another night's heavy drinking. Mr Tui lived with his family in a large new house built by the factory, but he was listed as the owner. He sent for a northern chef who cooked everything with pepper, from his native province of Shangdong. Liquor flowed freely in that household, and every meal was a banquet. The party leaders discussed urgent political issues with the help of Peking ducks, barbecued piglets, French brandy, and filtered cigarettes from Hong Kong. In the background the music of love songs, also from Hong Kong, played continuously to help solve the tricky political problems.

The boss's official monthly salary was about a hundred and fifty yuen, the equivalent of twenty U.S. dollars. But he made his real money the old-fashioned way, skimming a healthy percentage from individual mushroom producers. For every ton of fresh mushrooms sold to the factory, he took 10 per cent from the growers, that percentage coming from the inflated prices paid them by the factory. Happy growers worshipped him like a god, a horny little god who demanded sexual favours. The farmers would have the girls ready on demand, otherwise the mushrooms would just sit and rot and hundred of thousands would be wasted. Some angry farmers had reported his behaviour to local authorities, but he himself was, in essence, the local authority, and most of the reports landed on Mr Tui's banquet table. Those disagreeable farmers found themselves in bankruptcy shortly thereafter. A couple of farms had even been burned down.

In a busy season, mountains of fresh mushrooms were piled up along the cement pits. The whole factory smelled like a large mushroom-soup kitchen. Everything I wore to the factory, including my underwear, told the tale of my whereabouts. Most of the employees followed their boss's fine Communist example and had their own ways of stealing from the factory to supplement their income. A common one involved family participation. They invited family members to visit, and under cloak of night they ventured into the pits where the fresh mushrooms were stored. They bagged them, accompanied them through the side gate, and had the family member resell the mushrooms back to the factory early the next day, before the mushrooms yellowed. A brother of our one-armed division manager just lived in the factory while running an empty yet highly profitable mushroom-growing business. The factory drivers routinely unloaded mushrooms at their own houses and resold them back to the factory.

It was one happy family down there at the factory. The employees, about four hundred of them, lived in factory apartments and didn't have to work at all. They made the factory hire temps like my sister and me, thousands of us, while they all stayed at home playing poker and raiding the local food and fish markets. Some division heads and team leaders used their temps as cooks and nannies, while others forced sex on the young girls who were eager to make a buck in this freewheeling mushroom paradise.

The regular employees could be seen flying out of the factory door on their bikes every morning, going to the local market to buy the freshest seafood off the boats, while the miserable temps crawled in to take up the morning shift. Soon, temps were running the factory and the regular employees only dropped by to pick up their pay cheques.

To my surprise, I was told one day that there were five regular employees at the water-treatment division who never showed up, and that the reason why the division manager was here once in a while was due to his brother's mushroom business. The division had another temp who had never been seen. They said she was working at the division manager's home, coaching his son in maths.

One day I jokingly asked my manager whether he would consider letting me teach his son the flute. He said no thanks, the son was taking violin lessons. Oh well, it was a reasonable attempt to improve my lifestyle.

One of my biggest concerns, day in and day out, was food. The dried yams and rice I'd brought from home kept dwindling. I measured the portions of rice carefully each meal before putting it up to steam in the factory cafeteria. The portions got smaller and smaller. I found myself hungry all day long. I stayed away from the rest of the gang in the cafeteria because I didn't want them to know that I was eating cheap yams while they were eating white rice that looked plump and delicious.

I had another reason to hide. I had been cooking mushrooms in my room, eating them for three meals a day. At one point I became so sick of them that I threw up at the faintest whiff of steaming mushrooms. Yet all I saw in the factory were mushrooms. I smelled mushrooms and talked about mushrooms. Each day I carried a small bag of them tucked under my shirt when I slipped through the heavily guarded gate. I sautéed them, fried them, baked them, and steamed the suckers until I ran out of options. I tried cooking them with salt, sugar, vinegar, and wine. Eventually, after having eaten them three times a day for thirty days they all tasted the same. With the money I saved by eating mushrooms I used to buy rice from the local market. The rice tasted so good that sometimes I splurged and would have two pounds of rice steamed, then find a deserted corner where no one could see me and guzzle down the whole lot, plain. The others would have thought I was some starving Ethiopian, with my big head, skinny neck, countable ribs, and melon belly. I was sure I must have looked pathetic enough that my colleagues would raise a collection for me.

Fatty was the only one who noticed my dietary habits. He suggested we fish during our spare time, then I wouldn't have to worry about my food any more. We caught carp and yellowfish in the stream a mile from the factory. Now it was fish fillets sautéed with mushrooms every day. I tried it Hunan style, with spices and pepper, but it brought tears to my eyes and burned right through my stomach lining. I stuck to plain Canton style, simply steaming the fish with a touch of ginger and garlic, sprinkled with salt. My breath smelled unpleasantly fishy so I ate more garlic to cover it, which was a disaster. People stared at me and stayed away. Good thing I wasn't staying much longer or I would have had to start hunting game in the hills just for a change of diet.

One day I announced to Fatty that I was leaving to go back to school. He asked me to drop by his place before heading home.

When Si came to replace me one early morning, she looked so tanned that her teeth stood out, white like a crescent moon in a dark sky when she smiled.

'I'm glad you didn't lose my job.'

I smiled and told her that there was fish for her dinner that I had prepared, and plenty of rice left. She was very proud of me. Right before I took her bike and started my journey home, I brought her aside and told her quietly about the girl and the presence of a man. But that was all I said. Showing her a piece of thick tree trunk I had picked up from the roadside, I told her that she could use it to jam against her flimsy door each night and that she should hide the knife under her pillow just as I had.

Si looked at me oddly and thanked me, probably thinking that I had become affected by my solitary nights. I felt like a big brother, unwilling to leave my innocent little sister in such a horrible, dangerous place. Slowly, I climbed up the bike and rode off to Fatty's to say goodbye.

Not surprisingly, Fatty was waiting for me at his door. Two large bags sat at his feet.

'Here, let's load this on your bike,' Fatty said.

'What is it?'

'The driver, my friend, dropped this off last night. All fresh. Bring them home to your family and say "hi".'

I parked the bike and opened up one of the bags. It was full of red lychees, plump and fresh. It smelled like the Yellow Stone orchard that I had left behind. Each bag must have weighed fifty pounds. 'I can't take this.'

'Of course you can. You're an employee of the factory, so you're entitled.' He laughed. 'Everyone steals in this town.'

'I don't want to be chased by a bunch of factory security guards.'

'You won't. This is outside the factory's territory. Besides, you could have got them anywhere, and I couldn't eat the whole lot. They'd all go bad.' He rolled up his sleeves and helped me. When I opened my thin arms to give him a brotherly goodbye, my fingers couldn't reach all the way round. Fatty would always remain fat. He wore a confused look on his face, a little lost and sad. I asked him to visit me often and soon.

I rode all the way home against a head wind, not daring to stop for fear of getting caught with the loot.

My mum, dad, sisters, and brother were delighted to see me and the lychees surprised them. Mum wasn't quite sure about them but Dad said the choice was simple: either we ate them or we dumped them. We sat around our table and feasted.

I took ten pounds of the lychees to my four friends, who hugged me so hard I couldn't breathe.

We ate and chatted. Mo Gong was ready for another romance. I told them about my encounter in the night and they were all quiet afterwards. Like me, they didn't know whether to be turned on or off. They all wanted to know who the girl was, but I had to leave the story without an ending.

Yi, who was on holiday from his city job, related the last chapter of his own hopeless romance with his teacher's daughter. She had refused to come home for the arranged wedding with the town's

191

party chief, and instead had eloped with a fellow actor in the commune's troupe. He was a young and handsome man, whose father had fled to Hong Kong and had become a hotel owner in Kowloon. The newlyweds were building a big house facing a lake. We were all happy that this angel had flown out of her cage and was now gliding freely on her own wings.

'I guess she wasn't meant for you, Yi.'

He shook his head, smiling, while making his tobacco roll, thick and round as usual.

Just as usual, Yellow Stone was quiet. I felt glad to be home, but a small emptiness lingered at leaving a busy town like Han Jian. But soon all those young and lively faces became a memory, belonging to another time and age. They were people who were happier living in a more complicated world. I missed them, but on the other hand, I didn't have to sneak into my room early any more. I had my bunk bed back in the attic.

Before going to sleep that night, I stared at my textbook for a long while and wondered when Professor Wei was going to start my lessons. My heart beat faster at the thought of going to college, of maybe one day growing up and joining those young people out beyond the boundaries of Yellow Stone, and leaving this quiet, sleepy town that had no electricity.

In late August, the lotus leaves floated lazily on the calm surface of the Dong Jing River. The clouds seemed distant, and in the fields, drab after the harvest, buffalo ducked their horns and pulled the heavy ploughs, bearing the weight on their calloused shoulders, tossing up the flattened soil in readiness for the new plantings. They mooed – a sound the farmers interpreted as a prediction of rain for the following day. Their brethren, a few acres away, joined in, and soon the whole buffalo community were mooing, like foxes howling in the high western mountains on a night lit by a full moon. Autumn filled me with emptiness, as if my heart knew the bleak winter was near. The sound of the buffalo always seemed to me the lonesome song of Yellow Stone's autumn. I used to sit by the river and stare at the buffalo in the distance, letting their song take me back to the distant memory of the summer now behind me, leaving me forlorn and melancholy.

One morning, Mum woke me and told me to put on a clean shirt because Professor Wei would like to start her lessons with me. I jumped out of bed like a young fish frolicking in shallow waters under the sun. I washed my face with soap, brushed my teeth three times, with a double load of toothpaste, and combed my hair into neat furrows, parted on the right. I even looked into details such as nose hair and earwax for five minutes in front of the broken half-mirror in my room. My brother and sisters laughed at me as I walked into our dining room, but I told them that I now knew about manners after a stint in the big city of Han Jian. High-class people dressed nicely and behaved with dignity.

I ate my breakfast carefully, trying to prevent the soupy porridge from splashing all over my clean shirt or the pickled green vegetables from catching in the tricky cracks of my teeth. I brushed my teeth once more and put on a pair of plastic sandals, the most formal of all footwear, to my knowledge, to ever walk the street of Yellow Stone.

I carried my English book in my schoolbag and walked along the deserted alley instead of the broad street for fear of getting teased by my friends, who usually took up their positions at the bridge and laughed at every soul who passed. If they saw me, they would have roughed up my hair and tried to make me smoke until I smelled like a smokestack.

As I neared the western end of town, I became more self-conscious. My voice would sound too loud or too provincial. Even my toes seemed funny, sticking out of the sandals. The breeze had blown my way and no doubt my hair looked like a bird's nest by now. I touched it lightly with my fingers. It felt all wrong. I squatted by the river and checked my wavering image in the water. A few strands of hair were sticking up. I pasted them down with water, and opened my mouth wide to make sure no food was stuck in my teeth. Then I ran along until I stood in front of the forbidding door to the Weis' estate. Only after I had caught my breath did I knock, cautiously.

I heard the low rumble of a dog. It was sniffing away behind the door, becoming excited as it caught my scent. It seemed to say

'Welcome to the Wei estate, and could I have your ass for lunch.' I took a step backwards and almost peed in my pants.

I had long heard about this dog's reputation, how it would lurk behind the wall, ready to kill with those sharp yellow teeth. Thieves stayed away from the estate not because a couple of old ladies there said their prayers day and night, but because the beast walked the beat. In the daytime, he chased the birds in the garden. At night, he ran after the cats that ran after the rats. The guy was the man of the house.

'Shh . . . be polite.' A gentle female voice came from behind the door. The dog growled some more and barked grumpily. I took another step back. Politeness was not quite the issue here; he wanted to eat me.

'You are a naughty dog today, go sit in your house.' The voice became firmer this time. Gee, how about locking him up? He was only a flesh-eating animal. He dragged his feet away, shuffling along the ground, reluctantly leaving. No doubt his eyes still lingered on the door, no doubt he was still full of evil thoughts about having me for lunch. After all, it was a man-eat-dog or dog-eat-man world out there.

The door opened and a white-haired Professor Wei smiled like a white lily in full bloom.

'Come in, please,' she said in English.

My mind rapidly searched for an answer. I knew 'Sit down, please'. Our teacher used to say that sarcastically whenever I stood scratching my head, unable to answer any of his questions. Professor Wei wanted me to do something, but I did not know what. I didn't know whether to step forward or back, to nod or to shake my head, until she gestured with her hand for me to come in.

'Thank you, thank you.' I used up the only other two English words I knew in one single sentence, then cut my eyes left and right, looking for the fabled animal who was probably whetting his teeth on stone and racheting his appetite up for my skinny behind.

'It should not be "Tank you". It should be "Thank you", with the tip of your tongue between your teeth,' she said as I followed her into the garden.

194

It was the first time I had opened my big mouth and I had already tanked her instead of thanking her. This was going to be great. She might as well return me to the other side of the wall, where I belonged.

But she smiled, showing a shallow dimple in her lined face, like a sweet little girl trapped inside wrinkled make-up. 'I like your hair. Nowadays, kids just don't comb their hair like they used to.' I blushed like a mute getting smacked in the face. I understood her this time, she had switched to Chinese.

Had it not been for the river outside, my hair would have been sticking out like a sprouting onion garden. I was thankful. First impressions were important. I wondered what she would have said had my hair been less than perfect. Then there would surely have been nothing positive left about me in her eyes. She was doing this because she felt she and her sister owed my dad. That was it. I wouldn't be surprised if she told me after the first lesson that I was as impossible to educate as that dog out there. He probably understood more English than I did after all the eavesdropping he did from his own little house.

A narrow path paved with pebbles of various shapes and colours led us to the garden. It was rambling with shapely trees and wild flowers creeping all over the ground. There were arching trees and a gazebo covered with red flowers. At the lower end, some clear water had collected into a natural pond, where young lotus plants floated. Although the garden rambled, there was a certain discipline about it that was neat and orderly, just like Professor Wei herself.

She guided me to the white house behind the garden. I watched her tiny five-foot form move gently in front of me, admiring the knowledge she had stored away in that white head. She was a walking English dictionary.

Educate me, I prayed. Teach me, enlighten me. Make something out of nothing.

The red tile on the floor looked as if it had been swept and mopped twice a day, 365 days a year, for the last hundred years. The antique furniture was polished, and shone in the sunlight bathing the living room. The impression was of elegance, simple and neat. I stopped at the threshold, stared at the sole of my sandals, and thought of the dirty road I had just walked along outside the wall. Dirt or no dirt, I wasn't going inside wearing those sandals. But if I took them off, my naked feet would look vulgar and ugly, touching tiles where only pale uncalloused toes had been. I would leave dirty, sweaty marks everywhere. The cleaning lady would kill me.

'Come on in, don't worry about the floor, and sit down here.' She pointed to a cosy couch.

Good thing she spoke in Chinese or I would have mistaken it as an order to take off my sandals and crawl on my knees to avoid touching her floors with my dirty feet. I tiptoed across the living room, making my footprints as faint as possible. As I sank into the sofa, I was surprised how deep down I went. It wrapped my bottom snugly like no other chair I had ever sat in. I felt cradled by the touch of something soft and velvety. A sense of undeserved comfort swept over me.

Professor Wei pulled a chair over next to me. I straightened up from my own like a puppet pulled by its strings. She put her hand on mine to keep me from jumping out of my seat.

'I was very glad to hear from your lovely dad that you wanted to study English with me. What a refreshing idea!' She tossed her silver head and her eyes filled with a soft glow. Then her voice changed ever so slightly. 'Nowadays, kids out there only do bad things like smoking, gambling, fighting, and worse, talking about girls at such young ages.'

I shifted uncomfortably in my seat and felt the pack of Flying Horse in my back pocket; I was going to light a cigarette just as soon as I was out of here. The urge to smoke was alive and kicking.

'I'm sure you are not that type of a boy.' Professor Wei looked at me sharply and patted my knee as if to congratulate me. I sat in silence and gave her a nervous little nod.

'Now, why don't you show me how much English you know and I'll design a programme for you.' She crossed her legs and placed her hands one on top of another on her knees, comfortable in her role as audience.

I knew the time of embarrassment had come. I fumbled in my

schoolbag and fished out the untouched English book. I regretted not tearing out the second page, all scribbled over with caricatures of my English teacher.

'Read me the alphabet.'

That wasn't a bad place to start.

I cranked along with my rusty pronunciation, more and more unsure the further I went. I was red-faced at *G*, sweating at *H*, trembling at *I*, and lightheaded at *J*. The English sounds seemed to block my air passage and my lips went dry. I almost choked on those strange, cord-twisting letters. She stopped me just in time.

'It's hard, isn't it?'

I nodded, red-faced and mortified.

'I don't want you to pronounce those letters from your imagination. You made up some of the sounds as you went along, didn't you? Now follow me.' She half closed her eyes and read each letter slowly.

'*A, B, C, D, E.*' She stopped and looked at me. 'You made *E* sound like *A*. Now try again.' Her voice was like music to my ears. I wondered how different my life would have been had my goldfish-eyed teacher in school had one tenth of her elegance.

I imitated the movements of her mouth. She stopped at *E*, tilted her head, and listened quietly as I went over the letter until I beat it to death. Then she nodded reluctantly. We moved on.

The last letter *Z* took us a good three minutes. No matter how hard I stretched my neck, I could not get it. She looked at me patiently, with a slight frown, like a doctor trying to decide which remedy to use. I felt totally useless and stupid.

'So much for today.' She was declaring me a failure. I wasn't wanted back. Because of my dirty feet and ignorance, I was sure. She was going to give a weak excuse to spare me, but when I was gone, she would say to herself in English, *what a terrible kid*! Not only ignorant, but also impossible to cultivate. Perfect farmer material. My head went wild.

'You are very, very smart, I can tell from our first lesson.' She cupped her tiny hands, which were still beautiful, under her elegant chin. 'I am full of hope for you,' she said. 'If only you would come every day.' Her eyes were glowing with light as she looked at me. She was asking me to come back, I couldn't believe it. Hope filled me up again as if I were a sagging balloon. I was ready to fly.

'Goodbye, Da.'

I fumbled around for words, couldn't find any, and bowed several times.

I collected my bag and back-pedalled towards the door, where my dear old friend the dog was staring at me. He breathed angrily through his dark, wet snout. *You were lucky to stay that long and still be breathing*, he seemed to say. He looked disdainful, now. He had heard my terrible pronunciation, so bad that it had ruined his appetite. He, the defender of the elegant, wanted to kill me for mangling such a beautiful language.

You loser, don't ever come back again. His ears popped up, his eyes narrowed.

'Be a good boy, back to your house,' Professor Wei said gently. The monster dragged its bushy tail and shot a hateful look at me over his shoulder before heading for his house. What a character, did I have to deal with this grump every single day? When would it end? The day I lost my ass to him?

I picked my way gingerly behind the monster, darted through the door and let out a huge sigh as I fished out a Flying Horse. My eyes darted around, making sure Professor Wei wasn't witnessing another deadly sin from her lofty window upstairs. I would have waited if I could, but my vocal cords were screaming with desire to be smoked red and blue, and my heart throbbed with the excitement of surviving this landmark day. I needed to calm down or I would find myself jumping into the cool river. I was overcome with mixed feelings of joy and sadness. This was a new start to my boring and hopeless life, but it would be a long, uphill ride from the very bottom. The hill was Everest and I was starting out somewhere under the Pacific Ocean.

Seventeen

The school was without I-Fei now, and I had stopped going to the rehearsals. My classmates stared at me as though I were a dinosaur. Most of them hated me because I was arrogant, pompous, and too much of an artistic star. In elementary school, they would have ganged up and beaten the crap out of me, but times had changed. I was the big guy, sitting in the back seat, angry, ignorant, a fallen star of yesterday, a hostile sight to avoid. They cold-shouldered me. The rest of the school carried on as if I wasn't there. I watched them disdainfully and quietly. A few smaller guys in class still speculated that I had dated the most beautiful girl in the school's performing troupe. They winked at me when they saw her pass our classroom window. I said nothing, and kept them guessing in order to maintain the last ounce of respect I commanded among the students.

Dia was one of the guys who warmed up to me after he saw the vacancy left behind by I-Fei. He was a thin fellow who seemed to jump rather than walk. He had monkey ears and his hair was always a messy lawn that seemed as if it hadn't been mown for ages. He lived in a poor village ten miles west of Yellow Stone and walked to school every morning at sunrise, returning home at about eight each night. He was one of those kids known around the school as *walkers* to distinguish them from the students who bunked at the school dorm. He was the only person I knew who made thicker and longer tobacco rolls than Yi. And he used old newspaper to roll them. Sometimes when he ran out of old newspaper he would run around school looking for any scrap paper he could find.

This thin little guy carried a large schoolbag with him during the course of the day. Most of the space in it was taken up by the two cold meals he had to carry around, and the rest was divided up equally between books, a bag of foul-smelling homegrown tobacco, and an ugly pipe made from a twig. His nicotine addiction was legendary. He was the only person I knew who smoked before and after each meal and stopped halfway to squeeze in another thick, long tobacco roll.

The more time I spent with Dia, the less I felt like smoking at all. He was a great example of what happens to smokers. At the age of fifteen, he had a chronic cough and spat up sticky green stuff like an old man of ninety. His lungs wheezed loudly through his bony chest, outlined by countable ribs. His teeth were dark in front and back and he had a pale, lifeless look. The only gleam in his eye came from the reflected light of the matches with which he lit his rolls.

'How can you smoke like that?' I asked once, after we became better friends.

'Look who's talking.' Dia stared at me, puzzled. 'What's wrong with me?'

'Well, the shitty tobacco and the old newspapers you're using will kill you soon.'

'I'm not dying any time soon, Da. Grandpa rolled his first roll at the age of four and he's still kicking. He taught Dad to smoke at the age of five and *he's* still breathing. I didn't smoke till seven. The Dias are living legends. We'll live on.'

'Yeah, while wheezing.'

'That ain't funny.'

'I know. From tomorrow on, I'm going to bring you some of my dad's tobacco paper. That way you don't have to use the old paper any more.'

'No way am I gonna smoke with that pure white crap. It'll make everything as tasteless and plain as wax. The old ink on the paper adds a kick to the tobacco.'

'Yeah, so do bullets.'

One day I hid his tobacco bag under a thick layer of fallen leaves to see if he could do without a puff for a while. He couldn't. Dia ran around kicking the leaves like a crazy animal before attacking me and drumming my chest till I gave the bag back to him. He needed to smoke. In the end I felt sorry for him, watching him squat behind a tree trunk, puffing frantically as if there were no tomorrow. He had tears in his eyes.

'Don't joke like that no more.'

'I was trying to do you some good. I'm sorry.'

Every morning he made his first stop at my house, after his ten-mile walk. I treated him to some hot tea. He would sneak to our backyard for a smoke, and then reappear refreshed. Then we walked to school together. In the afternoon, he played with me for a while before the long journey home. Some weekends I would offer him my bunk bed so that he could stay for a night. He fought the invitations valiantly, but in the end never refused the offers. When he slept over, we talked about our lives and future late into the night. He wasn't a demanding guest, all he required was a chair to step on so that he could climb to the attic window-sill like a cat and smoke in the open air while staring at the bright stars.

The midterm exams came sooner than I liked. It was the first time I was paying attention to them. It had been a breezy school without serious tests for years. Now, the concept was arcane. The good students in class applauded and chatted excitingly about how they were going to review courses and score well. The losers put their heads on the desks and drummed the desktop, hating every word uttered by the good students.

The teacher enthusiastically answered questions the good students raised, and even threw in a smile or two when it came to the pretty girls in class. But when I raised my hand and asked which English book we would be tested on, the whole class burst into uncontrollable laughter. It was a big joke. The good students huddled together and laughed. Enjoying my humiliation, the teacher leaned back in his chair.

'What do you think?' he said slowly, tossing the chalk in his hands.

More laughter.

'I don't know.'

'Since when did you become interested in tests? Shouldn't you be in rehearsal at this time of the day?' He looked at his watch, smirking. 'For your information, it will be book four that you will be tested on. Are you sure you have book four in your possession?'

Continued laughter.

I felt Dia's eyes on me. He was the only one feeling sorry for me. The rest of them probably thought I was a drunk, just waking up to the glaring sunlight. I was human garbage in their eyes, victimized by changing times, with no idea of how to pull myself out of the hole I had sunk into. The talents I had, playing the flute and violin, were talents of yesterday. Now it was college, and whoever could jump the hoop and be that lucky 1 per cent to go on to college was the hero of the day. I still stank with yesterday's staleness. Most of them were happy to see me fall on my face, hoping I would break a few bones in the process.

I felt the presence of I-Fei, my hero of yesterday, outside the window, waving to me with the tip of his cigarette. For one moment, I wanted to jump out of the window, have a smoke, and forget about the class, the test, and these hateful people. Why couldn't people be more like animals and the creatures of nature? They didn't laugh at each other or kick each other's ass. Small birds sang the same tune on the same twig every day, and ants carried bits of food on their backs and passed them along to the next one in line, regardless of their sex, looks, background, or popularity.

The tests offered scant surprise. I stared at each paper for a good five minutes, scribbled down something, and turned them in. I answered half the questions on the maths test with ease, but the rest looked like a foreign language. And I only did one third of the physics test. History and geography were the hardest subjects to guess on, and whatever English I had mastered from the professor, a secret, was a mere scratch on a pyramid. Chinese was the only subject I excelled in. I had studied classics with my grandpa.

At the end of the week of tests, I felt as if I had gone to the Olympics and ended up sweeping the floor after everyone had left. I was sad, angry, and lost. What was I going to do with my life?

I thought about the buffalo pulling the heavy plough in the endless fields. Farming, Chairman Mao had once said, was the lifeline of our country. If I continued to stay at the bottom of the class, it looked like it would be the lifeline of Comrade Chen Da as well.

Eighteen

Dia and I found a new spot behind the school wall, where we met and chatted as he polluted his lungs with dark tobacco. He told me the secret of the Dia tobacco. Since his grandpa's time, they had kept a plot of land in their backyard the size of a basketball court, where they grew broad-leaved tobacco. The rich, bitter flavour was attributed to the fact that young Dia each morning watered the plants with the contents of three full night pots used overnight by the men in the Dia household. The thick, smelly piss nourished the young plants and added a special flavour not found with other growers. Thus Dia's brand worked like a double-barrelled shotgun, powerful and potent. It remained the only tobacco known to be able to quench their nicotine addiction, not a small feat.

One afternoon, I came to the spot earlier than usual. The leafy guava tree shaded the place like a benevolent umbrella. I took a short nap on some old newspapers and covered my face with my English book. The four lessons that morning had left me with minimum interest in life. The hovering flies didn't trouble me a bit. I didn't care if ants were crawling all over my sweaty, naked feet. My body lay limp on the rough ground, feeling the chill of the red soil beneath.

This morning, both the maths and English teachers had stared at me a little longer. As expected, there was sarcasm in their eyes and a sneer in their voices. What pissed me off was that not only did they not welcome me back to the classes I used to cut, but they also made snide comments that brought cheap laughter from the other students.

The young maths teacher never gave up until he got the girls in class to laugh. He was a fat fellow with drooping eyes and thick, floppy lips. Whenever he looked at the tall girls in the back row, his eyes shone with lust. He would lecture and walk around the class, intentionally rubbing the girls' backs, lingering there to drive a mathematical point home. He would touch their shoulders, and sometimes hold their hands a little too long, patting their soft young skin.

Dia kept count of all these rubbings in a logbook. One day, he said, he would report it to the authorities and have the fat teacher locked up for besmirching the purity of those lovely girls. Dia was a revengeful brat who was loyal to his friends and a pain-in-the-neck to his enemies. The fat teacher had snubbed him a few times, so Dia had declared him his enemy. The fat teacher often suggested we come to his dorm if anyone needed help. Young Dia had been there and the fat teacher wasn't helpful. In fact, he hadn't even opened the door after looking through the peephole. Dia had waited in the bushes by his dorm room; not five minutes later, he saw several girls being ushered in by the fat teacher.

As I dreamed away, snoring, I felt an intolerable itch around my nose and mouth. I twitched my face violently. I twisted some more. The itch stayed. I opened one eye and saw Dia smiling down, dangling an ear of wheat over my face. I grabbed the little brat and threw him under me. He slipped out and climbed on to my back and we started wrestling. The spot where we were was on a slope, which we rolled down until we landed in a soft bed of wheat. Then we laughed while trying to get to our feet. We helped each other dust off and climbed back up to our spot again.

'Have a smoke.' Dia sat down and rolled me a thick one.

'No thanks, not after you told me the piss story.'

'You'll need some sorta smoke for what I gotta tell you.'

It sounded bad. I looked into his eyes and he looked down. I took the roll and let him light it for me. Instantly, I felt the potent kick. The Dia piss worked miracles. I spat like a fisherman. 'What's the matter?'

'The midterm grades are out.' He had a dead man's tone, flat.

'How are ours?' I could feel my heart begging for mercy from the good Buddha. Make it presentable, I promised him, and I'll give you another thousand kowtows this very night.

'Well, mine are terrible.'

'And?'

'Yours are real bad.'

Kowtowing wouldn't be necessary any more. I had hit bottom and I deserved it. I puffed on the bitter smoke. For the first time, I felt good as I inhaled. I felt the rush go to my head; it was comforting, and I was satisfyingly numb. I leaned back on the red dirt wall limply, like a piece of smashed tofu. There wasn't an ounce of strength left in my body.

I was a failure, shaming myself, and my family. I should change my last name and never return home to beg for meals any more. Maybe I would take to the road like Mo Gong and Siang. The burden of failure made me despise myself.

'That's not all,' Dia added, stealing a careful look at me.

'What do you mean?'

'Someone pasted the results of all your exams on the wall outside our classroom. Now the whole school knows.'

'Son of a whore! It must be our principal teacher.' I gritted my teeth and slammed my fists into the soil. Now I was the laughing stock of the whole school. All my enemies, old and new, would be rejoicing over my downfall. Not only was I the son of a landlord, but I was stupid and lazy. Wise people could forgive the former but not the latter. I had shamed my whole family tree. My esteemed great-grandpa was at the top, and I was the loose, rotten screw at the bottom, the one who ruined the family's reputation. Dia shook my shoulder to make sure I was still alive and passed me another Dia-brand stogy. My hands shook from anger and humiliation; the only hope of steadying them any time soon was what my young friend was offering me.

I lay there with the afternoon sun caressing my face. The school bell rang like the call of a ghost. I could just see the smirks on the faces of my obnoxious schoolmates awaiting my entrance. I gestured to my friend to go to class while I lay unmoving, desperate for the sun to set so that the darkness would veil my shameful face.

Dia left his tobacco bag with me and said he would come to check on me. I managed a slight nod as he back-pedalled away from me. My hopes of going to college were dashed. I was a breathing dead body. There was no dignity, shame, or respect left in me, only regrets, tons of them. I had lived my life vicariously and now I was to suffer for ever.

When the sky finally darkened, I collected my books and took the small dirt road home, staying away from the street. I bumped into old farmers lugging muddy ploughs on their shoulders, walking behind their buffalo as they headed home after a long day's work. The narrow path between the green wheat fields couldn't accommodate both the muddy animals and me at the same time, so I had to wade into the wet field to let them through. I did this a few times, but it was better dealing with a mute animal than a dozen yelling boys and girls who took pleasure from another human's sufferings. I gladly gave way to the buffalo.

When I sneaked through our back door, Mum wasn't surprised or angry that I was late and all covered with mud. While getting a bowl of rice ready for me, she watched me silently. They knew. Dia must have told them.

As I sat on the last step to the river, I took my time washing my feet, dangling them in the warm water and letting the tiny fish nibble on them. I tried to think of a way to avoid the disastrous subject of midterm tests. There was no easy way.

My family of tired young farmers would have no patience when the only student in the household came home with disgraceful academic results. They worked their butts off in the fields, calloused their hands, bent their young backs, and lost their dream of being young. I had been wasting my time smoking, playing around, and not making use of the great opportunity offered me. It was a sin they couldn't have afforded to make.

With my head bent and eyes downcast, I stumbled into our dining room. The whole family stopped talking as I entered.

207

Silence.

I damned well deserved it. I slid into my seat and stared at the tip of my chopsticks, eating carefully so that they didn't clink on the edge of the bowl and anger anyone. I heard myself slurp the rice. The silence was getting heavier with each passing second.

Dad scooped a big spoonful of green beans into my bowl. It was a good sign. The head of the family had spoken with his action. I stole a look at him. He looked back.

'You broke a record, they say.'

I was quiet.

'It's time you do something about it. Your brother here wants to take time off to prepare for the college exam, but the commune won't allow him. Even if they do allow him, we're not sure we could do without his food rations.'

He pointed at the rice that was getting cold in my bowl. I stared at it and my guts twisted with guilt and sorrow. I wished I were dead. If I had been the older one, I would have been out there hustling. I witnessed the hardships my brother and sisters endured every day. They were in their late teens and early twenties. They had no new clothes, no friends, and no money, just a body filled with aches and pains such as only older folks should have. But the worst was that they thought they would be forced to be farmers for life, unable to marry anyone else but another farmer to bear another generation of lowly farmers, on into infinity. The sun would never rise in their minds. It was modern-day slavery on the farm, with the promise of little in return. In contrast, all I did was go to school. And what had I achieved? A shameful performance.

'You have a year and a half to get your act together; the farming tools will all be ready and waiting for you in the pigsty, just in case.'

It sounded like probation. No improvement, and I would be condemned to a life sentence on the Communist farm. I looked up at everybody after the sentencing, feeling a load being lifted off my back. They all wore mixed expressions of reproach and criticism, along with a touch of encouragement and even hope, the whole spectrum. I loved my family.

That night before going to sleep I asked Mum to wake me at five from the following day on and every day afterwards. I promised her that I would use the precious morning hours before breakfast when my mind was uncluttered to take a bite out of those unopened books of mine. She nodded thoughtfully, half doubting my sincerity.

I went to my room and knelt before the makeshift shrine to Buddha for a good ten minutes, not knowing what to beg from his benevolence. I was a total mess. Guilt ate away at my soul for goofing off what precious time I had before the national entrance examinations. I banged my head on the floor, swearing to work hard from now on. In the end, I became dizzy and went to sleep with a big smile on my face. I was sure that Buddha, my smiling, chubby spiritual light, had heard me this time. I'd banged hard enough.

At the crack of dawn, I heard a gentle knock at my door and saw Mum's nose sticking through the crack.

I moved my fingers slightly to let her know that I had heard her. She closed the door and went back to the kitchen to prepare breakfast for the family. My room was still dark and chilly, the morning sea breeze blowing through the window frames. A little voice in the back of my head sang the awful get-up song, while the rest of my body lay sleepily under the warm quilt. This was the time when the sweetest dreams were made. The birds were just beginning to sing, not too noisily yet, because they, too, had just awoken, and the insects from the surrounding fields were ending their nightly jazz session. Tired and dragging a little, a few hard workers still hummed along with the gurgling of the frogs. Their voices filtered down and thinned as light invaded the universe. I could hear their yawns.

Sleep took over and dreams knocked me on the head. I shrank myself into a little meatball, the cocoon of my blanket feeling like a velvet nest in which my dream ship rocked gently among the waves of sleep. Long live lazy autumn mornings. Let the sun be warm and the air cool for ever. And someone please shoot the commune team leader, who was banging the gong along the street, urging his members to hit the fields.

Knock, knock.

It was Mum again. She knew her son, and didn't trust me with a pillow. This time she stuck her whole head inside and tapped her finger on the wooden wall, a severe warning. I moved one limb at a time, slowly dragging myself out of bed like a rusty old machine. I could hear each drowsy part of me creaking and tearing. I slipped into the cool sandals that stood neatly at the foot of my bed. My toes curled and twitched. Good sign. The chill was waking my feet up. I put on my shirt and stumbled into the backyard and down the stone steps leading to the river. I squatted and splashed my face with the icy water of the Dong Jing. It was a shock to my system. Now I was awake.

I climbed back up the steps, took out my schoolbag and laid all the books on a small table in the backyard. I figured that with eighteen months left until the national exam, I simply had to use every waking moment of my life for studying. It would be four years' worth of work squeezed into eighteen months. My life was over for the time being. No friends, no movies, no chatting. No sitting in class passively awaiting the inept teacher to feed you. It had to be a flat-out attack on all the books I hadn't touched. I was going to breathe and live those books.

But which book did I start with? I looked at them, puzzled. I needed a scheme, a method, or I would never beat the competition. Only one out of a hundred made it in. I could easily kiss the books and my life goodbye and say hello to rice paddies.

A wise man once said that the difference between going to college and not going was the difference between wearing genuine leather shoes and going barefoot. To me, it was more like life and death.

In all the books I had read, college men were tall and handsome, wore western suits, ties, and glasses, and had their hair well oiled and neatly parted in the middle. All the girls dreamed about them, they kicked ass in society. If they happened to be from a rich family, they were the rebels who ran off with the sexiest, prettiest maid in the household. If they were from a poor family, they ended up marrying a rich girl, but were still rebels. It was only their due.

Girls, money, with no need to shovel manure or plough the fields. They simply moved their fingers and out flowed the most romantic poems, words that moved people's hearts. They were the intelligent and privileged winners. All others were born to the destiny of mud and manure, working in the same fields as the cows and the buffalo.

A cold breeze swept across the fields. I shuddered at the thought of getting up this early, rolling up my pants, and wading into the chilly fields to weed the wheat. Many had lived like that for generations. I'd rather die. Quickly I opened my English book and attacked the first thing that appeared before me.

A big official poster about the new college system was posted conspicuously on the wall of the commune's headquarters. Hundreds of young people travelled miles just to stand before it for hours, half believing what it said in black and white. Some copied it down on a small piece of paper and brought it back for others to see, as if they couldn't trust their memory. Confusion reigned among the people of Yellow Stone.

Only months ago, Chairman Mao was alive and kicking on his sickbed under the loving care of his young nurses, who saw it as a heroic, patriotic act to mix their business with his pleasure. School was bad and revolution was good. Young people had got used to it. They liked it that way. They beat up the teachers, burned down schools, marched out of classes, and drank and smoked as they saw fit. There were no tests, no grades, no good students, no bad students. They were all bad, therefore all good. Everything was fine because Mao said so.

Now everything was upside down again. The announcement explained nothing. It didn't make any distinction between the children of the politically good and the politically bad families. It said the tests were open to all and that admission into college was based purely on performance.

One day the team leader of the commune took my brother aside and asked what he thought about the new policy. Brother Jin said he dared not think that such a policy applied to him. The team leader, a Communist party member, slapped my brother's knee and said he was smart for thinking that way. He added that if Jin believed the policy was what it said on paper, he was too naive. The landlords were still the landlords, there was no future for them. After the party member left, Jin gave him both fingers.

Within days, there were rumours that some cadres of the commune had co-operated on an open letter to the government of Fujian province, showing their indignation over the admissions policy. Emotions were running high at the inequality; the fate of the Communist country was at stake. They said they were worried about the revolution, not themselves. They also said that to educate children from the Black families would sabotage the revolutionary cause.

In a month, the education commissioner of Fujian replied, in a letter that was published in the *Fujian Daily*. It confirmed the policy as presented. The Red families felt left out, deserted. They felt betrayed, and were willing to do anything to block the Black families from participating in the examinations.

My cousin Tan, the son of my mother's brother, had taken the plunge and signed up for the first examination. He hung up his tools, skipped farm work, and hit the old books. He locked himself up in the family attic with only the alarm clock for company. He lived on three hours of sleep and some sporadic meals that were passed through the opening on the floor. He lost five pounds in ten days and grew a long rough beard on his narrow chin.

Unfortunate things happened. The team leader was incensed when he heard the reason for Cousin Tan's disappearance. The leader ran to their house and cursed and shouted names until the whole village could hear the racket and a crowd gathered before their house. Then the leader threw a stone at Tan's window and made him come down. Tan hadn't seen the sun since he disappeared into the attic several days ago, and blinked at the sunshine, while the crowd shouted as if they were seeing a rat crossing the street in broad daylight. The team leader called him the son of a landlord and questioned his sanity. He humiliated him, and made him go to work on a chore that could very well have waited till the following spring. Tan was in tears, and swore that if he was ever admitted to college he would take the admissions letter and shove it up the guy's ass. The team leader threatened to withhold the food ration to Tan's family if he was ever absent again without approval. During the next few days, he was assigned to tedious, unnecessary jobs, while the rest of the farmers on the same team rested at home doing nothing. It was off-season. Tan had to hide his books in his pockets and read them during long water breaks.

The matter reached the Putien county education commissioner. He quietly sent a letter to the team leader, calming him down. My cousin was finally allowed some time off. The team leader, however, withheld the food ration for Cousin Tan, notwithstanding the commissioner's order. He swore that he would screw the revolution before it screwed him, a true revolutionary martyr.

Suddenly, everyone was talking about college. People gathered in knots, swapping gossip about who would be the most competitive in the tests. The bridge where my friends used to sit and gossip about women and gambling was now a forum in which they discussed who the next maths or English wizard might be. War stories about some legendary teachers from our high school began to circulate among the people of Yellow Stone.

There was the fat maths teacher, Du, with bushy eyebrows and a birthmark as ugly and prominent as a dark cloud on a sunny day. Before the Cultural Revolution, each year on the day prior to the national college exam Mr Du would call an emergency meeting for all the graduates, flip open a portable blackboard, and show the lengthy solutions to a few complicated maths questions he predicted would appear as major score-gainers. He would come in and talk briefly but importantly for ten minutes. The meeting was over when he lit his cigarette. Nervous students hurriedly jotted down all the details and committed them to memory. Du's track record had been consistently eight out of ten. Marginal students had been brought to tears when they saw the questions appear on the real exam.

Then there was the history teacher, Mr Wa, who was no pretty boy either. He looked frighteningly like someone from the Pleistocene age, minus the thick body hair. All he needed to do to give us a living picture of the Peking Man was bend his back a little, walk slowly in front of the class and let his long arms dangle on both sides. His head had only two parts, the forehead and the chin. His eyes gleamed wildly under a steep cliff of a forehead, and his small nose flattened out above a set of teeth so big that he had a hard time closing his mouth. He spoke in a stutter, spattering everything around him with saliva. His voice roared like a Peking Man's must have done, seemingly unaccustomed to the gentility of evolution.

And then there were the super-students, who had attended high school before the Cultural Revolution and had a solid foundation in all subjects. Among them were my Cousin Tan and a neighbour by the name of Li. Candidates worked on old college exam questions; these guys breezed through effortlessly. In the eyes of youngsters like me, they were heroes.

As the first national examination drew near, the talk of legends stopped. Everyone watched silently as the candidates nervously awaited their date of trial.

On the first day of the examination, pale students walked towards the test sites, quiet and anxious. Mr Du called for a meeting. So did the Peking Man. The meetings were open to all. Thousands of students crowded into the high school's open-air gym and listened through crackling loudspeakers to the two legends at work. The atmosphere was as sacred as at a religious event, and hearts were just as pious.

At nine a.m., I put down my books and joined the rest of the crowd to watch the uniformed county police ride into town on three-wheeled motorcycles, carrying the examination papers. The street was quiet as the police honked their way noisily through the thick crowd. Hours later, some of that crowd would be winners and many would be losers. I held my head between my hands and sneaked back to my room. I felt weak in the knees just thinking about those poor guys who opened up their papers and registered a blank. One of them could be me. It had definitely been me at midterm. I buried my head hopelessly among my books, then stared out of the window.

I was getting ready to go to my fifteenth lesson with Professor Wei. I had got into the habit of combing my hair and scrubbing myself neatly before leaving. Having no brain was something you couldn't help, but having no manners was unforgivable. Besides, I was afraid the dog would chase me if I looked any different from the day he first saw me. He didn't have to like me. All I asked was that he get used to me, which he didn't seem to be doing. He had to bite his tongue each time my dirty feet shuffled in front of his eyes.

Professor Wei opened the door with the same smile she'd given me fourteen times before. The dog gave me his usual glare, sleepy, bored, and mean. *Here comes the loser again*. If I did anything different, like walk a little faster or snap my fingers, he would frown like an old man and growl a warning. *Don't piss me off, you brat*, he seemed to be saying. It was he who set the tone of the day.

But this time Professor Wei didn't give me her singsong 'good-afternoon' in English like she always had. She walked a little faster guiding me through the garden, and didn't say a word about my hair. I sensed something was wrong, but what? I had scrubbed the soles of my sandals clean before entering her living room. The carpet shone in the afternoon sun like on any other day. My seat on the couch felt like velvet, hugging my skinny bottom as it had always done.

Professor Wei sat rigidly in front of me, her eyes icy, her mouth set. Something had upset her terribly.

'My friend saw you smoking in school. Is that true?' She came right to the point. 'I am shocked to hear this.'

So was I. Who was that little friend of hers? I had been smoking for ages, but I didn't mind keeping it a secret from the professor. I didn't want to hurt her. What went on beyond the serene wall of her security would surely be too harsh for her gentle, loving heart to bear. She would faint, not once but many times, if she were allowed access to the list of my terrible evil-doings. But now some-one had broken the unfortunate news to her. She had probably been crying and praying to her god the whole night. I fought the temptation to lie. She seemed so trusting and believing, but the thought of her western god, Jesus Christ, invisibly hovering over us made my heart skip a beat. I could fool her, but not her god. All I needed was another sin to add to my troubled record.

'My friend in school makes me do it occasionally,' I said weakly. A half-lie was better than a whole one. 'It was for fun.' But there was no such thing as fun when it came to nicotine. Either you were addicted or you were not. I hoped she didn't know that.

'It is an evil thing, and a curse to men. It broke my heart to hear about your smoking. God made you healthy so you could be useful. Don't ruin everything,' she preached. She spoke calmly now that I had confessed. Her smile returned. She believed me completely. What a relief! I relaxed and sank back into my seat, ready for a lesson, when she suddenly grabbed my schoolbag and said firmly, 'Let me see your bag. I think you carry cigarettes with you.'

I held on to the bag tightly, surprised by her quickness. 'I swear I only smoke for fun.'

'For fun! You tell me it's just for fun. Your teeth are stained beyond recognition. You think I am naive? That's all right. I think you are a hopeless addict. There!' She stuck her hand into my bag and came out with a handful of Flying Horse. She shook with rage and seemed totally disgusted by the tobacco in her hands.

My face went pink, red, and pale at the same time. What a feisty lady! I had underestimated her by a big margin. I felt shaken with embarrassment.

'Aha! Little old lady knows.' She gave me a sly smile. 'Now why don't you take these poisonous cigarettes, dump them in the trash can for me, and wash your hands with soap. Then we can start our lesson.' Like a little girl, she almost danced across the floor to wash her own hands.

I did what she ordered me to do, like a puppet, still numb.

When I got back from washing my hands, she was in her usual seat, peaceful again, as though nothing had happened.

We carried on with our lesson as we had many times before, but I found it hard to concentrate. My mind kept thinking about this new person inside nice Professor Wei. Who was she? I had a lot to learn.

Nineteen

I was making slow progress. Maths, physics and chemistry were hard. I was behind a couple of years, and the formulas seemed to have got longer since I last studied them. The teacher was lecturing on calculus and matrices, while I was still struggling to catch up on geometric equations. I attended the classes. The teacher and the good students treated me as if I didn't exist. Each time I raised my hand, there was an uncomfortable hush in the room. Another stupid question. My maths teacher would roll his eyes and reluctantly give me the chance to ask my question. Then he would ask his protégé, the Head, to answer it.

'The Head' was a nickname we gave to the class president, who had this huge shiny forehead. He was also the school's Young Communist League president. He was the kind of guy who made exaggerated speeches in public meetings and shouted slogans while parading on National Day. He walked with a stiff neck and a pair of duck feet. He looked at other lowly classmates with disdain, and was considered the biggest snob on campus. He was doing fine among other equally snobbish high-flyers until the day he was caught writing a love letter to a girl in class. Now he was in another league, a womanizer and a snob.

When the Head was done, the teacher applauded slowly, nodding and smiling. Another superb performance by his young talent. The teacher himself was distantly cool. He openly avoided talking to me, such a lowly student. Once was enough, but again and again? I quickly lost interest in his class. My mind wandered off on dangerous paths. Ideas flitted around inside my head about how to best torture such an evil being. It would have been fitting to have him and his protégé tied up, butt naked, to the old pine tree at the school entrance and let them beg for mercy as the chilly sea wind nipped at their skin. I hated them and I hated myself.

Dad suggested that I study with neighbours who were just starting school. That way I could slowly work my way up and would soon be on the same footing as the guys in my class.

Jon was a little fellow in junior high, a maths wizard. I went to his home and we worked the questions for a few nights until we called it off. His parents fought in their spare time in the room next to us. His dad was an old grump who complained about everything. His mother, highly temperamental, could curse like a sailor. And she did, every night. You would think that they would kill each other, but they didn't. They lived on happily and fought again the next day. The verbal volleyball and occasional banging of farm tools made my head ache. I moved on.

I lugged my schoolbooks back to another neighbour, Gan, who was a teacher at an elementary school. He was willing to go over the science and maths courses with me. The first few nights were a success. I was a natural at maths, and a helping hand went a long way. I was just beginning to enjoy it when his younger sister, a tall, skinny girl a couple of years younger than I, began to hang around the study. All my dreams of peace and quiet were dashed. She would get her books and sit opposite me. She played with her hair and admired herself in a hand-held mirror, murmuring like a baby. Then she'd sit there, bored. I would bury my face in the books and work on my studies, pretending to be unaffected. Occasionally, I caught her staring at me. Whenever our eyes met, she would bite her lip and run out of the study. The next night was a circus. She brought a couple of her noisy girlfriends. They nibbled each other's ears and laughed. And they had these mouths that went on and on and on. All the while, they cast their eyes in Gan's and my direction. One minute she came over to borrow a pencil, the next minute, a piece of paper. Gan was a patient man and a doting brother. Understandable, he had to live with the child. He went on talking and coaching. All was peaceful. It had nothing to do with him. I got the feeling he might miss the fuss if she weren't around, heaven forbid.

My previous study hole might have been the Middle East, but this was no Switzerland. My brain screamed SOS. I quit the place that very night and swore never to return. The next day I went down to our storage room, which was decorated with spiderwebs and housed hundreds of unknown, lethal, crawling creatures. Flashlight in hand, I kicked and fumbled among legless, armless pieces of furniture. It was my cave; there were treasures to be explored. I had Grandpa's old gambling lamp in mind. It was a huge, infamous object with ornate bronze designs, and had been given to him as a gift from his gambling buddy to prevent cheating in the dark. It was put in storage because of its gigantic appetite – it burned a whole bottle of oil a night, and its smoke stained the white mosquito nets black.

I flashed the light around the dark room; in the corner my old friend glistened like a beacon at sea. As I stepped over cautiously, my big toe caught a round thing that rolled until it hit the wall with a healthy clang. I turned the light on to it, and there, standing on its bottom, was an aged, elegant pot shaped like a short, flat pumpkin. It was Grandpa's liquor jar. It used to sit on his lap and sleep by his pillow. He sipped blissfully from it when it was full and whistled into it when it was empty. It was his other child, the child Grandma didn't have any part of bearing. Nor was it one she approved of.

I scooped up both Grandpa's legacies and dodged my way out, without ruining too much of the webs guarding the room.

'What are you doing with those things?' Mum asked. She had been standing by the door waiting for me.

'Well, I decided to study by myself in my room in the evenings, so I need a good lamp for light and a teapot.' I clutched my two treasures.

Anything for my studies. Mum could have objected but she didn't. She knew my ways of tackling a problem. If I danced around something long enough, I would eventually give it my total attention. Mum was a little goddess that the big god had sent into our lives. She understood my vices and tried to forgive me as much as her limited powers allowed her.

I let the old treasures soak in the river for a few hours, and then rubbed them roughly with the wild grass that grew along the riverbank. The lamp shone in the afternoon sun, but the liquor jar still carried the heavy scent of alcohol. Grandpa had told me that the jar was the work of a gifted potter from the mountains of Fujian. He had used the local soil in creating his pots, and if the jar was filled with liquor long enough, the cells of the jar wall would become saturated. For ever after, one could just pour water into the jar and out would pour liquor. I hoped the cells hadn't become saturated yet because otherwise I would be hallucinating all night, whistling into its tiny mouth, and college would for ever remain a dream.

That night after dinner I officially locked my door, lit my big lamp, and filled up the old jar with dark, steaming tea. I made sure a night pot stood by, prepared to take a larger than usual output. I was ready to burn.

But as I picked up physics, I thought about chemistry. When I leafed through chemistry, the maths book screamed for my attention. I fought the temptation of the green English book, which by now had become my favourite, and there were the books on history, geology and philosophy moaning and groaning at the bottom of the pile like step-children. Only Chinese history was a given. My midterm results in that subject put me legitimately at the top of the class. I juggled all these books like parts on an assembly line, finally dropping them and resting my head in the cradle of my hands.

Four years of work, and only a year before the biggest exam of my life. Not an ideal situation. I could probably handle half the material and be mildly successful, but not all of it. And the horror stories of how difficult the examination questions were flooded my mind. You had to really know your stuff. The most perplexing, complicated questions on each subject appeared on the tests. The government made sure that 30 per cent of the test-takers fainted upon seeing the questions. Another 40 per cent puked at their own ignorance. The remaining 29 per cent would climb the cliff, but only 1 per cent, their hands bleeding, would make it to the top. It was equality. It was even democracy, compared to the previous system. It was a hundred times better than Communist slavery.

Finally, I settled for the English book. I was showing decent progress, I was told. There was the usual vocabulary, grammar, drills, tests, and conversations. The simple conversations were silly, but thought-provoking. I often wondered why Englishmen greeted each other with phrases like 'good-morning', 'good-afternoon', and 'good-night'. Simply 'good' everything. If I walked around the dirt street of Yellow Stone and greeted people with the 'good' formula, they would think I was crazy. Some might even knock my teeth out and ban me from the town for ever. Those folks were content asking each other, 'Have you had breakfast [lunch or dinner] yet?' After all, nothing was 'good' about a day till your stomach was filled.

Then there was this 'thank you' for this and 'thank you' for that stuff. Being thanked by Professor Wei for not smoking gave me goosebumps. Was that the same as not thanking someone for doing something?

I thought about the 'thank you' word in my own dialect. We said 'bua' to show appreciation and gratitude. *Bua* was the word for a shallow bamboo basket. In the old days, you would put some food in the basket, kneel before the local official with the basket raised above your head, and present it to him to show gratitude for governing the town effectively. Thus *bua*, the tool, became *bua*, thank you. If you were very grateful, you would say a very big *bua*.

As an experiment, I once told Dia that I would give him a little *bua* for not lighting that foul-smelling tobacco roll of his in my room. He stared at me long and hard like I was crazy, and lit a jumbo nonetheless.

But all this interested me tremendously. I often thought about the people who actually used the language every day. What a controlled way of speaking! In my mind, all the men were gentle and moustached, wore tall hats, carried a timepiece and a cane. In the crook of their arms leaned ladies, snake-waist thin, with long dresses, yellow hair, and blue eyes. They didn't walk, they strolled, and the men's canes measured their strides as the hems of their long dresses swept the floor. Clark Gable and Vivien Leigh. London. New York. I had no idea it was the time of the hippies, gangsters, druggies, rock 'n' roll; that Gable was long gone and that Leigh was in a wheelchair with wrinkles even on her toes.

The burning question, which I found impossible to ask my professor, was how the Englishmen and women cursed. Or did they? How very naive of me. I later came to know that a thick encyclopaedia could be made of all the curse words used in that great language.

I was awakened by Mum's knock on the door. It was five in the morning and I was in my bed, my English book still on my desk. The lamp had used up the whole bottle of oil. The teapot was empty. I had no recollection of undressing myself or putting the light out.

'How did I go to sleep last night?' I asked Mum, whose face was now inside my door.

'Dad saw your light still on at two and found you asleep with your face on the book.'

I must have drifted off.

'No more irregular hours like that. You are going to ruin your health.'

'But Mum, I need to study longer hours to catch up.'

'You won't catch up that way. You need to have a good, healthy schedule.'

Such intense conversation made my head throb. I slipped under the warm quilt and had another fifteen minutes in bed before I kicked off the blanket and splashed my face with icy water from the river.

One afternoon, as I was on my way to Professor Wei's house, the rain began to penetrate the thick foliage that covered the narrow road. It was so loud and urgent it sounded as if a machine-gun were spraying the leaves with bullets. It saved me the trouble of bending down in the river to wet my hair. I combed my mop with my hands as I saw the thick clouds gathering on the western horizon. A storm was coming.

I skidded along the wet road and was happy to finally arrive at Professor Wei's door. It had been left open, and as I ran upstairs I could hear her voice coming from the second-floor window. She waved to me. I smiled back.

Not surprisingly, the dog was standing in the rain, greeting me with his mean dark glare. He dug his back feet firmly into the ground, as if warming up to attack me. He gave a throaty rumble, a weak threat that I had got used to, and blocked my way. There was something different in his eyes today, a knowing look. I checked the second-floor window for help. Professor Wei was gone. It was just me and the dog, and he had the upper hand. I wished I had a rifle. The spot between his eyes looked very tempting.

He sniffed my thoughts and shook his head in defiance. Water splashed all over me. I shook my own head. Not as much water. The cunning animal was enjoying seeing me get drenched by the storm. He wanted to see me chilled, sneezing, then on the floor begging for mercy, at which time he would walk over and sink his teeth into a juicy part of me. A dinner in the rain was better than no dinner at all.

Sudden lightning cleaved the dark sky, followed immediately by deafening thunder no less than half a mile away. The loudness brought me to my knees. I closed my eyes, and plugged my ears with my thumbs, waiting for the imminent attack from both the thunder and the dog, but nothing happened. The thunder trailed down to spasmodic firecracker mutterings, and vanished. I opened my eyes and saw the dog crawling in the mud towards his house, his tail tucked between his legs. At that moment, I lost all respect for the animal, and wanted to shoot myself for having put up with his cruel, unfair treatment.

Professor Wei greeted me with a dry towel as I sauntered towards the door like a real man for the first time, fearless and dignified. I could feel the weak look in the dog's eyes now that he had been brought to his knees by the thunder. I had withstood the uproar. I took the towel and gave my head a good drying. Professor Wei found me a T-shirt and I was once again comfortable. But no feeling surpassed the sweetness of winning.

That dog was for ever crossed off my fear list. It was, after all, a man's world out there, pal.

'You look happy today,' Professor Wei said, rather surprised.

'Thank you, I'm happy to be here,' I said in English.

'Maybe you know something already,' she said in Chinese.

'What do you mean?'

'Well, I heard from my friend in Putien that for the next college examination, if you choose English as your major, you don't have to take tests in science or maths at all.'

'Is that right?' I pinched my thigh, almost jumping out of the seat. I tried to imagine life without maths, chemistry, and physics. It would be like a honeymoon for ever. I felt like standing up and singing an aria. 'Oh, but why?'

'Well, the government lacks English majors in all the major universities. I think you should shoot for a college in, say, Beijing.'

Beijing! Only the best went there. Yes, ma'am, whatever you say!

'You think I am going to be that good?'

'You will be if you work hard. You have shown tremendous progress.'

'Really?'

'I am going to cram you until you are full.'

Cram me, please. I never felt emptier.

'Here you go.' She pulled out a bagful of books and printed papers. 'These are the exercises and all the English vocabulary that you need to know to pass the test.' She patted the stack like an insurance man talking about a rainy day.

I rushed over and touched the pile with a shaking hand. This would be my salvation.

It was getting late. The storm persisted outside and the sky remained dark. My heart was pounding with excitement. I couldn't wait to run home and tell my family the wonderful news.

'Would you like to stay and join me for dinner?' Professor Wei asked. Her sister was away visiting.

An image came to mind of my stomach looking like the cracked Sahara desert beneath the baking African sun. I banished the image quickly and said, 'Thank you for your invitation, but I eat late.'

Who was I kidding? I could eat any time, any place, anything.

'You look hungry.' She could be blunt when it suited her.

A hungry man was after all a hungry man. It probably showed, either the sunken midriff, or the hunger in my eyes. Maybe it was my pale face. But it would be highly improper for me to stay for dinner. I should be the one bringing food to my teacher, not the other way around. Mum would think I was greedy. She had taught us that no matter how poor you are, you should never covet another's food. There was more. My reputation as a gentleman would be at stake. I was afraid of letting go of my horrendous appetite and eating up her meal as well. In the end, I wouldn't even burp. I could just see myself guzzling down a whole bowl of rice at the speed of an Olympic skater while she, a rabbit, nibbled away at a carrot, both of us embarrassed for our own reasons.

'No, thank you. My family is waiting for me.'

'I know what you are thinking. But it isn't a shameful thing to do. In our faith, it's called sharing. I entertain my church friends all the time, thank God.' She dipped her head and showed deference to her god even as we spoke.

Judging from the weather, I would be here for a long time. It would be even more inappropriate to sit here and watch her eat. 'Thank you, I'll have a bite then.'

The little lady clapped her hand joyfully and said, 'Thank you.'

Soon the helper in the household came by to tell her that dinner was ready; we walked to the dining room. It faced the flower garden, and some blossoms were still doggedly smiling at us in the rain. The glass dimmed the sound of the raindrops and water poured off the roof in a cascade. It was a simple room with elegant wicker furniture. On the wall hung a picture of a white man with kind eyes, long hair, and a white robe. He must be Jesus Christ. Hanging opposite was a much smaller picture of Chairman Mao, with his Buddha's face. It was clear who was the boss and who was the altar boy.

'New religious freedom,' she explained as I studied the room. 'As long as I have Mao's picture, we can have God's picture on the wall as well, they say.' The days of no religion were over.

225

Professor Wei was very much the leader in the fight for more freedom.

Dinner consisted of simple sautéed vegetables from the garden and well-simmered chicken with a lot of rice. The maid had already set the food out on the table and it smelled heavenly. My stomach growled loudly. I had to clench my stomach muscles to make it stop.

'A young man like you should have three bowls of rice.' She pointed at the monster of a bowl. She wasn't too far off the mark. On a good day, I wouldn't disappoint her.

She took the ladle and scooped the steaming rice into my bowl. Professor Wei, the hostess, beamed at me. She piled up my bowl to the height of the Ching Mountain while her portion was only two dainty spoonfuls. I felt like a mountaineer, saddled with bags and tents, ready to climb to the top.

'Now, shall we pray?' She closed her eyes and her head hunkered over the table. I ducked my head a little and left my eyes half open. I saw her lips move fast and she swallowed her words. I couldn't understand any of it. I caught her god staring at me and shut my eyes instantly.

'Now we have thanked God for what we have today. Dig in. I can't wait to see how you young people eat so much.' There was mischief in her face. I felt like a rooster before a chicken fight.

Dig in I did. Soon the mountain began to lower. She ate her rice grain by grain and spent more time shovelling food into my bowl. She told me about the gatherings she had here for her church friends and about the joy of having young people around. She always cooked tons of food on Sunday; her house was a sanctuary.

When I was down to the third bowl, the setting sun dangled under a thick cloud. She scooped the dishes' last spoonfuls on to my plate. I had never seen anyone have more fun than she while watching someone else eat.

'You are a healthy, hungry young man. I am so glad you finished it all. No leftovers tomorrow.'

I thanked her many times for her delicious dinner. Professor Wei leaned against her door like a loving grandma and waved goodbye. Only after I turned the corner did I let out a gigantic burp. If the breeze hadn't been making the leaves sing, she might have heard it.

The news about the college examinations worried my parents a great deal. It meant that I would give up my science courses. Was it premature? The government was changeable on policies like that. You were talking about a country that had changed the constitution more often than its meals. There was intense conversation between them. I felt it necessary to drop in the keywords.

'With this policy, I might be able to apply to study English in a college in Beijing.'

It was a showstopper. They were silenced. They looked at me with doubt. But Dad thought about it for a second, then nodded with approval. 'I like the sound of it.' He was the man who had made me the first violin player in the history of Yellow Stone, however bad I was, and he was ready for me to major in English and send me off to Beijing. He would share every bit of my progress over tea with his many friends for the rest of his life.

Dad was the dreamer. Mum was the practical enforcer who knocked on the door at five every morning to wake me and shake the mosquito net, making sure I didn't take too long a nap in between studies, or waste time dreaming.

'Wouldn't that be a little too fancy and exotic for us?' Mum asked. You bet it would. Think mud, think manure, think digging the hills, that would be more appropriate for us, but I wanted to be special.

Dad shook his head, always a step ahead of me, now more sure than I was.

'Why not?' he said. 'Maybe some day he will be an English-speaking diplomat or our country's representative to the UN.'

Dad was always somewhat too ambitious and loved his young son for being like him. There was such certainty and conviction in his voice that it scared me.

'Are you sure you want to study English somewhere in Beijing?' Dad turned around, asking the question to which he already knew the answer.

Nothing sounded better than that to a farm boy, crippled by political mumbo-jumbo, a kid who was facing the prospect of shovelling mud for life and living way below the international poverty line. Are you kidding? It would be my dream, something to die for.

I managed a nervous nod, unsure of the honour the question had bestowed upon me. It was like being asked, 'Would you like to be ruler of an empire?'

The answer was definite, nervous: 'Yes. Please show me the throne.'

Twenty

Cousin Tan locked himself up again in the attic on the day the results of the examinations came out. The pressure was so great that he hadn't eaten for days, and he had been suffering a mild depression since taking the test. He had tried alcohol. It didn't help. Then he had slept and slept, with the team leader laughing outside his window, calling him crazy. We were all worried. Then one day Tan had emerged suddenly, throwing himself into farm work. He kept silent about the test, and shut his mouth whenever anyone talked about college. He was an angry mute, immersed in his own world. He had lost weight and looked forty, even though he was only in his early thirties.

His excellent scores sent shock waves through Yellow Stone. Tan cried as the results were slipped under the door of his hide-out. He at first refused to open the envelope. When he eventually did, he let out a piercing scream and danced downstairs to meet his beaming family. He was the sort of guy born for college life. Nerdy, wearing thick glasses, he read everything, including the microscopic directions on the backs of chemical fertilizer bags. He wrote poetry and dabbled in fiction in his spare time. He was dreamy and romantic. Way beyond the marrying age, he had refused many matchmaking sessions with sorry-looking country-side girls. His vision of a wife existed only in books. Considering he came from a landlord's family with no prospects whatsoever, he was lucky anyone would even consider him. The situation didn't trouble him a bit. He had made peace with himself. Why bother with marriage? Wait until you could afford it, he used to say, which frustrated the heck out of my uncle, who believed that by now he should have been surrounded by demonic grandkids.

Two days after the results came out, cousin Tan fell into another bout of depression. He said the high scores would only worsen his disappointment in the end. The scores were nothing but a cover-up. One's political background would take precedence. Such a drop from a staggering height would crush his soul. There were again rumours that candidates from the wrong families, despite high scores, would be placed at the end of the admission line. When all the slots were filled, they would be left holding an empty bag, just another way of finishing off the Black families. Tan retreated into his attic and stared out of the window all day long.

At the end of the summer, Tan became the first college student in Yellow Stone after the Cultural Revolution. Amoy University, finance major. When the certified admission letter arrived bearing his name, the whole town was stunned. Amoy University, located on the beautiful subtropical island of Amoy, was the best in Fujian. It trained the cadres for the province. It was an old boy's club. Tan would fit in beautifully.

This time, the whole family was teary. Many years of suffering had suddenly come to an end. The sun had risen and that night the stars would shine. Tan was now the happiest of men, giving Flying Horses away as if he were getting married. I eyed his slightly bent back and tired eyes. It wouldn't surprise me if some professors were younger than he. Maybe he, too, would become a professor and marry one of his female students. I was so happy for him.

From that point on, his fate changed dramatically. Tan received three wedding proposals in the next three days from the most eligible girls in town. They came from good families and had solid bodies that could plough the fields like oxen. Their families even agreed to forgo the standard marriage fees. One of the fathers promised to throw in two farming cows as part of the dowry. Not a bad deal, we joked. Cousin Tan laughed at them all and rejected their offers. He was our hope. We celebrated with him at a big banquet before he left. He encouraged my brother to take the plunge and cautioned me to concentrate on my major, make a reasonable study schedule, and persevere.

That night I sat in my room facing a tall stack of books; I assigned a time slot for each subject. In order to cram everything into a single day, every day, I had to get up at five and go to bed at ten-thirty, allowing only short breaks for lunch and dinner. No entertainment, no goofing off with friends, no daydreaming, only hard-core studying. My heart beat with the excitement of the challenge; I couldn't close my eyes. I tried to imagine what a college classroom looked like, occupied by sharp professors and leggy city girls wearing sexy skirts. The stars blinked from a clear sky and the moon shone through my window. I made up my mind. College was the only thing for me. I'd get out of this small-town hellhole. If Tan could swing it, so could I.

Beijing. The word split into four parts that split again, winking at me like stars as I fell asleep.

Suddenly, school had a purpose. College was the goal, and ancient teachers like Mr Du and the Peking Man paraded the street of Yellow Stone attracting many admiring looks and greetings. Only a few years before, shamed, they had walked the same street, wearing tall hats and with thick plaques hung around their necks on which their names were smudgily written in red ink. Their heads had been shaved and their hands tied behind their backs. Kids had thrown bricks at them and adults had spat in their faces. They were stinking intellectuals. Society had had no place for them then.

Mr Du's former wife, who had left him a few years before, now begged to come back to him. Du didn't want her. He married a young teacher who fell under the magic of his mighty mathematical talents. Genius and youthful beauty: the people of Yellow Stone could live with that. There were serious debates as to whether he would live longer or die sooner, given his new, energy-consuming marriage. Different schools of thought came to different conclusions. In the end, he was the superstar teacher who had guessed correctly the answers to two big questions that had been on the national mathematics exam. He deserved to enjoy his new wife.

Peking Man didn't have any problems with his Peking woman, but luck also came his way. He was honoured with Communist party membership. He called himself a fossil newly unearthed by the party. It was a mixed blessing he had difficulty accepting or rejecting. A cynical historian, he had his doubts about the party. But he also knew enough not to refuse such an offer. The Cultural Revolution could come back any time and then he, the Peking Man, would be the one who had rejected party membership, thereby rejecting the party itself, maybe even rejecting the country. Then he would have to change his nationality or they might lock him away in some cage like they had the real Peking Man. They said he shed tears at the swearing ceremony. Many suspected they were tears of pain and suffering, not joy. Poor guy. As for my goldfish-eyed, wheezing English teacher, he retired after his wife became bedridden and incontinent. With him gone, the school didn't lose much. I could attest to that.

The finals for the fall semester loomed before us, and hard-working students were found lurking behind closed doors, hitting the books late into the night. And the students who boarded at school clutched their books and went off to find a quiet spot in which to study.

Rotten students like my friend Dia dragged around like lost souls searching for meaning in life. Although still smoking his thick rolls, nowadays Dia was motivated enough to discuss college and the good life beyond it, but not enough to whip his skinny ass into action. He was sarcastic about my efforts and bitter at those students who weren't his friends. He came to my house every day as usual, sitting on our back doorstep, listening to me read English or quietly smoking while I studied other subjects. I tried to involve him in studying, but it wasn't as easy as getting him to roll a big one for me.

'What do you want to do with your life?' I asked him. He leaned back and yawned.

'No idea.'

'Why don't you study with me?'

232

'I can't. I ain't cut out for that sorta stuff. Looks like I'm stuck here.' There was a sadness he wouldn't admit. He avoided my eyes. 'Son of a whore, a few years ago, even my fucking dad would tell me books were bad and ask me to tear out pages so that he could roll his tobacco in them. He would tell me to go be a carpenter, blacksmith, or something, or just hang out. The teachers didn't care. Fucking Chairman Mao told everyone to screw your teachers, burn the schools, and just kick ass. College was bad and all that shit. Now suddenly, they changed their minds on us who'd followed their great, stupid teachings.'

He looked helpless, then sort of let it go and started humming his favourite revolutionary song, the one that was called 'Our Hope Is in the Green Fields'. The roll dangled from his lip and the notes emerged a little out of tune. He was pathetic and hurt, and unknowingly represented the bitter class that had obviously enjoyed the Cultural Revolution and detested its abrupt ending. The changed world was a little too much, and too soon in coming.

The school announced that teachers would use the results of the fall semester finals to help determine which majors the graduating students should concentrate on. I abandoned the leaking compartments of my ship, the science courses, and steered the good parts along the misty coast.

The teachers noticed I'd stopped going to science class, but didn't express concern. They took it as a sign of my total surrender. Dia still hung around those classes, not sure which major to take. Every day he would pass on to me statements made by the geeky science teachers. Science was the future, liberal arts students were doomed because the enrolment was much smaller. The whole science class had a kind of cult following. Students came out of the classes red-faced, excited, and excitable. They thought they could conquer the world with the little they knew. They were the cool bunch, the talented, and we, the liberal arts students, were the leftovers who couldn't crack it in the big league. I hated them all, especially the Head, who was now the ace of the graduating class, only a small percentage of which defected to liberal arts. Dia followed me without much conviction.

The phenomenon only pleased me. Fewer heads meant less

competition. I had done some research. Most of the science students would end up being lab workers, agricultural researchers, industrial engineers, or worse, geologists digging for oil in the remote desert at the edge of China's sprawling landscape. But liberal arts majors had a future in management on college campuses and in government offices. I figured that at worst I would lead them and they would work for me, and if I was successful as an English major, some day I might even be a star in the hall of international diplomacy, where champagne, cigars, limousines, hotels, and exotically beautiful women abounded. The dream was dizzying.

I stopped going to Professor Wei's for two weeks and reviewed the subjects within the liberal arts field. I was up at five in the morning, and dragging my hurting body to bed at eleven. Teachers held review sessions for every subject. I skipped all the sessions, sequestering myself in my private spot in the wheat field outside the school's low wall, where I banged away at my books on my own.

Lunch was dried yams; I would take breaks by spreading a small blanket on the soft grass and sharing a nap with Dia under the soothing sun. The school wall blocked the sea breeze, and the ripening wheat danced in the wind singing a busy song. Dia hogged the entire blanket. When I'd wake up half an hour later, he would still be snoring away. I reopened my books and attacked each of the untouched chapters before me.

I loved the endless wheat fields, which were turning golden as the new year approached. There was calm here. I sat with my legs crossed like a monk and spread my books on the ground. There were chapters of history so beautiful that I couldn't help reading them out loud again and again. This was another time, with totally different people. There was so much I didn't know about my own country, my own race. Geography had its own charm. It gave my imagination wings. The world appeared on those pages. The Amazon, the Nile, the Himalayas, and the thirteen colonies of America. The red leaves of New England. I sat on a small piece of Yellow Stone, but the world was within me.

This new knowledge filled me with joy. I read and read until the sun quietly fell below the horizon and daylight gave way to grey darkness. I jostled my faithful friend, who had ignored me the whole afternoon. He rubbed his eyes and followed me home like a man who had lost three days' sleep. He complained about how I should have awakened him. Now he had lost another afternoon of precious time.

I feigned anger, turned around and caught his thin neck in a grip and pinned him to the dirt road. He grabbed a handful of dirt and threw it at me. I let him go and he jumped on me and started tickling me. To please him, I played along. He was a dear friend who needed a push. I felt bad about not having spent time playing with him. Then I threw him over, picked him up, and threatened to throw him into the nearby Dong Jing. He begged and begged, I put him down, and we laughed all the way home. It never took much to please my best friend.

The finals for the fall semester took three full days. At each test, I swaggered into the classroom empty-handed and chose a seat apart from everyone else. It was just me and the paper. I wanted the teachers to know that there was no possibility of cheating for this born-again student. My message was loud and clear; the teachers looked at me suspiciously. I scribbled quickly and answered all the questions in my best handwriting. Good presentation counted for a third of your score, Dad had cautioned me. I did the best I could. This was a defining moment: I was declaring my intention to join the race for college and if anyone had any problems with it, I couldn't care less. I had been at the bottom before, crawling on my knees. Now I was limping along. Soon I would be running. I wanted the world to know that I wasn't born in order for someone to step on me.

I handed in the papers early. The teachers kept calm, their curiosity at bay, pretending not to look at me. As I left each classroom, I could feel their hands grabbing my papers and checking the answers. I knew they would be shaking their heads in amazement. It wasn't just my imagination, for my faithful Dia was never far behind with his on-the-spot reporting of what happened after I left each test.

'The teacher grabbed your paper and did this.' He rolled his large eyes and froze them in comic astonishment. 'I think you're real cool.'

'I hope so.'

'I'm sure so, pal.' Dia ran in front of me, blocked my way, and said with two thumbs up, 'I'm damned fucking proud of you. You're so cocky, but I love it.'

The results of the final were significant, because the college entrance examinations were only seven months away. If you didn't make this one, you might as well go home, sharpen the farm tools, and register as a proud farmer for life, just in time for spring harvest.

The howling wind would give you a hell of a welcome as your shoeless feet sank into the freezing mud. The memory of digging the hard, cold soil with a blunt hoe was still fresh in my mind. The harvested wheat and fava fields had to be softened so that rice could be planted before it was too late in the season. The cold, piercing wind had slapped my face so that I couldn't keep my eyes open, and had left bloody cracks on my face and hands. My feet had sunk into the wet furrows and the cold water had shot up my ankles, stinging like an attack of pins and needles. No one in the entire town of Yellow Stone wore shoes to the fields. Barefoot was the norm, summer or winter. The farmers were proud of their big, calloused freezable feet. They had worked this way for generations. Why change?

Admiration was an understatement. I feared their heroism. After three days in the cold field, I swore I'd rather be a monk, with nothing better to do than dream about nuns in the next monastery than be an unwrapped frozen chicken like the farmers of Yellow fucking Stone.

I sweated through the semester finals and the results blew me away.

On the public announcement wall on campus, my name hovered at the top in every liberal arts subject. My proudest achievement was English. I scored 91 per cent, putting me head to head with a guy they called the English Wizard, Cing, an apple-headed rival of mine since first grade.

Silently I thanked Professor Wei, my secret weapon.

236

Dia was busy trumpeting my victory like a pimp. He hung around the wall, smoking his thick one, shouting to anybody passing to look at the results, particularly mine. When the Head came by, Dia showed him my glories. The snobby science major sneered, and told Dia that no one in the history of this lowly high school had ever dared dream of majoring in English. It was a major for the privileged city boys, not farm boys like us, who smelled like manure. It was an elegant major for high-class people: it had to do with the mysterious western culture and capitalism: it had to do with America. The Head knew how to hurt a fragile soul. Dia spat at his feet, cursed like a sailor, and walked back to me like a loser.

'Is that true, that no one in our school has ever made it as an English major?'

'It's true. Why?' I asked.

'You gotta make me proud. I was out there happy for you and the Head trashed me left and right. Now I'm totally busted up inside.'

'Let me ask you, was there anyone in the history of this lowly school who ever played the violin before?'

He blinked and cocked his head for a second before shaking it slowly. A broad grin spread across his sad face. 'Right, you're the first one.' He straightened up and hugged me violently.

'You could do it, man,' Dia spat out excitedly, 'and you gotta do it for me and the fucking school. Then when you pack up and take the fabulous Fujian–Beijing train, I'll load a shotgun and shoot the fucking Head right on his shining skull, that son of a whore.'

'You got to study with me. Maybe, just maybe, you'll have a chance, too,' I said.

'Forget it. You're the real genius. Remember a couple of months ago I had to pass the answers to you through the window. You knew nothing then. Now you worked hard, and you've scored high. I know this ain't the big one, but it shows you can do it. I ain't got it. You gotta keep up. I'm ready to do anything for you, carry the bags, roll cigarettes, get water, anything. In fact, I'd even marry you if I were a girl and you fancied me. Just let me tag along, don't desert me. I feel awful lonely nowadays since you changed.'

'I'm sorry. You could stay overnight at our house any time you want,' I suggested. 'You know my mum loves you, so does all my family. We could always spare a bowl or two at the dinner table.'

He nodded, almost in tears. I rolled him a thick one from his bag and he was as happy as a goldfish.

Mr Ka, my new English teacher, was a dark-skinned young man with a head of feathery curls.

He summoned me into his office. 'Congratulations,' he said. 'You finally woke up.' He jerked his head violently. His curls were bothering him.

'I heard mixed things about you from some people, but it doesn't matter what they said any more,' he continued. 'I like what I see now. You have potential.'

A brilliant opening line. He made a friend of me on the spot. It was us against them now.

'We have work to do to get you where you want to go.' He was good with abstract terms. 'I'll give you what I have and help you with what you need. Do you know what I mean?'

I was clueless. I shifted in my seat and nodded ambiguously.

'First thing to push for is membership in the Young Communist League. I checked your record and it's pathetic. You weren't even a Little Red Guard in elementary school.'

Not the memory of my miserable elementary school again.

'Someone screwed you up badly. It was wrong.' He narrowed his eyes and looked out of the window.

Damned right it was wrong. It was criminal. I was the only one in the whole fucking school who wasn't a Little Red Guard because I was from a Black family and was personally on the suspect list as a counter-revolutionary. I still had nightmares about it.

'It's time someone stood up for you. I'll get you the membership before you graduate. It'll enhance your chance of admission into a top-notch college like the one I went to. You don't want to be second-guessed on such a minor point, do you?'

'No, sir, and thank you, sir.'

'No problem. I had the same conversation with Cing, another talented potential. You two are my only hopes for the year. I'll personally involve myself with your growth. Together we'll give it our best try.'

It brought to mind the pep talks from my Ping-Pong coach. The pep talks meant nothing, but they made you feel real good. A sort of national anthem in words.

Mr Ka was doing what was commonly known among teachers as fishing, claiming credit for students who made it to prestigious colleges and using it to enhance their status and gain a promotion and a higher salary. Teachers at Yellow Stone High dropped names of former students now in college, and talked about their roles in propelling them there. They peppered their conversations in class, after meals, over tea, and even in bed with their wives, with these names. They believed they'd made those kids college men, and they lived for the glory.

Mr Ka had more at stake. He was new, and needed to establish a record. What a challenge he faced. No one in the history of the school had gone on to study English at a good college. He was the right man at the right time to do the right thing for the right person.

Within days, a small red poster was pasted on the school wall. It attracted almost no attention. It stated that I was belatedly being given the glorious title of Little Red Guard and had been admitted into the Young Communist League. For a brief moment, I felt like the Peking Man, tickled by the emptiness of such a title. Communism had become a commodity with a price tag, its value plummeting a notch each time it was sold at a garage sale. Soon the membership would become a tradable commodity, one you could pick up for a penny with a cold drink thrown in.

I went to Mr Ka's office to thank him. He slapped my shoulder and grabbed me with his strong hands.

'Congratulations, young comrade. You are the future of communism.' He spoiled the serious words by winking at me. Then, in an un-Communist gesture, he threw me a Flying Horse and said, 'Let's celebrate.' He put a match to the cigarette before I could refuse. We smoked in silence, staring out of the window.

Professor Wei did the soprano thing when I told her the results. Her hands cupped beneath her chin and her silver head tilted to

239

one side, she shook her head, speechless. She was in heaven. Her happiness for me was genuine. God bless her.

The school authorities regrouped the entire graduating class, which amounted to just over five hundred students. They were now formed into six science and two liberal arts classes. S-One, which was what Science One was commonly called, comprised the best of the science students and was where the Head and other snobs were. The school placed the best of its faculty into that class. The rest of the science classes were left to rot. Students held strikes against the school, threw rocks at S-One, and some snobs were even beaten for showing off their exclusivity. But the separation stayed.

L-One, or Liberal Arts One, also got the best Yellow Stone High had, which included the venerable Peking Man and an assortment of liberal arts buffs. It wasn't much, but it was all they had. Apple-headed Cing took the back seat on the right; I took the one on the left. Poor Dia was regrouped into L-Two, where he claimed to sleep through most of the mornings without being disturbed by the teachers. They didn't care. Students smoked in class and propped their feet on the desks. Teachers found a warm sunny spot and read novels.

L-Two was the Siberia of Yellow Stone High. Students there settled their daily intellectual disputes with fists. The school principal had joked about putting shackles and handcuffs on the podium in case of extreme violence. Dia was considered a good student and became a leader. He actually felt fine about it and often snubbed his followers in my presence. I liked the change in him. A good student in a bad class, he became more responsible. I was happy for him. I tried to get our English teacher, the hustler, to reconsider Dia's case and have him moved to L-One, but he said he would wait until Dia showed some real progress on paper. I fed him with the crumbs from the Peking Man, and he didn't miss much. He just had to face the fact that he might be stuck in a loser's hole.

Cousin Tan returned home for a visit. His hair was longer and his shoes would be shiny if he'd bothered to polish them. His sunken cheeks had filled out, and he sported a few ballpoint pens lined up evenly in his jacket pocket. He crossed his legs and his right foot languidly tapped. His speech came easily, filled with college jargon. He was on his spring break, with not a burden in the world. He sat in our living room, surrounded by my whole family.

'It's all good meat they serve there at AU.' That stood for Amoy University.

'Even for breakfast?' I asked.

He nodded. 'Pickled meat.'

What a luxury. I had never heard of such a thing, but I believed him.

'But I stay away from pickled meat for breakfast for health reasons.' He shook his head ever so slightly. It was a shake we should feel rather than see. The movement was at least fifteen degrees gentler than that of a typical Yellow Stone farmer.

My mouth watered and I had to swallow a few times at the delicious thought of meat steaming on a plate. My lofty goals about going to college vanished, and my desires became very basic. My whole body yearned for meat. Simmered, roasted, sautéed, boiled, fried, smoked, or pickled. What difference did it make? The bloody flesh tasted good whatever you did to it.

'We spent a whole long month on MT,' he said casually.

The whole family shrugged. MT? What was that? Meat Truck?

'Military Training, that is, for all AU students,' Cousin Tan explained.

'Look at my hands.' He stretched out his hands for us to see. 'They're all calloused now. See how hard the rifles have made them.'

It wasn't AU or MT that had made his hands rough, I thought. It was FFW, Fucking Farm Work.

'I heard you are preparing for an English major,' he said, fingering the callus on his right hand.

'Yeah, what do you think?' Mum had urged me to seek his advice; now I was all ears.

'How should I say it?' He recrossed his legs and leaned back. 'I've met some English majors at AU. They were all rich kids from the large city of Fuzhou and, of course, Amoy. You know, the kind

241

that wear expensive clothes and watches, ride fancy bikes, and have lots of spending money. They're artistic and romantic.'

His eyes narrowed as if he were staring at a mirage, close but untouchable. 'There was one pretty slender girl, jeans and all, who was so talented she could speak English more fluently than some of the teachers there. She was from HK, you know.' Hong Kong. 'I wouldn't try for English. You have all the disadvantages. Those guys have big, foreign tape-recorders complete with American-language tapes. Have you seen a recorder before?' He shook his head. 'Of course not.'

I still didn't believe it was humanly possible to preserve a human voice once it had spoken. It was like trying to gather water once it had spilled.

'Those guys have beautiful, perfect accents. It's talent. You have to be artistic and musical. I don't think anyone at YSH [Yellow Stone High] could teach you that. And even if they could, we would be stuck, given our thick lips and slow tongues. If I were you, I would consider something else, maybe agricultural management.'

I saw my dad lose interest in talking to this new city man. He rolled a thick one and offered it to my cousin. I knew Dad was being funny. He should know that they wouldn't do thick ones on the AU campus. Cousin Tan refused it, pulled out a Wind cigarette, and offered it to Dad and my brother.

'What is it?' Dad asked.

'Oh, it's the most popular brand on campus. Even the chairman of my department at AU smokes these.'

Dad shook his head like a Yellow Stone farmer, violently from side to side. 'Not my type. It's too light, it'll make me sneeze.' He broke the cigarette in half and dropped it on the floor. 'Why don't you stay for lunch?' Dad's way of saying goodbye. Mum frowned warningly at him.

'No, no. I have to go to Putien to see some AU classmates, you know.'

Sure, we knew. Socializing. It was a part of high society. We had no meat for lunch in any case. We watched him comb his longish hair with his hands and walk with a straight back down the narrow street of Yellow Stone, greeting people with a wave of his hand like a victorious Napoleon.

I retreated to my room after he left, taking two hours to rebuild the spirit he had so gently and carelessly dashed. But no matter how tacky he had become, I still liked it better than seeing him locked up in his attic. He had the freedom to vent his airs now. That was what it was all about. I renewed my determination, wanting to be in his shoes, if not necessarily like him.

'Do you still want to pursue the English major?' Dad asked me later.

'Yes, even more so.'

'Why?'

'Because I think they've got a bunch of losers and playboys at AU. I'm not afraid of city folks. They're wimpy, I'm tough. They already have everything without college. I don't. I'll work my butt off and beat every one of those pompous spoiled brats. Don't you think I can do it?'

Dad smiled, and nodded confidently. He blew a perfect smoke ring. I caught it with my index finger, cutting it in half.

Twenty-one

Firecrackers filled Yellow Stone's narrow street with thick smoke. It was Chinese New Year again. Farming was halted and half the town was into serious gambling. The well-off smoked their Flying Horses and bet with cash; the stingy made do with grains or animals as bets; and the desperate smoked their thick handmade rolls and even put their wives on the betting table. Time-share concept at its most basic. A villager fifteen miles west of Yellow Stone was heard to have lost his wife twelve times at one sitting. When she got word, she drove him out of their house and had the commune arrest him, disclaiming her association with such a shameless loser.

The burning smell of firecrackers filtered through the window and the sound, similar to the beating of hollow bamboo poles, woke me up at the crack of dawn. I opened my eyes; it was still dark outside. Superstitious townspeople believed that the firecrackers scared the devils and demons away. No New Year's celebration could start without a lot of ghost-chasing early on New Year's Day.

I stared at the remaining stars, still twinkling in the east. I badly wanted to snuggle under the thick cotton blanket and sleep until the sun smiled through my window, to dream a delicious dream of the long, tender noodles with succulent meat, oysters, and crispy eggs that I knew awaited me at the breakfast table. I dozed off, only to be awakened by another burst of noisy firecrackers.

'Wake up, I'm ready.' It was my mum at the door. Her voice was gentle but firm. By now, I had become her regular sidekick in this yearly kowtow ritual. I wondered how she managed before I became her self-appointed altar boy. What had happened to my four able-bodied siblings? She must have been busy since midnight preparing the food for sacrifices and arranging them before each of her dozen gods. Dinner last night hadn't ended until midnight. That meant Mum had skipped a whole night of sleep, maybe dozing off in between her preparations.

'Another half-hour,' I declared from under the blanket.

There was a brief lull. Then she said, 'I want to start early this year, for you and your brother's good luck.'

Somehow Mum believed that the earlier you knelt before the gods in the morning to thank them, the more luck it would bring. This was going to be a big year for us. It was her way of making sure that Jin and I would go as far as Tan had done. Ever since the day Tan had mentioned his college life and all the meat they ate, Mum had been dropping hints. Her favourite was, 'If you like meat so much, you should try to go to college like Cousin Tan.' She was a smart woman, and her little hints worked on me better than ever. Only she could see that a lofty idea like going to college could be reduced to the simple word *meat*. She mentioned it whenever I was hungry and stuck my head into the kitchen in search of food; it would send waves down to my empty stomach, making me even hungrier. Soon, when I was bored with studying, I'd lick my lips and imagine the devilishly good taste of meat in my mouth. Then, sighing, I'd struggle on, just like the cows of Yellow Stone thinking of the delicious hay awaiting them when the ploughing was done for the day.

The word *luck* jerked me out of bed. I wouldn't want to second-guess Mum's wisdom. Besides, all those good gods must be watching. I put on the New Year's attire that had been neatly folded on my bench and walked downstairs quietly so as not to awaken the rest of my family. I splashed my sleepy eyes with icy water, scrubbed every inch of my face, and brushed my teeth extra carefully, using a new tube of toothpaste. Mum wouldn't let me near the little shrines if I wasn't considered clean.

It was time to hit the floor in front of those who held my miserable fate in their invisible hands. I stretched my knees and my back in preparation for the torture to come, then rubbed the skin on my forehead and massaged my temples with both thumbs. I knew that my head would ache, my knees would hurt, and my back might break, but I was willing to do it anyway. I told myself if I didn't have the brains to crack open the door to college, I surely had the thick forehead to kowtow my way there. Nothing could stop me once I had a dozen gods behind me.

As usual, we started with the God of Earth. Mum, on her knees, said her words of gratitude, followed by wishes for the new year. In her rapid, almost unintelligible chanting, the word *college* was squeezed into the flow. She had said those prayers morning and night, and they slipped in and out of her mouth like well-oiled noodles. The prayers were for the general welfare of the whole family, for health and prosperity. And then there were the special requests. The order of importance and significance were pre-determined in her mind. There would be no mistakes, no faltering. This was where her expertise lay. She was the voice of the Chen household. By now, the gods should have no problem recognizing her.

I looked at her humble, pious face. Her eyes were closed for maximum spirituality. There was both joy and peace in her gestures. She was begging before her forbidding gods. At that moment, Mum was a little girl pleading for candy. I had never really seen her in this light before. Finally, she opened her eyes and smiled happily, as though she had just got what she had prayed for. She gestured to me.

My turn had come.

I took the burning incense from her, cupped it in my hands, then, taking a deep breath, I sank to my knees. A thick cushion had been laid on the floor for me, and I started silently counting the many thousands of kowtows I had promised the gods in exchange for numerous petty favours in life. Again, it was payback time. I began with complete gestures: kneeling, hitting my head on the floor, standing up, then kneeling again. Slowly, as the numbers got into the hundreds, I began to remain kneeling. My head didn't hit the floor nearly as hard as it should have. Silently, I made a pact with the god to whom I was kowtowing that as I was going to be doing so many, I would need to skimp on the formalities a bit. My kowtowing in the end became reduced to an up-and-down motion of the head. Eventually I would just be sniffing the floor with little jerks, sweat stinging my eyes.

Dad had suggested another option. He said if you promised any god a thousand kowtows, you could actually just do a hundred really big ones and tell the god that each of the big ones stood for ten. I knew he said it to try and rein in my suicidal zest. At times I was tempted, but then I thought about the formula of input and output: what you put in was what you got back. If I aimed at a fancy college in Beijing, I had better be doing some serious banging with my thick skull. No discounts. No hanky-panky. After kowtowing to twelve gods, I dragged my exhausted body to our living room and sank into a chair. By this time, my sisters and brother were up, and I extended my sore hand on the armrest as they willingly dropped their monetary contribution into my hand in exchange for the hundreds of kowtows I had done on their behalf while they had snored away the early hours of New Year's Day. They smiled at me and I kept curling my fingers to indicate more contributions. I felt like a boxer, bruised and raw, back from fighting for my siblings. I was worth every fen they gave me and more.

When I'd eaten the noodles that were traditionally served as the first meal of the year, and after spending the kowtow money on five packs of Flying Horse at Liang's black market, I headed for Yi's workshop.

The gang was already there. They roughed up my hair and pinched my ears and nose, paying me back for all the times I had been too busy for them. I loved these guys. They were always the same: gruff, sincere, and caring in their own very charming way. When they felt jealous or neglected, they shouted at me and slapped my head, then their irritation was over. Like the Dong Jing, full to its brim with pure rainwater, their hearts were generous with love.

'Fucking piece of shit, you look pale and weak. What's the

247

matter with you, college man?' Mo Gong made the welcome speech for the gang. Sen, Yi and Siang searched my coat pockets, split up the cigarettes, and laughingly enjoyed their first good smoke of the year.

'I brought these for you guys because I wanted to apologize for all the neglect.'

'Shut up and have one yourself.' Sen threw me a pack of Wing cigarettes with filters. I lit one. It felt good to be back.

Nothing in the room had changed much. The tools were still hanging on the rough dirt walls. There were traces of sawdust. A bunch of tobacco leaves still dangled in the dark corner, hidden away from the sun. And the place still smelled like a school dorm, except now there was the added smell of mould. The place had been shut up since Yi had left for his job in the big city. It was opened once in a while, whenever Yi was back in town. Mo Gong, Sen, and Siang had been on the road a great deal. Old habits were hard to kick. Gambling, stealing, travelling on the old bike, they were still outcasts. Sen patted my shoulder and sat next to me on Yi's old work stool. 'Brother, you missed out on a helluva lot of fun when you were hitting those books.'

'What the hell have you guys been doing?' I asked.

'Take a look.' Mo Gong threw a thick heap of money on the bench and nodded. It was supposed to mean something to me. I had never seen that much money before. The butcher next door always carried a wad to the commune bank at the end of every day, but this neatly stacked pile was twice as thick.

'Where did you get it? Did you steal it?' I couldn't believe my eyes.

The four gave me another roughing up and pinched my ears and nose again. I struggled free before any more damage was done. They all smiled the same Buddha smile, silent and mysterious.

'We went to Yi's city for ten days and won it,' Sen said.

'How?'

'Well, we set up two gambling tables in a rented hut near Yi's factory. Half of Yi's colleagues came, just for the entertainment. Those rich city folks! We robbed them raw and stole them blind. Yi played stranger, and we three ran the two tables. Before word got out, we moved, and here we are. Nine hundred and thirty yuen!'

I trembled. The figure was so large, it was almost criminal. I knew my rich cousin Yan made thirty-two yuen a month. My friends had raked in two-and-a-half years of profit in just a few days. That was stealing at its best.

'You don't believe me, do you?' Sen asked, smiling.

'It's so much. You know, we could build an eight-bedroom house with that much.'

The four nodded. They'd probably been smiling ever since they got the money. Why not, who wouldn't? If it had been my money, I would smell it every second, smile at it all day long, and slip it under my pillow to dream about at night.

'But we're not building houses. Here,' Sen took half an inch from the stack and threw it to me. 'Listen, this is our money. Let's use it wisely and clean everyone out. Then we'll have tens of thousands.' Sen was good with numbers. He meant the sugarcane fields, where we had met for the first time.

'What do you mean, ours?'

'The money is ours, yours as well as mine. You're still our brother. We'll use the money as seed money to gamble some more, and soon we'll all be rich and maybe buy ourselves some wives,' Mo Gong said, lights dancing in his eyes. He winked at the end of the sentence. Money first, then a wife. It was Mo Gong being totally honest about his worldly outlook.

I felt touched by the inclusion. The brother thing still caused a tightening in my gut. We were bound by our sworn allegiance, but when money came into it, things changed somehow. I felt uncomfortable. We were meant to stick together in friendship and love, not for money. No one had inserted any clause about money. It was a spiritual alliance, not a financial one.

Something about them had changed. These guys were no longer kids. They had all begun to wear rough beards. Their voices were deeper and huskier. They were grown-ups with grown-up desires and ideas. They had seen the city and gambled there with the big guys. Now there was this pot of money. Who knew what was next? Maybe the cops were after them.

'Are you sure this money is clean?' I asked, stern-faced.

'Smug little rascal.' Mo Gong grabbed my neck and planted a wet kiss on my forehead. 'Don't worry about a thing. Money is always clean.'

He picked up the stack and planted a kiss on that, too. 'We're rich. Let's hit the fields. The losers are waiting for us to wipe them out.'

'This time we're the big guys,' Sen said. 'Only big hands are welcome from now on. The penny business is over. Da, you come with us, even if it's just for a day or two, then you can go back to your studies.'

'You have to come. Just spend some time with us, okay?' Siang said. 'And we've got some love stories for you to hear.'

The temptation was high. It was New Year's Day. No one could say anything about my taking a day off from my studies. God made this day for men to play. I deserved it. Four pairs of eyes were waiting for me.

I bit my lips. 'I really need to study every night to make it to college, I swear. I'd love to come with you and wipe them out, or even just be with you guys and boast, but I really can't go.' It was the pact I had made with my family and Buddha. I had better stick to it.

There was disappointment in their eyes.

Sen was a man of reason. 'Well, we're all grown-up now. If you gotta do it, then go do it. Let's have a drink tonight, though.'

'I'll be here with all the food you can eat. You guys go make big money, and we'll celebrate tonight.'

'You better be hitting the books or else I'll crack your skull,' Mo Gong threatened affectionately. He would have made a great law-enforcement officer.

Yi and Siang both kicked my behind as I left them.

On my way home, I thought about them and the money. Things used to be simpler. There had been no college to dream about, and my friends had just been lightweight neighbourhood hooligans, walking their beat on the street of Yellow Stone. A puff of smoke would have made them content and a good joke could last for days. Tobacco had been sweet and liquor charming. Now I was

250

turning down their offer of adventure to hit my tedious books, while they headed out on a mission to clean up the whole town. The thought wedged in the middle of my heart. I sighed as I entered our house and crept into my room, where my books were waiting patiently for me. I closed my eyes before opening the first book to study the first item on the agenda for the day. There was peace within me. The excitement of the New Year belonged out there, on the street of Yellow Stone.

I was going for the English major, so I acted like one. I decorated the walls of my room with English words and phrases. I also made cards with English words on one side and Chinese on the other. I carried a thick stack in my coat pocket wherever I went. I'd mumble to myself, trying to memorize the words. It was a way of immersing myself in the world of English. I'd do it while shopping, walking, eating, and doing the big one in the bathroom.

Once I stopped by a peanut stand for some hot fried peanuts laced with brown sugar, a favourite of mine. I leaned over the old man's cart and pointed at the smallest bag, the only one I could afford, still muttering an English word from my card stack. The sweaty old man stood there with a puzzled look on his face and asked me what I meant. I said I wanted a bag of peanuts. Why was that so hard to understand? He said I had said something funny. I asked him to ignore it, it was an English word. He handed me my peanuts and said I was crazy. Another time I walked through our crowded living room, which was filled with my dad's patients, absentmindedly practising a difficult English phrase I was studying. Later a concerned female patient took my mum aside and asked earnestly whether I was all right up there, pointing at her own head. 'Not all the time,' Mum said.

On that New Year's Day, I took Dad's constant advice to review the old lessons before heading for the new. What better time than today to go over all the word cards of the past year? I searched around my study. The cards were scattered around my room – under the pillow, on the window-sill, in matchboxes. There were hundreds of them.

I laid them out on the desk, the Chinese characters face up, and painfully searched my memory for the English words to match them. To my joy and relief, my young mind still cranked along the way it should have. For a long while, I had been afraid that my brain had aged into a fossil from all the liquor I had soaked it with and all the smoke I had sucked in. But no, the brain was still a heaving pile of jelly, alive and bubbling. I could remember 99 per cent of the long, strange English spellings, months after my first encounter. I slipped to my knees and gave my many gods a deep, head-banging kowtow, which I was sure spilled a dozen words from my memory. By noon, I was done reviewing and I reported to Mum, who was dozing off on her kitchen stool. It was the custom, on New Year's Day, for humans first to thank gods for their good deeds, then humans to thank humans to whom they felt grateful. I needed to bow my New Year's greetings to my saintly Professor Wei.

I touched Mum's shoulder and woke her. She smiled guiltily. 'Did I fall asleep?'

'No, you didn't.'

'Yes, I did.' She rubbed her cheeks and shook her head. 'Let's go to the backyard.'

In Mum's book of virtues, sleeping was no minor felony. Her life was about work, work, and more work. The only time she slept late was when she was rolling in bed, crying her guts out from the pain of her ulcer. It happened twice a year, when the weather changed. Then the whole family would stand around her bed gloomily.

I followed Mum to the backyard, where the hungry chickens surrounded us with high hopes of lunch.

'You take that one.' She pointed at the tallest rooster. It studied me with an intellectual chirp. I called the rooster *Leader* because he had stood out from the rest of the flock when he was young. Only the best for Professor Wei.

I whistled to him and he moved towards me with trust, his stride awkward. Leader was my pal and hero. Last summer I had sent him to fight for the honour of all the Chens' chickens against our neighbour's roosters. Not only did he defeat all his male counterparts, he also victimized all the desirable females in the wake of his victories. I could have laid claim to all the eggs that afterwards appeared. Leader's legacy lived on the lips of all who had witnessed his feat. But it had cost him something: Leader lost a big chunk of his red comb, which made him look even more rugged and handsome. Soon, he didn't have to fight for the females any more. They came to him willingly.

But today Leader the Stud was going to become a gift to my dear teacher. It would be a totally different world out there. No more wars against other roosters, lots of space to run around among flowers, plants, and fruit trees. Who knows? He might turn artistic and start singing like some of the females he used to hump. His only opponent would be the dog. But Leader was the top choice for the job. He could run faster and jump higher than the dog. There wasn't a thing to worry about. And with any luck, his sharp beak would poke the dog's eyes out and make him a visually challenged animal. Wasn't that a happy thought to start the new year with? I wouldn't have to worry about the evil, sniffing hound any more. A blind hound was as good as a dead hound. I needed to put in some good words for Leader, so that Professor Wei would delay his arrival on the dining table.

When Leader shoved his head under my hand, I patted him gently, then grabbed his wings and tied them up. In the meantime, Mum got hold of a fat hen and tied up her wings, too. I caged the pair in a bamboo basket with little windows, added two bottles of fine locally brewed grain liquor and was on my way.

In our neighbourhood, live chickens were at the top of the gift list. Liquor was sent to wash the meat down. When a man asked a girl to marry him, he had to carry a pair of chickens tied with red bows when he went to the girl's family to ask for her hand.

I bowed deep and long before Professor Wei and greeted her with 'Happy New Year' in English. The two chickens made a big fuss. I had to kick the cage twice to quieten them.

Professor Wei returned the greetings in her gentle voice and asked, 'What are those chickens doing here?'

'I hoped that you would teach the chickens some English and some manners.'

'The dog will take care of the manners,' she said, smiling, 'and we'll see about English. You really shouldn't have.'

'Mum and Dad said that you have turned me into a good student. We are grateful.'

'You did it yourself, Da,' she said. 'It's all within you, and of course, God has blessed you.'

I nodded in agreement, not quite sure which god we were referring to, one of the local ones or her own god. But we both took comfort in the thought that there was someone up there guiding our lives. That was enough to bring a smile to our faces on that glorious first day of the year.

As we talked, the dog slouched over with disdainful eyes. He stuck his black, twitching nose into one of the cage's windows, investigating the basket's contents like a customs officer. He poked around, stiff-legged, with his ears and tail stuck high. He took his time, exercising his sovereign power over the territory. Suddenly, he let out a painful yelp and jumped back. Crouching low, he stared at the basket warily. A bead of blood welled on the tip of his nose, getting bigger and bigger until it trickled down the side of his mouth. He whined and pawed at his snout. Stifled anger was mingled with fear at the alien animals inside the bamboo basket, who had wounded him.

Yes! I caught myself cheering for Leader's first victory, even before he had set foot on this new land. *Way to go, sailor. Next time, go for the eyes. Then this piece of splendid paradise will be yours for ever and you can start a family of Leaders, all with that sexy, red, crooked comb and gorgeous feathers that you love to show off to your female friends.* It was worth fighting for.

'That's a tough chicken you have there,' Professor Wei said curiously. No one had ever brought the dog to its knees like this before. 'I want to keep him to chase the birds around here.'

'Oh, he would be very good at that,' I said confidently. 'There's a hen in there, too. I thought they could make a nice little family here.' I sneered at the pathetic dog, who was still squatting on his hind legs.

'Oh, they'll love it here and I promise I will never use them as food, if you know what I mean.'

I was overjoyed by her promise. I untied the knots on the

chickens' wings and they ran off happily without even casting a glance at the old dog.

'You can do whatever you want with them. You don't have to make that promise,' I said.

'Now that I have seen them, I am even more certain that I want them around as pets. Look at those feathers.' She studied Leader, an eye-catcher wherever he went. 'What happened to his comb?'

'Missing in action in World War Two.'

She laughed.

'Now you wait here. I want you to take something to your dad for me.' She disappeared into the white house and came back with two kicking and quacking ducks, their wings tied.

'I can't take them. Dad would not allow me.'

'Don't be silly. Your dad cured my sister's illness. I wanted to send them to your family some time today, but here you are now. Please take them for me.'

I carried the ducks home in the bamboo basket. I wish I could have made the same promise about keeping them alive, but who knew whether tomorrow they might become Peking duck or roasted duck. Each part of their greasy bodies would play an inevitable role at our dinner table. Dad's favourite part was the liver. Mine were the juicy thighs. My sisters loved the greasy skin. Brother Jin always had the wings, and Mum loved chewing the bones. And duck soup suited everyone's appetite any time of the year.

I whistled all the way home, with the ducks quacking as I walked along the quiet Dong Jing River.

At home, Mum and Dad smiled helplessly at the ducks.

'You shouldn't have accepted the present,' Mum said.

'But Professor Wei said it was for the treatments Dad gave to her sister.'

'Next time, run,' Dad said, but he seemed pleased. 'Now let me free them in the courtyard for a day or two.'

I followed his order and untied the ducks.

'But leave the red bows on their wings,' he added.

I looked up at him and tried to swallow a smile.

Dad had an ego the size of Ch'ing Mountain. He wanted the

traces of gifts to remain, like leaving the price tag on an expensive present, so that curious neighbours and friends would ask about the two noisy creatures and Dad would be forced to reveal the source of the gifts. The inquirers would be so impressed that they would talk about the givers for another two days, prolonging Dad's glory at being the doctor for the Wei sisters.

'Join me in the living room after you wash your hands,' Dad said, still smiling ear to ear.

'Okay.' I scrubbed my hands, which smelled like duck feet, and ran into the living room.

Dad had brewed a tall pot of strong tea. He sat comfortably in his old cane chair with his feet on a stool. The well-wishers of the New Year had gone home. It was quiet family time. My brother sat in the corner lighting a cigarette, while Dad poured a cup of steaming tea for him, and filled another for me.

'It's New Year's Day and we have made a new decision about your brother. He is going to take time off and start preparing for the college exam. What do you think?' Dad sounded confident. Once he had made a decision, he considered that 80 per cent of the job was done. He believed that by his believing in us, we could swim the ocean and climb mountains. No hurdle was too hard to overcome, no glory too high to obtain.

I looked at my brother, who was smoking quietly, then at my dad. 'Dad, why didn't I hear about it sooner? I'll go make room for him in my study; I know I'll learn a lot from him.'

Pleased with my response, Dad rolled up his sleeves. 'Now here is the strategy for you two. Da, you are still fresh. You're going to help your brother. You'll make a schedule and study together.'

I was surprised. Jin, who was two sisters away from me, had been in first grade when I was still crawling around in my diapers fighting for food with the chickens in the courtyard. Now I was to help him. My heart beat with pride. With a little hard work and a bit of determination, I had won my dad's respect.

'That will be great,' I said, turning to my brother. 'I have all the books.'

'I'm not really sure about college, I've been away from books too long.' Jin sounded pessimistic. He had always been my

256

opposite in many ways. He was always calm and wise, never the one to want to take centre stage. When it came to a major decision, we always had to push and shove a little. I hoped for victory, while he worried about failure.

'You can do it,' Dad told Jin. 'You were the maths wizard of your class in junior high. You will devote your time to learning the other subjects over the next seven months. 'Don't worry, son, I feel lucky this year.' Dad looked at the two quacking ducks, now depositing droppings all over the courtyard.

It was superstition. Things were coming in twos.

Dad was an amateur fortune-teller. There were many tricks to the art of predicting the future. His speciality was judging facial features. Each day, the first thing he would comment to Mum about in the morning was the colour of his face.

Holding a mirror in his hand, he would say, 'Rosy. I wonder what good things are coming our way today.'

Mum would squint and say matter-of-factly, 'I don't see any rosiness there.'

'There.' Dad would twist his face, trying to squeeze colour out of the pores. 'A little there, huh?'

Mum would have to agree with him or he would keep looking in his mirror the whole morning.

'Is it the colour again?' I asked.

'Yes, the colour is good and my right eye is twitching like crazy,' Dad said, pointing to his face. 'Son, this is the chance of a lifetime. I thought you guys would never have the opportunity to dream about college. Now Mao has gone west and you're given a chance to try. The Chen men have never been known for lack of talent, only for lack of opportunity.'

He turned to my brother, lit another cigarette for him and said, 'Jin, you have the advantage of being more mature. Da, you have the energy. Work together like brothers should, make up for the disadvantages, and both of you will win this time. All you need is hard work. Jin, if you as a teenager could farm like an adult to support this family, then there is no college, I mean no college under the sun, that should be too hard for you to get into. We are behind you all the way. And you, Da, have no reason to even have to consider anything other than your first choice of college. Beijing. Shanghai. Anywhere your heart belongs. Young man, you don't know how lucky you are. Look at your sisters. They weren't even allowed to finish elementary school.' Dad finished his speech, his eyes fiery.

The conversation turned from father-son chitchat into an admiral's final order. The enemy was at the front door. Now go get them, sons.

Jin quietly put out his cigarette and said to me, 'Tomorrow, wake me when you get up. Let me get a feel of what's going on, then we'll sit down and talk. Make me work hard if you see me slack off, little brother. We'll work together.'

'Sure thing.'

Dad filled our cups again and symbolically drank his in one gulp. He had said enough. Now it was up to us.

'Bottoms up.' I toasted my brother and rose to leave. When I pushed the door open, Mum was right behind it and had probably been listening to the whole conversation.

I climbed the stairs to my room, and sat down at my desk, which was covered with piles of books. The sense of a sacred mission swept through my heart. Just before this pep talk, college had been a young man's romantic ideal. Now it was a reality full of emotions. If I failed, I failed the whole family, all the way back to our earliest ancestor, whose tombstone had long become sand. If I won, the family's ship would sail again. It was about pride, humiliation, revenge, dignity, and vindication of the family name.

I shivered as I recalled how often Mum had been casually dropping hints about the good things that had happened to Cousin Tan's family ever since he became an AU student. More marriage proposals, better treatment by their neighbours, and his father's visit to the glorious AU campus.

I knew she wished this were happening to her; that brother Jin was the one receiving all those proposals and she was the mother reviewing all the girls with a magnifying glass, passing along her well-reasoned, tactful rejections, while inwardly gleefully witnessing their disappointment, especially that of the families who had spat at her in the past. She wasn't mean or cruel, but suffering made you see things differently.

I compiled two lists. One was a checklist for my brother of everything needed to catch up with me. The other was my own list of dos and don'ts, a sort of New Year's resolution. On it were no movies, no plays, no sports, no more time off until after The Big One. Tonight would be my last night out with my friends.

A popular, local melody was being badly distorted by a whistler just below my window. The nightingale was Siang, the designated messenger from the gang.

I closed my book, went to the kitchen, and picked up the food basket Mum had prepared for my friends. When I had asked her for the food, I had promised her that it was my last night out with them, that from now on, I would shut my door and bury my head in my books.

'What a terrible whistler,' Mum said. 'Why don't they come in?'

'Because they're afraid of you.'

'Why?'

'Because you're a good person,' I replied.

'How strange.'

'Well, my friends aren't afraid of bad people, they deal with them all day long and beat them up all the time. But when they meet a good person like you, they don't know what to do. They turn shy and stay in the dark.'

Mum shook her head and wiped her hands on her apron.

When I pushed the door open at Yi's, no one jumped out to throw me to the floor or pinch my neck. It was quiet. Four heads, a cloud of smoke rising above them, slumped between legs.

'Hey, brothers, the food is here. Why is everyone so damned quiet?'

'We lost half our money,' Sen said in a low voice. His eyebrows were locked together, a hairy mess.

'How?' My heart dropped. Five hundred yuen gone like the wind. 'That's impossible. You guys are the quickest hands north of the equator and east of the western world.'

I shook Mo Gong's fuzzy head. His neck was boneless, like a

259

rubber pipe. The picture of prosperity only hours ago, he was now a deflated balloon.

'We were doing fine at the beginning, wiping out people like a typhoon. I mean big hands. Then someone snuck from the fields and reported us to the commune. They sent in a battalion and cleaned our pockets. Good thing we made for the sugarcanes, that's why we're not sitting stinking in the commune jail.'

'But the police got our names,' Siang said. 'It's only a matter of hours before they come and knock at our door.'

'What? Who reported it?' I asked.

'Some guy from another village. We'll take care of him sooner or later.'

'So let's eat first and then run,' I said.

'I don't think we have time to eat. But we need some money, we're broke,' Sen said.

'What about the other half of the money?' I asked.

'In the field. We buried it. We'll get it later. Now ain't a good time,' Sen replied.

'Here.' I dug into my pocket and took out about ten yuen. 'Not much, but take this for now.'

'That's a lotta money,' Yi said.

'Don't worry. I have no place to spend it,' I said, pushing the money into Sen's hands. He took it slowly.

'Thanks, Da, you're a real pal. We'll borrow it,' he said, his head low.

'It's nothing, and it's not enough for you guys. Hey, if you wait, I could go home and get some more.' I was thinking of borrowing from my brother.

'No, no, we're leaving now,' Sen said.

'Do you have to?'

All four heads nodded in unison.

'Listen, if we go now, we'll be in Putien in a few hours. We'll stay at Yi's and make another living there. If we don't, it'll be jail time.'

'Eat the food up, please, or you'll be hungry.' I opened the basket. The smell of fried fish, roasted pork, noodles, and New Year's rice cakes permeated the room and opened their eyes.

'Here, use your hands. Eat.'

Four pairs of hands fought for the juiciest pieces. Soon Mo Gong was licking the bottom of the meat plate and Siang was burping. Sen wiped his greasy hands on his hair, a habit he had since he was young, and Yi picked his teeth. A perfect last supper.

The four of them touched me with their greasy hands before leaving. Sen whispered to me, 'Work hard, college man. Make us proud.'

I carried the empty basket home, feeling like a fugitive myself. My friends had vanished into the darkness. All I could hear was the clanking of the old bike.

Twenty-two

The first day back from New Year's break, Dia sported a brand-new, army green Mao jacket. One of the pockets was already missing a button. He stood outside our door and looked as dopey as a bridegroom.

'Hey, happy New Year, and how the hell did you make the girl marry you?' I faked a frown and crossed my arms across my chest.

Dia rubbed his reddened face. 'This thing?' His hands smoothed the wrinkles on his jacket. 'Mum made it for my elder brother and the stupid guy washed it in boiling water. It shrank two sizes. Now, I gotta wear it. I took the button off to look more casual.'

I studied him for a few seconds, prolonging his agony. 'You look really stupid, but I love you, pal. Why didn't you come out for a visit or something?'

'I was too busy. Mum wanted me to go to the temple with her to beg for luck with the college entrance exam. You know what I told her?'

'What? Something witty?'

'Yeah, I thought it was hilarious. I said that to get me into college, a decent one, Buddha himself would have to do the exam for me.'

I thought about the thousands of kowtows that I had done to beg for Buddha's grace and felt a mild temptation to kick Dia's ass for insulting my good old Buddha.

262

He slapped my shoulder and shouted, 'What, you don't think it was funny? My dad still can't get over it. He's probably somewhere telling it to the villagers and smoking his huge pipe. Oh, and I went to a smoking contest.'

'Did you win?'

'Did I win?'

'Sorry. Did you win big?'

'I didn't win.' He seemed disgusted at my poor judgement.

'Sorry, again. So who won then?'

'Who do you think won? Grandpa!'

'Grandpa?'

'It was amazing,' Dia said, warming to his tale. 'Grandpa walked into this smoky, hazy spot, the oldest contestant. You know, a little wobbly. I sat at his side, sorta supporting him. The young, aggressive guys laughed at his shaky frame, but soon they began to fall outta the contest. Smoked out! Ha, ha, ha. Couldn't take it. Grandpa just went on and on with his pipe like a busy chimney. His eyes were smiling, and I kept pouring him hard liquor to quench his thirst. In the end, he won first prize, a whole year's supply of matches for him to burn.'

'Hell of a story, Dia. I think you should take him to the smoking Olympics every single year. Even when he's blind and in a wheelchair, he'll beat the hell out of those young craps.' I shook my head, swung my bag over my shoulder, and we were on our way to school.

'Well, Dad is a little concerned. He said smoking like that, Grandpa might die an Olympian during the contest one of these days.'

'I don't think that'll ever happen to any Dia man. You guys just wheeze a lot but never perish.'

'That's the Dia men, you got it.' Dia patted his own chest with pride. 'Hell, come to think of it, if he croaks, it would be another record to add to his long and glorious smoking life. To die smoking. Wouldn't that be something to put on your tombstone?'

'Shut up, you.'

We chose the narrow path between two green wheat fields, still wet from the melting frost. The morning sun gleamed through the fog. The trees, road, and endless fields looked like an Impressionist painting.

'I feel ashamed walking beside you, you know,' Dia suddenly said.

'Why?'

'I heard that you locked yourself up in your room and banged your fucking head against the wall studying, and that you didn't even take New Year's Day off. You didn't, did you, you son-of-a-gun?'

'That was pure rumour. I had a great time this holiday.'

'Not true. I have my source.'

'I wouldn't rely on it entirely,' I teased him.

'Wait.' Dia ran in front of me. 'I heard something you might wanna hear.'

'What?'

'About your friends.'

'What about them?'

'You haven't heard anything?'

'No, I haven't heard from them since they skipped town on New Year's Day.'

'Don't pull my leg.' Dia stopped me in the middle of the narrow road. His small eyes seemed to dangle from the midst of his sockets, radiating sincerity.

'I swear to Buddha,' I said. 'Tell me what you heard.'

'Okay, here's a clue. Money.'

'Money? What money are you talking about?' My heart sank. Even Dia knew about their fortune.

'You sure you don't know anything about this? Okay, the rumour out there had it that Siang stole about a thousand yuen from the commune's shoe factory his father runs. That's why he's been hiding out with his friends.'

The news hit me like a fist. Siang, a thief? On the run? I recalled the glee on my friends' faces on New Year's Day. They were so full of joy. That one thousand yuen had to have been money they'd won honestly. Siang wouldn't steal. My sworn friends wouldn't lie to me about where they had got the fortune. It hadn't been in their eyes. There had been no fear. It was money that had come from courage, bravery, and their ability to take a calculated risk at the gambling table.

'You don't believe me, do you?' Dia asked.

'No, I don't. They told me a different story.'

'What? They told you about the money?'

I realized my slip of the tongue. 'Forget it, Dia. We didn't have this conversation, okay?'

'Hey, slow down. I'm your best friend. Trust me. The commune is investigating the whole thing now and they can't prove whether Siang really has the money that he was accused of stealing.'

Holy shit, I could have given the truth away. I was glad I was only talking to Dia, someone in whom I could confide my darkest secrets. 'What else did you hear?'

'That he stole the money to gamble, but there's another rumour that the shoe factory's one thousand yuen might have been stolen by its bookkeeper or someone from the inside. Someone knew that Siang was in possession of a fortune and framed him. He was easy pickings. You know he hangs around the shoe factory and is good friends with the treasurer.'

My heart sank deeper. There was a scheme out there to frame and ruin Siang and his friends, and possibly me.

'Did you hear anything about me being involved in any way?'

'No, everyone knows you're a born-again good guy who was recently honoured with the Young Communist League title in school. You've been making quite a name as being a top contender for college.'

'How does your small village know so much about the things happening here?'

'My neighbour, the baldy. Remember, I told you about him. He's the head of the commune's militia command. He was drunk last night, boasting to my dad. I got the whole scoop. He's heading the investigation.'

'What's he doing now?'

'Nothing concerning you,' he told me. 'Relax.'

I had never felt so relieved. I prayed a quiet thank-you to Buddha that I hadn't followed them to the fields to gamble on

New Year's Day. I could have easily been implicated. Buddha had been watching over me.

A dark shadow clouded my mood. My friends were in trouble. I should do something about it, but I didn't have a clue about what. I truly believed that they had gone to Putien and cleaned Yi's colleagues out. They were self-made, rich men, unjustly put on a short-list of suspects. It would have been easy. They were social outcasts. Someone had probably known about their money, swiped the cash from the shoe factory, and laid the crime on them, just in time to get away clean. The whole town would believe it was Siang, of course. It was the holidays, gambling time, and he just happened to be back in town on the day the crime occurred. He probably went to see his dad at work and someone saw him and heard about the money they had won in Putien. Bingo. What better motive, what better timing!

'Wake up and have a thick one.' Dia stirred me from my troubled world and passed me a made-by-Dia stogy, the very thing needed to calm me down. I took the lifeline and inhaled a mouthful of dark blue smoke into my lungs. The nicotine made my blood race a little.

'I have to do something about it,' I murmured.

'No you don't, pal. Don't look for trouble.'

'What do you think I should do?'

'Sit on your skinny ass and hit the books. Remember, you don't know nothing.' Dia stared at me, sending a message with his eyes.

I swallowed my fear with the bitter smoke. 'I know nothing,' I repeated a few times. It made me feel safe.

Dia was a street-smart, disillusioned, lazy guy. But he was loyal to his bones. In my book, that one virtue covered all his sins. He was a hero and a buddy to me, but he also annoyed the heck out of me. I grabbed his hair and roughed it up again. He reached out and tousled mine, then we chased each other up the steep stairs of the school.

I heard Dia's lungs wheeze with each step he took. He had to slow down a few times to catch his breath. I stopped and looked at him with sympathy. The pride of being a Dia man, smoking and wheezing, and living a long life. It was such a stupid belief. He would probably die young.

Inside the school, the Head walked by us with his nose up in the air. He sported a new jacket, as well as a new hat for his formidable pate. He hurried by, sneering and ignoring us as if we were a couple of stinking bugs he wouldn't mind stepping on and grinding to death.

'That guy annoys the heck out of me,' I said to Dia.

'My feeling, exactly. Watch this.' Dia cleared his throat and shouted, 'Hey, Head, there's bird droppings on your new hat.'

The Head stopped without turning around. He knew where the voice came from. He thought for a second, then took off his new wool hat and checked the top quickly.

'Oops, I lied.' Dia laughed.

'You little rat.' The Head was angry. He rolled up his sleeves and walked up to Dia, who stood his ground.

I inserted myself between them and said, 'There's no reason to get angry here. Dia just wanted to see your head, that's all. It's a joke. Can't you take a joke, big boy?'

'I can take a joke, but not from you two losers.' The Head gritted his teeth.

'Hey, watch your mouth.' I felt like shaking the guy. From the corner of my eye I saw Dia reaching into his bag, ready to do some serious damage to the self-acclaimed top intellectual of Yellow Stone High. I quickly put my hand on his arm.

'Why are you wasting your time in school? You guys belong in the fields. There's no future for you two in school.'

'Says who? You?' I stepped closer.

'Says everyone. Haven't you heard? Liberal arts is just a dumping ground for waste like you guys. Don't think a few good scores will get you into college. No way.'

My anger was reaching its peak. You could insult my looks, my character, and my honour, but no one was allowed to tear apart my dream. I pulled back my right arm, ready to shove my fist down his throat. This time Dia dragged me back.

'Hey, Head, let me tell you something. This man' – Dia pointed at me – 'is gonna be an English major at a top college in Beijing, while you, the engineering major, will end up in a corner of this freezing country, spending your miserable life sawing lumber in the snow. And you're gonna get so lonely, you're gonna start thinking about fucking a sheep while this man will be the translator for the Minister of Foreign Affairs, touring the beautiful western world. Wake up, Head, and think.'

My anger subsided at Dia's rousing speech.

'In your dreams.' The Head put back his hat and walked off proudly.

We looked at each other and laughed. There was a reason why we liked each other. We worked well together, unrehearsed.

'How did you come up with crap like that?' I asked Dia.

'Well, that's what I think is gonna happen to you, man. Don't disappoint me. Work your bony ass off if you have to and do honour to our friendship. I have high hopes for you and low expectations for that creep. I don't get it. How can such a big head be so stupid? I think the best thing for him to do would be to hand over his head to some scientist, who can study it and find out what's wrong with it. That would be his biggest contribution to science.'

We had another good laugh.

'You know the way you reason and talk really impresses me sometimes. I think you could do well if you worked hard with me. You're just too lazy and negative.'

'Thanks for encouraging me, pal. That's why I like you, for thinking well of me when everyone else trashes me as if I'm a dog or something.'

'Hey, no problem. But think about what I said, okay?'

'I will.'

We slipped into our classrooms after promising to see each other at first break. Good friends were like family on the first school day.

The classroom was half full when I came in. There were some changes. The broken windows were fixed and the wall was repainted with rough white paint. There was a large slogan about studying hard, a quote from the dead Chairman Mao. Students buried their heads in their books. Some stuck their heads out of the window and puffed their tobacco rolls. There was a sense of seriousness that hadn't been there before. A fellow was actually reading an English lesson out loud. Only a year ago, his teeth would have been knocked out for doing that. I sat in my old seat, in the corner of the last row. The corner was no longer for the convenience of jumping out of the window whenever I felt like it. It was an island. It felt safe here, I could survey everything and everyone, yet no one could see me.

It was ironic to bring Mao into this drive for intellectual excellence. If Mao had known what his Little Red Guards were doing, he would have howled like a lonely wolf in his icy coffin and cried his smoke-ridden lungs out. Mao, the dictator, was the friend of the devils. He wanted China in perpetual turmoil so that he could rule for ever. He had a simple philosophy: peace and leisure bred unrest and resentment against leaders, while a sense of crisis strengthened his own leadership. That was why, ever since the Communists took over in 1949, Mao hadn't stopped making fake smoke over fake fires. One political movement had followed another. And strewn down his long path lay the bones of millions of angry ghosts. He hadn't cared about the young generation, whom he had ordered to walk out of school and into the countryside to get re-educated by the poor farmers in their muddy fields. He had simply wanted them to be ignorant, so they wouldn't be aware of what a fiend he really was.

Young people loved it. Since the big guy didn't want them in school, they packed up and moved to the countryside by the millions, singing the Red Guard songs and waving their Little Red Books. But soon, they found that all they could learn from farmers was back-breaking labour and antiquated farming techniques dating back thousands of years. So they started insulting the farmers, stealing their daughters, and stopping going to work. All day long the youngsters smoked, drank, gambled, and fell in love. There was nothing else out there to do. The lonely countryside became their trap. They roamed around the hills, but it was too late to move back to the cities they had come from, because of China's population control system. A city person could easily give up his registration to move downwards into the country, but not vice versa. They cried, and some committed suicide. Now they understood what their leader Mao had meant by finding your roots in the countryside. He had meant it literally. Go marry someone there, breed a litter of ignorant farmers, and never come back to the city to bother me again.

At eight sharp every morning the old bellman wobbled to the bronze bell that hung under an old pine tree. The sound of the bell echoed far and wide. In the school hallway, Peking Man snuffed out his cigarette and shuffled into our classroom. He smiled like a gorilla at the new slogan on the wall. He tried hard for a few seconds to conceal his laughter, but his thin lips were unable to cover his big teeth.

'Who put it there?' Peking Man asked. 'Is that a joke or something?'

The class was very quiet.

'When Mao said study hard, I don't think he meant the kind of stuff we're studying now,' he stuttered. 'You should know that he was referring to his Little Red Book, but I doubt any college would give you credit for that.'

The whole class rocked with laughter. Only Peking Man could open the first class of the year that way. What he said was brave, because Mao's ghost still haunted the nation, but Peking Man was fearless and angry. He had been beaten and sent to labour camps not too long ago.

He snapped his fingers and the class calmed down. 'About learning history, let me tell you a story.'

We were all ears.

'When I was at the university, I roomed with a medical student. Every night before going to sleep, the guy stuck his hand into a wooden box under his bed and mumbled things. Day in and day out. Finally, I couldn't contain my curiosity and I asked him what he was doing. You know what he said? He had a whole collection of human bones in that box. He was trying to develop a feel for the bones blindfolded, because he wanted to be a good doctor.

'What are the bones of history?' He paused and looked at us. 'From that day on, I did the same thing with all the historical facts: dates and names of the dynasties, all the important little things in

270

the study of history. I had flash cards, stacks of them, under my bed next to my stinking shoes. Before we turned out the lights, he would be busy with his bones, and I with my cards. We had a grand time. We both graduated with honours.'

Peking Man didn't ask us to do the same thing; he simply inspired and challenged us to follow in his footsteps. He was the perfect teacher for us to follow. His hairy chest, long limbs, formidable face, and that mountain of a jaw all attested to a man who knew the past well. 'Now I heard that you guys are going to take the Liberal Arts examination. We don't have a lot of time left. Thousands of years of history have to be learned and relearned. I am here to guide you, but you have to do the rowing. Do you have any special requests before I begin?'

'How many questions did you guess right on the last national history examination?' one boy asked.

My question exactly.

'I would say I guessed them all, because I taught them all.'

'No. I meant in the final days, when you gave your cram session,' the boy persisted.

'Oh, that. Three out of the five essay questions. I gave my last graduating class the exact answers two days before the test. I considered it my gift to them. The smart ones went home and committed them to memory, and they came out of the test smiling from ear to ear.'

Another point driven home. Thou shalt heed my words. Peking Man had the mentality of a god, and we were brought down on our knees in the presence of his achievement.

'But,' he said, 'my guessing is just a bonus. Sometimes I guess correctly, other times I don't. You need to go home and chew up this thick volume.' He waved his textbook as if it were a Bible. 'Digest this and make it become part of you. Every word in here, every fact, is a building block to your dream of a college degree. Young people like you belong there.' His eyes swept across me, and my heart warmed up ten degrees. 'Remember, for the next few months you have to sleep, eat, walk, and talk with these books. And you students who are behind, you had better dream about them as well.'

271

I repeated the whole thing to Dia during the break and he was spellbound. It was exactly the kind of motivational speech he got excited about. He started hopping up and down the quiet hallway, cursing the teacher who had assigned him to L-Two, the Siberia of intellectual stimulus. He had spent the first class fighting for a good seat, then sleeping and waking to the foul smell of the guy in front of him who farted throughout the whole morning.

'Hey, calm down. Like the Peking Man said, you just have to study hard yourself. He can only do the guiding.'

'You don't know how hard it is to be among those losers. Thinking about it makes me sick.'

Dia's attitude surprised me. He was changing. He no longer saw himself as a loser the way he used to. I saw hope in him.

'You know, let's study together tonight and see how effective it is.'

'How?'

'Well, I have a plan.' I whispered into his ear and he smiled.

After dinner that day, I told Mum that I was going to study in school until late at night. I asked for a key to our door and got a bag full of food for Dia, who had sent word home that he was sleeping over at my house.

The school was locked, so we found a short wall and threw ourselves over. We ducked our heads and moved swiftly towards our classroom. The night guard was a middle-aged man who was still trying to impregnate his wife. He had been married for many years and had no kids. A monk from the Ch'ing Mountains had a secret recipe. He urged the night guard to drink a glass of grain liquor every night before mounting his wife. The guy had a natural aversion to alcohol. The taste of liquor drove him crazy, but his wife, a big woman by any standards, was said to pin him in the crook of her flabby arm and force the liquor down his unwilling throat. The man had passed out a few times, but the wife didn't care. All that mattered was what was coming after the liquor took effect on her subdued husband. She had been heard singing lullabies at midnight on a good night.

The drinking drill took place every night. Through their window, you could see the silhouette of the little man facing a glass of liquor with a woman the size of a hill looming over him. The man had nightmares when darkness fell, rumour had it.

Dia stopped at the guard's window. He was curious about what went on in there, but this was not the time. I kicked his bony behind and we lifted the window of our classroom like a couple of thieves and sat at our seats.

I planned to study history every night with Dia. It would save the oil my huge lamp at home burned, and Dia could smoke his lungs rotten while studying, a thing my mum despised. We would use candlelight to illuminate our books.

Dia took out the candles I had given him money to buy. All four of them gave off a mystic light, soft and calm. He rubbed his eyes and mumbled something to the effect that he could not see well with the tiny candles. I whacked his head and told him that once upon a time there was a scholar so poor yet so committed to his studies that he poked a hole in his neighbour's wall to borrow the light coming through it. In the winter, he would sit by a large pile of snow and study in the silver light coming from the icy surface of the snow at night.

'All right, all right, enough of the historical bullshit. I need a smoke.'

I whacked him again playfully and opened my history book while he lit his thick one with the candle.

During the winter holiday, I had finished my history studies. They included Chinese ancient history, world history, and the stupid history of the Communist party. The subjects were contained in a thick volume of one thousand pages. In the beginning, I had been stunned by how many dynasties China had. The names of all the emperors and their successors piled up like endless waves of the Dong Jing River. Gradually, I developed a method of study. I charted them into a family tree and gave them funny names, like those I used to give to my dogs, chickens, and ducks. I carried the charts with me at all times and reviewed them again and again, even when I went to the bathroom. Every minute was quality time in my schedule.

'Have you read through the book at least once?' I asked Dia.

'I'm trying to, but I can't remember a thing. All I remember is how many wives the first emperor of the Tan dynasty had, and how one of his wives eventually took control and ran the country. You know, I actually fell in love with her. I think I need a wife like that to run my pathetic life.'

I shook my head hopelessly, unable to help but be amused by him. I wished that everything we had to learn in school were that interesting. I bet our hero, Peking Man, must have had a blast studying the personal lives of those corrupt emperors. He had probably wished he were one of them. The emperor was above all law. He could have as many wives as he wanted. A lot of them were discarded after one night and locked in the back of his palace, forbidden for ever to leave, left to entertain themselves with the eunuchs.

'Well, that's good,' I said. 'At least you remember something. Why don't you try to think of the whole book as a story about us and the people who lived before us in this land called China. It will be fun.'

'Nah, the fun is just reading about the female parts. If I were living in those feudal times, I'd definitely apply for a job at the palace as a eunuch.'

'And have your balls cut off?'

'It would be worth it. I'd be in charge of the rejected ladies in the back of the palace and could enjoy every single one of them every day.'

'Come on. Let's study. We're not here to talk about girls. You read the first chapter and I'll test you later tonight.'

Dia ducked his head and forced his eyes back to his book. I moved my two candles to the corner of the room and started reviewing my chapters. I normally began lightheartedly, then, as I thought about the big test just around the corner, every single fact in the thick book became important. Finally, I became paranoid and began to memorize the tiniest details. I even remembered the birthdays of each emperor. My brother, who had just started his preparation, was totally shaken when he found out that I could even remember the name of a small village where one emperor had stayed at the humble shelter of a blind villager when he was chased out of the capital city. It had appeared in a footnote.

The night was quiet and cool.

At first, I could hear Dia's feet tapping the floor. He smoked a few times, then I became totally absorbed in the book. Dia was forgotten. A couple of times, he tried to get my attention with his out-of-tune whistling. I ignored him as a matter of discipline. When I finally turned to look at him during my break, Dia was sweetly snoring away in a puddle of drool. His candles had fallen to the table and burned themselves out.

I shook my head and walked over. Yanking a long strand of my hair out, I spun it in his nostrils. He frowned a few times, then suddenly woke up. 'Shit, I drifted off.'

'How many pages did you do?'

'Three.'

'That's it?'

'I need electric light. Candlelight makes me sleepy.'

'You numbskull! You don't even have electric power in your village. How can you say that?'

'I'm a new Dia man and I don't do well under candlelight.'

'Well, it should be safe now. The guard's window is dark.' Dia ran and flipped on the light.

'It means something, you know?' Dia said.

'What means something?'

'That I can only study under this big light.'

'Yeah, it means something. It means you need some serious spanking right now.' I picked up our teacher's stick and chased the lazy lout around the room until I nailed him down on the floor. I whipped him lightly and he begged for mercy.

'Admit that you're lazy and don't ever talk like that any more.'

'Forgive me. I was just playing with you, pal.'

The next three hours we spent quietly studying. I could see him fighting off a yawn a few times. He pinched his nose, twisted his monkey ears, and at one point spanked himself with the stick I had used on him. I was proud of him. If I could discipline him like this every day, he would probably do all right.

'Now it's test time,' I announced.

'No, it's quitting time,' Dia retorted. 'It's eleven. The electric light is going out.'

'We're just beginning.'

'Mercy, what's the questions?'

I gave him three simple questions. He missed only one. Then he questioned me. I got them all right.

He was hyped about his performance and we went on testing each other. When it was my turn again, Dia knelt on the floor and said, 'Hey, stop it. I can't take it any more. College is yours, man.'

'Come on. Let's do some more.'

'No, I'm dying right now. If I don't close my eyes, I'll drop on the floor.'

I was really in the mood. Nothing could stop me. Dia fell on the floor and started snoring while I walked around, repeating what I had just learned, telling the stories over and over to myself until I remembered them well. The big test was only months away. I was scared and didn't need sleep.

Suddenly, I heard a knock on the window. It was pitch-dark out there. Who could it be?

I immediately turned off the light and squatted on the floor, pinching Dia's ear to wake him up. The beam of a flashlight pierced through the window and swept around the room a few times.

A deep voice shouted, 'Get out of there before I fire the rifle.'

'Wake up,' I whispered into Dia's ear. He was sleeping like a dead man. I had to do something. I kicked him. He scrambled up like a shocked animal.

'The night guard's up.'

'Shit, let's run.'

We collected our things in the darkness and climbed out of the window like rats. The flashlight followed us until we'd got over the wall, where we collapsed, panting like hunted beasts.

'He said he would shoot us if we didn't move. Do you believe him?' I asked Dia.

'Nah, the only gun he's got is the one between his legs and it ain't very effective as his wife could surely tell you.'

We laughed all the way back to my home. It had been a tiring night, but I felt satisfied because I had done a lot of studying and remembered everything perfectly. And Dia was making progress.

The fright of being chased by the school guard was easily forgotten.

The next day, during the compulsory morning exercise, the principal stepped up on to the stage. Something was up. He never appeared, except for very special reasons.

'Last night we had two intruders on our campus. We only have one of their names. We are still working on the other. They climbed the wall to get in. I was furious when I heard this.' He paused, frowning.

My legs were shaking and my knees felt weak. I didn't need this public humiliation any more. I silently begged the principal to forget it. Dia stole a look at me. The whole school was now in the field, busily guessing who these two guys could be.

'As I said, I was mad until I was told what these guys were doing in our classroom. Studying! I said to the night guard that I was shocked to hear that. It was a beautiful story. If I have my students studying until three o'clock in the morning, then I am looking to be the principal of a very promising school here. These guys are a good example, you all can learn from them.'

I was totally stunned by the twist. Dia was smiling at me now.

'To these two young men, I say continue working hard, but watch your health, and don't climb the wall. You could break your legs, or worse. I praise you, but I ask that you don't come to school at night any more. We will keep our school open until midnight for you, but no later. That's my message. Now everyone, go back to your studies.'

It felt good being praised for our efforts. I was sure Dia felt the same way. He badly needed the boost. Maybe now he would pick himself up and start to run with the others.

Twenty-three

Every morning I rose with the sun. Then I shuffled to my brother's room and woke him up. I would see a few books lying beside him. He had fallen asleep again, worrying about the exam. Each morning, he jumped out of bed, rubbed his red eyes, and stared at me as if I were crazy. I was.

I went through our backyard, opened the squeaky gate, trotted down the steps to the river, and squatted by the clear, cool water to check my reflection. I had lost weight since I had begun rising at sunrise and going to bed at eleven every day. I splashed my face with water and wiped it with my sleeves. Six hours of sleep every day. I needed a lot of cold water to keep my eyes open.

It was already late April. The smell of summer was pungent everywhere. Our backyard was a colourful garden with red roses, yellow ga-gai blossoms and white lilies. Mum had planted some lima beans, which had flourished in the most imaginative way and now crawled overhead along the wood frames of the doors and windows. I found a spot beneath the thick leaves away from the scorching sun, placed my favourite bamboo chair there, and munched on some bean pods as the gentle breeze ruffled my hair.

Every morning I woke up to tackle political studies, the most boring of the five subjects required in the big exam. It was all about the twisted philosophy of the Communist party. Some of the theories were so involved, they sounded like sophistry at best, and that was what they were.

It was like a carpet-cleaning salesman raving about this great revolution taking place in the carpet-cleaning industry, when actually none existed. And the machine he was trying to sell you wasn't one bit as good as what he claimed. It was tedious self-promotion, mixed with a little bit of lying. Many times I wanted to throw the book into the river. What was this? Marxism combined with Mao's superior thoughts? It was simply some foreign garbage, stir-fried with local flavour until it became a dish called communism, Chinese style. Moo goo gai pan with ketchup.

Some of the questions and explanations given were so far-fetched I felt like spitting. Like why in the beginning of the revolution Mao had ordered his armies into the countryside instead of starting a revolt in the big city. The book said Mao was applying Marxism to China's unique circumstances. That was bull. Mao was just running for his life. He hadn't even had time to wipe his ass. The Nationalist army was after his head and he had had to flee into the woods. There had been no Marxism in his mind at that time.

I almost puked as I read a whole chapter talking about the virtue of Mao's one-liner: 'True knowledge comes from practice.' Yeah, right. Well, he'd had plenty of practice, starting with dumping his ugly country-bumpkin first wife and crawling into bed with a chic Shanghai actress, while his army was chewing tree roots and getting their asses frozen in northern Shangbei, a hiding spot in which they were eventually able to revive.

But reality was reality. Political studies stayed, accounting for one fifth of the exam's total five hundred points. I swallowed the sawdust and tried to keep my sentiments to a minimum.

Jin took another spot under the lima-bean foliage, sipping his tea and smoking as he buried his head into his own studies. After three months of intensive work, Jin was making amazing headway. I fed him all that I had and gave him my best guidance. He didn't need much help. Neither did he need any motivational pep talk.

For ten years, since the age of thirteen, Jin had been a full-fledged farmer. There wasn't any kind of farm work at which he wasn't an expert. He was a quiet guy, one who had learned to be cunning just to survive. When he first left junior high to work on the farm, the farmers had laughed at him and let him do all the heaviest jobs. They sometimes even doubled the load. My parents weren't there to protect him. And had they been there, they wouldn't have been able to do much. They were landlords, guilty humans who could not argue with anyone. They were just supposed to lower their heads and slave away until the day they died. My oldest sister, Si, who joined him on the farm at the same time, often came home crying about the unfair treatment. But Jin never cried or complained. He just grew quieter and firmer. He had to be the man. He began to hang out with the boys, and picked up smoking and drinking at the age of fifteen just as a way of blending in. Soon he became a respected farmer, skilled in some of the hardest tasks. He could carry more weight on his shoulders than anyone else, while running for a long distance uphill, taking no breaks. There were still times he had to fight against unfair treatment and discrimination, but he had thrived and made us all really proud.

Now his mentality was totally militant. If he could handle the back-breaking farm work, school should be easy. He wanted to go to college. It was his only future. Cousin Tan had paved the way for him, and I was right behind, pushing and shoving.

While we studied, our three sisters toiled under the sun, taking over the workload for my brother. Each day, they came back sweaty and exhausted. My brother and I would come to the door to greet and thank them. They would just smile and ask us how much we had studied that day. We would tell them, and they would be happy for us. There was such hope and caring in their eyes. Brother Jin couldn't wait to jump back into farming again as soon as the tests were over. He couldn't stand the thought that someone else was bearing his load for him. He knew how gruelling the summer heat was, how sore your back could get, and that no matter how calloused your hands were, cutting the rice with the ancient, blunt sickles gave you raw, open blisters every year. It was life at Yellow Stone we were trying to escape from.

On the farm, sarcasm surrounded Jin. They were the same familiar taunts that had been used against Cousin Tan. That he was old enough to be a college teacher. That his family background was politically incorrect. That he didn't have the knowledge to succeed. Jin had been in junior high when he left school. None of the taunts bothered him. His buddies came by every evening to check on him and wish him good luck.

After a light breakfast – three bowls of rice porridge for Jin and two for me – we studied geology and history together at a long table in the living room, facing the lush garden. We drew history charts on our makeshift blackboard and more were spread all over the floor. We examined every detail of China's long history and pored over every exotic city in the world.

Jin sometimes offered me a cigarette during our five-minute afternoon break as we talked about our dreams and desires. His were practical and comfortable, while mine were whimsical and somewhat far-fetched. He wanted to go to a solid college with a good economics department near home, become a manager of a company, marry a pretty girl with a solid temperament, and raise a family. I wanted to go to Beijing, the pearl of China, which was a fifty-hour train ride from home and study English. From there, the sky was the limit.

Jin would nod with amusement at his younger brother, and offer candid advice, never a word of discouragement.

'You're very young and the world is yours,' he would say. 'Dream all you can dream.'

Once he told me he believed I could achieve anything and distinguish myself in anything if I applied all my energy towards it. That moved me, coming from my quiet, distant brother who was eight years older than I. He said that even as a very young kid I had dared to do things that were out of most people's reach, such as becoming a Ping-Pong champion, playing the flute, and learning the violin. He had done none of those things. I hadn't known that he had watched and been quietly proud of me. We had never talked much when we were growing up. He had been too busy playing the man of the house and I, the baby of the family.

Mum would bring in our lunches, rice with some meat soup. I knew that we didn't have any money, so I asked Mum where the

281

money to buy the meat came from. She was quiet for a bit, then said we needed nutrition to study, that I was not to worry, just to continue the good work. I knew that our family was probably piling up loans just to feed our two non-performing mouths. Jin and I talked and we decided to tell Mum to stop doing it. It was getting a little too luxurious for us. We just wanted simple soup made with vegetables from our garden, and a lot of rice. April was when the green couldn't meet the yellow, a phrase used in Yellow Stone to describe the time right before harvest when the food from the last harvest is about to end. And we didn't know where Mum got all that long-grained white rice. By now we should have been eating just cheap yams three times a day, but that was something we didn't want to concern ourselves about just then.

I told Jin I would try to make some money after the exams and repay the debts we had caused the family, but he told me the best thing to do was keep studying and make it to college. Nothing would mean more to the family. So we ploughed on like the buffalo of Yellow Stone, furrow after furrow. In the evenings, we separated and studied our favourite subjects. He tackled maths, and I did my English exercises. To keep us awake until eleven, we drank lots of tea and used the night pot a great deal.

One night, Jin accidentally knocked his teapot over. He came upstairs with his head hanging and told me that it was a bad omen, and that he probably wouldn't make it to college this time. I told him it was silly to think that, and that my many kowtows for him should cover this insignificant mishap. We laughed; it made us feel better.

I decided we could save a lot of time by not going to school any more. Everything was in the books. There was no need to sit in classes and waste time. By April, most of the real teaching had been accomplished.

Soon Dia began to do the same thing and found his uninterrupted sessions extremely useful. He would drop by sometimes, but mostly he stayed in his village and locked himself up in his room. The whole village thought he was crazy. He actually enjoyed it. In the villagers' eyes the old Dia was just another harmless, smoking Dia man who quietly grew tobacco in the backyard and would eventually marry a decent girl and set up a nest for another generation of smoking men. Not this Dia. He wanted to be thought a dreamer in a village where dreamers were a laughing-stock. He said he wanted to look like Einstein and be as great and crazy as he was, so he kept his hair long and dishevelled. Staying indoors all day made him look pale in sharp contrast to the permanent tans of his fellow farmers, who got sunburned every day digging and shovelling their lives away in that nameless village. Some thought Dia was suffering from an incurable disease.

Despite this busy schedule, I managed to jot down a short letter to Yi at his factory address, asking for an explanation for my friends' disappearance and the truth about the money. In the letter, I enclosed another sealed letter to Siang, begging him to somehow return whatever money he had taken from the shoe factory, if indeed he had taken it from there. I offered a long explanation about why I had even assumed his guilt. I told him I was being frank with him, that he needed reasonable advice like this, and told him that whatever he did would never affect the way I thought of him, and of course, to forgive me if I was talking total nonsense. It was like throwing a stone into a lake. My buddies were travelling men and they were probably in another province doing something else by now.

Summer arrived, with its unbearable heat and millions of mosquitoes. The golden rice fields were harvested and the flying insects lost their homes. They flew into our rooms like jet bombers, low and fast. Even in the dim light of Grandpa's oil lamp, I could see their pointed, thorny noses, diving for my vulnerable, salty pores. The smaller ones made you itch. The big ones poked you with long, sharp needles. Mum had made us both a huge palm-leaf fan with which we swatted busily as we tried to concentrate on our books. The exams were a month away. Every day I walked around the house with a lump in my throat, thinking about them.

Jin and I stopped talking about dreams and instead tested each other on everything, the more detailed the better. We became so involved that when we took a bathroom break at the same time, we still tested each other through the thin partition separating our stalls. Every minute counted.

Soon we began to lengthen our days by two more hours, adding an hour before sunrise and an hour in the evening. We lived on four hours of sleep. Our appetites diminished. Dad was concerned, and gave us a brief lecture. We shrugged it off. The exam was only a couple of weeks away. What more harm could such a short time do?

When Jin was tired, he stared into the empty space before him, deep in thought. His cheeks were sunken, his face was wan, and he'd grown an unruly beard. Each time I took my eyes off my book and stole a glance at him, my heart went out to him. He was a man consumed by his quest for the only way out of this hellhole. He wanted only to give it one try. If he failed, he was going to burn those books and be a farmer for ever. Each minute of his time was precious. I prayed silently for us every night before going to sleep, even on my most exhausting days.

I wished that I could just sleep in for ever. But when I woke up and splashed my face with cold water from the river, I bounced back to another day of cramming. When I grew tired, I closed my eyes and leaned back in my chair, trying to imagine that I was on the train to Beijing, surrounded by the fresh faces of young college kids. Outside was the most beautiful scenery. There goes Fuzhou, Hanzhou, Shanghai, the Yangtze and Yellow River, and finally, the capital of China, Beijing. Then I would rush to the platform and see the flag of my college flying high in the wind as I ran into the arms of my new teachers.

After that self-administered shot of adrenalin, I pushed on. I thought of cows, those great cows, which ploughed and ploughed for ever, never complaining. The books were the endless fields. The thought made me feel a little better. I felt recharged, and plunged back into my studies. Before I knew it, it was time to sleep again. No days had been longer or shorter than during that time. We stopped worrying about everything else. We were in our own world, and it was completely filled with our desire to excel.

We smiled and encouraged each other. I never felt closer to Jin, nor he to me. We were a couple of marathon runners, each taking inspiration from the other. We kept saying to one another that, yes, we were nearing the finishing line: hurry, hurry, or it would be for ever too late.

Immediately after the Cultural Revolution, going to college suddenly became the rage. Poet, scientist, Commie-sucker Mr Guo Muo Ruo called the period 'the Spring of Science'. Nerdy scientists such as Chen Jin Nuen became national heroes. Chen Jin Nuen had worked for twenty years on one mathematical formula, finally proving it. He was a single man in his late forties, a little crazy, and suffering from bad health, who had lived in a miserable tiny studio, cluttered with papers. He would forget to eat, to sleep, and was often so deep in thought he would bump into a tree and sincerely apologize to it, not realizing that it was just a tree.

Thousands of suitors sent marriage proposals to him – beautiful actresses, doctors, teachers, and nurses. The president of the Communist Women's Federation at the institute where Mr Chen worked took it upon herself to go through all those letters. She chose twenty finalists, and, along with a committee, picked a kind, caring nurse to be his wife. He began having three meals prepared for him daily, and put on a dozen pounds. He eventually moved into a spacious, four-bedroomed apartment facing a park. He spent his days smelling the flowers, and walking arm in arm with his new bride, whom he didn't really know what to do with, his mind being occupied with another maths problem.

He went on the lecture circuit, and his story moved audiences to tears. Millions of young people wanted to be exactly like him. He was a Chinese Einstein. There were students who imitated Chen's lifestyle, staying up all night and going to school the next morning red-eyed, hoarse and pale. They walked around absent-mindedly, bumping into chairs and tables and apologizing in a whisper.

The radio talked about young heroes who had overcome severe difficulties and had made it to prestigious colleges. There was heroism, glamour, money, and cushy jobs awaiting those who crossed the threshold. A college education was money in the bank – getting there was as rare as hitting all six numbers in the lottery.

In China, from the moment you were admitted into a college, no matter how low-level it was, your life would be totally taken care of by the government. There was no tuition to pay. They gave you the train ticket, a food stipend of thirty-six pounds of rice a month, a bed, all the books you needed, and a guaranteed job, a prestigious, white-collar job. It was the best college deal in the whole world.

But for Jin and me, it was more than that. We were out there to make a point. The Chen family had been dragged through mud for the last forty years and Mum and Dad had been through hell to raise us. Now it was time to pay them back, and to make them proud.

I drew a flag in red ink on the calendar for each of the three examination days in July. Each day, as I looked at the flags, I felt a lump in my throat. My blood would begin to boil, my heart would race, and the exhaustion would vanish as my energy returned. I would rush back to my books and read for a few more hours.

Finally, the big exam was only ten days away. Jin began to have difficulty sleeping. No matter how early he got up and how hard he studied, he still couldn't find peace. He would stare at the top of the mosquito net and listen to the mosquitoes hum their war songs. Dad had to find some sleeping pills to help calm him down. There were times when he would simply sit quietly, staring at his book, his eyes unmoving, thinking and thinking. I knew the pressure he was feeling.

He began to claim he couldn't remember anything. I made him some tea and told him that we were not going to waste all the work we'd done. We hadn't slept enough, had seen no friends, and had hardly been outside the house in weeks. Finally, I tested him on a few tough questions and he answered them beautifully. I slapped him on the back and he returned to his studies. At this point, we were bound together like a couple of soldiers in battle. My words meant more to him than anyone else's.

In the back of my own mind, however, there was always the fear of opening the exam paper and not knowing any of the answers. I had nightmares about my mind going blank. I woke up sweating and shaking.

We ploughed on, whipping each other with words of

encouragement and sometimes letting ourselves think of the sweetness of having a dream come true. It was about the family. It was about a lot of things. It was vindication for Jin personally, a junior high school dropout, trying to make it to college. I assured him that there was a school eagerly awaiting his arrival. I cheered for him and he cheered for me. He said that I could make it to the top, the very top. I thanked him, strengthened by his confidence. It wouldn't be long before this whole thing would be over. We would look back and laugh.

Twenty-four

Yellow Stone literally got a shot of excitement five days before the national examination: electricity. From that day on, hydro-powered electricity would be provided twenty-four hours a day. Not that Yellow Stone had never seen the magic of electric power: for the last ten years, a limited supply of electricity, four hours a night, had been generated from a small station near the commune. Noisy, inefficient, and expensive, only one fifth of the town could afford it, but everyone could hear the old generator as it cranked along. It added a thrill to the quiet nightlife there, as it spat out steamy hot water into a pool right outside the power station. On a cold day, we would climb into that pool naked, and have our hot baths. Even though the water smelled like oil and sometimes had traces of grease floating on the surface, there was always a long line of people in various stages of undress waiting for their turn to dip into the pool. At times, when the manager of the station was drunk, he would use his powerful flashlight to illuminate the unruly bathers and scare them away. Startled, they would run for it naked, clutching their clothes.

The old generator became such an important part of people's lives at Yellow Stone that you often heard a mother say to her children, 'Where have you been? The generator has already started.' It came on at seven each night, and people scheduled their lives around it. And when it was turned off at eleven, kids had no business being up any more anyhow: it was curfew, when the small town of Yellow Stone returned to its prehistoric silence and darkness. At that time, only the moon was supposed to shine.

Now everything would change. Even though there were only five days left before the exam, Dad decided it would be good for us to have one electric outlet. Jin and I were to share a fifteen-watt bulb that dangled from the ceiling. The first night, we stared at the bulb for a good minute after it was turned on. Then we shook our heads in disbelief and smiled at each other. There would be no more need for Grandfather's smoke-belching oil lamp. I could wave my fan to chase the deadly mosquitoes without having to worry about dowsing the light.

As the sacred days slowly approached, the atmosphere in our household changed. Mum prayed a little harder, and rose earlier in order to say longer prayers. Meals were more lavish. There was always meat on the table, just for Jin and me. We no longer argued with Mum about the unjust inequality among family members, we simply shoved the food down and returned to our studies. Our sisters lowered their voices when they talked and walked past our rooms quietly. But the biggest change was in Dad. He actually bought some Flying Horses and slipped them into my room late at night. No words were needed. He badly wanted me to succeed.

It reminded me of a story about a father who was carrying his son on his shoulders one day. A wise guy asked the son, 'Why are you riding your dad like a horse?'

The son smiled and said, 'Dad does it in the hope that some day I will become a dragon and glorify him.'

Two days before the exam, the whole town of Yellow Stone gathered, to gossip and watch the candidates. Every third family had someone taking the exam. Few public events mattered as much to the townspeople. A militiaman from the commune paraded through the street with a loudspeaker, shouting about the virtues of the exam and yelling encouragement. 'Don't panic, be brave, have a strong heart, and be prepared for both failure and success.'

The slogans roared through the speakers, which had been mounted on the front of a muddy tractor. People listened quietly as the tractor drove noisily by. It was wartime, and the young people were going out to do battle.

Food vendors loaded up their supplies and rented spaces near the test sites. Yellow Stone's high school and elementary school, where some of the tests would be held, were swept, mopped, and dusted by hundreds of temporary workers. The desks were all numbered, and schoolteachers were called back from their breaks to be monitors. The commune had several thousand exam applicants, all of whom were going to crowd into the town of Yellow Stone, the seat of higher learning, and take the tests that would determine their futures. Word was out that Peking Man was going to give his final predictions on the history questions. Since entrance to the school was sealed, he would hold court in the commune's auditorium. His moment of glory had finally arrived. The site of much political significance was turned into his shrine.

I strolled along the street for the first time in months and headed for the commune. Jin felt ashamed to be among the younger crowd. He stayed at home and took a nap. Only the graduates of Yellow Stone High were allowed in. Hundreds more stood outside the hall. Peking Man had set the rules; he was a tribal type, loyal to his own kind, and nasty to all others.

In the hall, Dia quickly spotted me. He looked sick and still had the Einstein hairstyle. His eyes were red, with dried yellow crud in the corners – which I don't think Einstein had.

We hugged and laughed.

'You're still alive. So which college are you shooting for?' I asked him.

'The way I've been doing, I think I'm heading for the agricultural speciality in my own backyard. I'll end up learning tobaccogrowing. Da, I'm thinking of taking the science tests.'

'Are you crazy? With just two days left? You know nothing about science.'

'I know nothing about liberal arts either.'

'There's no time for that sort of wavering, Dia. Weren't you studying at home like me?'

'I was, but it got to me. At first, I was so good. I read for eighteen hours and burned the oil all night. Naturally, I began to sleep in the daytime and get up at night. Then I got hungry, so I ended up cooking. After I ate, I got sleepy, so I went back to take a nap. But instead of a nap, I slept for twelve hours on end, and then it was fucking night-time again. I was totally screwed up. I couldn't tell night from day.'

'Now you're studying for the science tests?'

'I don't know what I am doing, I'm finished.'

I slapped his unruly head and he shook it like a lion. 'All right. I'll do liberal arts.'

'Good. Let's find a good seat for ourselves.'

We sat on the crowded floor with the rest of our sweaty classmates. The surface of the street could have grilled a fish and the temperature within the auditorium would have made a baker want his job back. Hundreds of eager faces were waiting for Peking Man to perform his annual ritual. Everyone was solemn, pressured by peers, family, and society to succeed. What was usually a rowdy crowd now sat quietly, as if awaiting sentencing.

Peking Man strolled in, sporting a T-shirt two sizes too small that revealed a couple of inches of his hairy pot-belly, and a pair of loose shorts that were cut too long. His legs were more bent than they appeared under long pants. That explained his unique side-to-side rolling walk.

The crowd took a deep breath. It would be our first brush with the examinations; it brought a raw awakening within us.

Peking Man was silent and serious. He gazed at us with the look of a saviour, a doctor. *I know your pain and I am here to take it away*.

His eyes sparkled with those wild lights so rare among modern men. He opened his mouth a couple of times, but no words came out. A stutterer was a stutterer. On the third try, he made it. A loud sound filled the hall with echoes; it sounded like a cry from some ancient creature, but our hearts responded to it. It was a war cry.

'My students!' he called. 'This is a battle and I am here to give you the weapons!'

Any other day, the house would have rocked with laughter at so silly a declaration, but not today. Today we believed him. It was wartime, us against the world, and it felt good to have Peking Man on our side. I felt like standing and saluting our hairy commander, the Monkey King.

'I have made my decisions after a long and hard search.' He rolled his sad eyes, then refocused them on us.

'Here are my top selections for the year.' He threw open a portable blackboard. Written on it were four long essay questions. The crowd scribbled furiously. There was only the sound of pen fighting paper, and the noisy breathing of Peking Man, who seemed to have a loose valve somewhere, another of his unevolved organs.

He then went on to explain the tricky points hidden in the questions, piloting us through them like a seasoned sailor in troubled waters. He dodged, turned, and twisted. His logic was clear and his delivery forceful. His face gradually wrinkled into a smile. Normally when he smiled, we ducked our heads, for no one wanted to witness the display of his big yellow teeth. But this time, it was comforting, in a devious way. To us, those teeth were weapons.

'Each of these questions could be worth twenty-five per cent of the score. Nail the answers in your brain. If any of you comes out of the test missing these questions, any part of them, you will not call me your teacher any more. Now go.' He leaned on his elbows and nodded his huge head, indicating his farewell to all our miserable souls. We rushed out of the hall for some fresh air. Another five minutes and some of us would have been carried out on stretchers.

Hundreds of others waiting outside surrounded us for tips on what had gone on inside. I dodged a few money-waving questioners, and went to say goodbye and good luck to Dia, my tortured friend. He patted my shoulder and gave me a firm hand-shake. We understood each other, and parted silently. As I was turning the corner, I saw Dia giving his notes to a guy waiting to buy information. The man gave him a one-yuen bill for the notes. Dia pocketed it, then turned to another eager soul. Dia would sell the questions until no one wanted them any more. And he did, ten times.

The day before the tests, the street of Yellow Stone was alive with thousands of applicants coming to town to see the test site so that they wouldn't get lost in the next day's frenzy and confusion.

Stone-faced militiamen walked the sealed sections of the school. The test-takers nervously looked beyond the yellow ribbon. For the well-prepared, today was the day to rest. The three long days of test-taking would be exhausting, to say the least. I saw Head, the snob, dribbling a basketball absentmindedly, like a girl. Silently, I wished him luck: may he open his paper and not know a thing.

Others were just sitting around chatting, killing time. Han, my elementary school enemy, wasn't one of them. He had been studying, but the stuff was coming out from his granite head, his mum said. Today, he was sitting before a tall pile of books, not knowing which one to read. His mum said he wouldn't eat, talk, or sleep. I also wished him luck, and hoped that he would faint on the floor of the test site and never wake up.

Since early morning, Dad's friends and neighbours had come by to wish us good luck. Ar Duang, whose son was Dad's patient, carried a large basket of fruit and insisted that we eat it all so that we would have fresh minds. Jin mingled with our guests in the living room, taking it easy. I knew he would do well. He was smiling and looked relaxed. I had got up at five and had washed my face extra carefully. Mum and I had prayed and kowtowed before every single god in her shrine. She had just unearthed a new one called the God of Wisdom and wanted me to beg hard before him. I had slammed about ten big ones to him, and I was sure every one of them would be worth something.

I'd long been expecting this day, yet was a bit fearful now that it had finally arrived. I had been studying an average of fifteen hours a day for the last ten months. Now it was coming to an end. The lump in my throat grew bigger. When Mum asked me how I felt, I pumped up my confidence and said that if I kowtowed a little harder, some of my knowledge might spill out.

She smiled.

I was the only one from the town of Yellow Stone to register as an English major; only eight others in the commune were taking that major. So the National Examination Commission decided to lump us together and have all nine of us take the entire three-day exam in the city of Putien, where our final subject exam, English, was to be given.

Mum carefully prepared a large plate of fried rice noodles with leeks, oysters, and eggs, along with some meat soup, for my breakfast. She said the rice noodles were crispy, and so should all my tests be. Dad slipped a roll of money into my pocket tightly held by rubber bands, about ten yuen in total. It was surely the last pot of money left in our family, unless it had been borrowed. I looked at Dad. His wizened face had the kindest smile. He searched for something to say but was at a loss, and so he squeezed my shoulder, then turned away. I felt my eyes moisten.

Everyone in my family silently watched me pack a foldable bamboo mat, a sack of rice, my chopsticks, a rice pot, two bags of books and some clothes. My youngest sister, Huang, was pumping air into a borrowed old bike. She would be giving me a ride to Putien. It felt as if they were sending me off to the battlefield, a place so far away that my family couldn't be with me. There was an inner sadness, but I didn't show it. I was sixteen. I threw my luggage over my back, pushed out my chest, and smiled broadly at everyone. I wanted to tell them by my actions that I was brave and ready to take on the enemy.

Right before I stepped into the street, I turned and ran upstairs to my window. I knelt down and begged my grandfather to come with me to Putien and watch over me as I wrote the answers. He had loved me so deeply and had expected so much of me. It was he who had taught me the first strokes of calligraphy, his hands over mine. I needed him now more than ever. I told him that I would do honour to his name and that all his sufferings at the end of his life were not in vain because they had given me strength and would be the basis of all my success. Tears filled my eyes as I called on his spirit again and again.

On the way to Putien, Huang and I talked for a while, then I took out my flash cards to review the English conjugations. I remembered them so well I was sick of them, but I was terrified my memory might suddenly fail and all that knowledge disappear without a trace. We arrived at Hillside High School at the edge of Putien after three hours of hard pedalling against a head wind. The school was temporarily converted into a camp for the test-takers from around the county. I followed the sign and found my name on the door of a dark classroom. I settled in and sent my sister home before sunset.

It was a zoo. At least a thousand students were bunking there for the next three days. The kitchen was overcrowded. I had put my rice pot in the steamer in the afternoon; it took me half an hour to locate it at dinnertime. I ate my cold rice with dried fish on the lawn in the playground and stared at the stars. I had intended to do some studying before going to sleep, but it was impossible. There was no light, no room, and I was constantly surrounded by a mob of mosquitoes. Like the city people, the mosquitoes here were sleazy. Their snouts drilled like needles and their sting stayed with you for a long time.

My room had a dim fifteen-watt light bulb, two tiny windows, a dirt floor, dirty walls, and thirty sleepers. We were a bunch of strangers, but our backs were rubbing against each other. Lying there, we looked like a raft stitched together with old ropes. The guy on my left came from the mountains and didn't believe in washing his body too often. Sweat was the least of the foul smells coming from his body. The diminutive guy on my left farted throughout the night, and had the runs. And the mosquitoes buzzed all night long. When I woke the next morning I found numerous bites all over my body, including two on my eyelid.

Daylight finally came. I crept to a quiet spot and knelt down for a brief prayer, then fought my way through the kitchen, this time easily finding my rice pot. The trick was to put it in late and get it out early. I slowly swallowed half the rice I had steamed and left the other half uneaten.

The first test was Chinese. I was ready.

At seven-thirty, a man led the nine of us English majors on a mile-long hike. We found our test site at the top of a hill and waited outside like runners at the starting line, ready to dash as soon as the bell rang. Rich kids arrived with their big-shot daddies in cars that left a dusty trail. City boys had long greased hair, fashionable clothes; the girls had long silky legs, partially covered by flowing skirts. I wore a yellowed cut-off shirt, a straw hat, shorts, and was barefoot. Nobody looked my way, as if they had sized me up in a second and immediately dismissed me as an ignorant country bumpkin in the wrong crowd. But I stood there, bare feet and all, sure of what I knew. Nobody said I couldn't take the test because I wore shabby clothes and had no shoes. Before the test, all were equal. Besides, I was dressed in my Sunday best.

It was fifteen minutes to test time. I saw frightened looks on the faces of hundreds of test-takers crowding beside me. White-robed nurses were walking around, waiting for people to collapse; they were ready to scoop them into a waiting ambulance. The cops were wearing loaded firearms to quell possible unrest. I wondered why? Did we look like a bunch of looters?

I felt thirsty, dizzy, weak, tired, and felt the need to go to the bathroom again, despite having visited it only five minutes ago. I closed my eyes and prayed in silence as I waited in agony for the time to pass. Grandpa, dear Grandpa, help me now.

The bell brought me back to reality. I ran into my test room, sat in my numbered seat, and closed my eyes again before opening my sealed questions. I felt like puking. My hands were trembling.

The proctor, a bespectacled bald man, nodded at me with a kind smile.

'You may start now,' he said.

I broke the seal with my pen. As I focused my eyes on the first question, there was a sudden rush of blood to my head. My mind went blank suddenly, and I had to grit my teeth and grip my table to let the feeling pass. No wonder some people were carried out by ambulance. I didn't want to be one of them. Slowly, the darkness receded. I read and reread the question and wrote down the first answer of the day.

The test lasted for four hours and ended with a long composition that was worth 45 per cent of the test. I came out smiling to myself. The first thing I did was head for a quiet corner to kneel and thank all the good gods who had helped me through this first test.

I saw others, strangers to each other, chatting and talking excitedly. I didn't want to get involved. It was over.

I stayed on the hilltop under a tall tree, munched on some dried fish, drank some water, and reviewed my history flash cards.

There was a guard sitting near me. I gave him a Flying Horse and asked him to wake me if he found me dozing off and to make sure I wasn't late for the test. At ten minutes to two, I put away my history book and looked for signs of the guard. He was snoring away like a buffalo, his lips twitching. Obviously he was having an erotic dream of some sort. Too many young females taking the test were wearing too many enticing skirts.

I smiled from ear to ear when I opened my history paper. Peking Man had guessed two of the four questions. Each would bring me 15 per cent of the total score. I let out an animal cry of ecstasy as I left the room, then danced down the stairs. Others watched as though I were crazy. Long live the Peking Man!

I knew all the answers and had had plenty of time to check every nuance of the questions, as Peking Man had taught us to do, analytically and clearly. I wanted to take a picture of him and frame it above my college bunk bed and pray to him. He was almost a god. They should at least make him a local god of Yellow Stone High and give him whatever he wanted from life.

That evening I ate twice as much as the day before. I was halfway through, only three more subjects to go.

I sailed through the second day like a sleek sailboat. At noon, Mum and Dad dispatched my sisters, Ke and Huang, to bring me some fruit. They went to my dorm. Since nobody knew where I was, they kicked dust and hiked uphill to the top, inquiring around and asking the lazy guard.

'The barefoot boy?' he asked my sisters. They nodded and he took them to my spot under the tree.

I was so glad to see them. There were tears in their eyes, they had been terribly worried when they couldn't find me. Now they had discovered me studying at high noon under the hot sun. It hurt them to see this, because they loved me. I told them I was having a ball. They laughed at seeing me so happy about the tests. I asked them about Jin. They said he was doing all right. I ate half a delicious watermelon at their urging, slurping it down quickly. They were pleased when they left.

The English test came last, and it came as no surprise. I knew every word and irregular conjugation. There was a long translated

297

article about a magic ring story. I had never felt as confident in an examination before. The large bag of exercises given to me by Professor Wei covered all the questions and more. I wanted to hug her and tell her she should become a goddess too, and that I would frame her picture and worship it every day.

When I walked out of the test room for the last time, my burden dropped to the ground. I was free.

Even the city folks began to look okay to me. I was ready to hug and embrace anyone, when I saw my brother looking for me. I ran over to him and we shook hands frantically.

'How did you do?' he asked.

'Couldn't have done better,' I said, out of breath.

He had come to pick me up and share all the details of the experience we had come through together. We forgot about our fatigue and talked, laughed, smoked, and talked some more. We compared answers, thinking that we had got about 85 per cent right. We were ecstatic.

We rode home in the fading sunlight. The breeze was gentle, the air cool. Our hearts were light. My brother had become my best friend. We had fought together and won. At least, in our hearts we knew that we had won.

When we finally reached home that night, the whole family had been waiting for us. I didn't realize how much I had missed them till I saw them again. I quickly ran upstairs to thank the gods, jumped into the river for a brief swim, then sat with the whole family around our large table and chatted until midnight. That night the moon was so big and round, hanging only a few feet above the treetops, that I felt as if I could reach out and touch it. The gentle moonlight filled me with hope and warmth. With a thankful heart, I went to sleep smiling.

The next day I woke up to the painful twisting of my ears and nose. I tried to get up but my legs were pinned down. I opened my eyes to see my four friends, making ugly faces as they tried to wake me up.

'Hey, what's up?' I rubbed my eyes.

'We're taking you hunting, college man,' Siang said. 'I heard you did well in the tests.'

298

'Yeah, everyone's talking about it.' Mo Gong gave my ear another twist.

'We're gonna take you out for a day of fun.' Yi pulled my quilt off and lay beside me.

Sen was nudging my behind with the butt of his hunting rifle. 'Wake up. We've got catching up to do. Who knows, you're probably gonna be outta here in no time.'

I was surprised that Mum and Dad had sent them to my room, which was in the innermost recess of our house, and also by the fact that my buddies didn't seem the least upset about the letter I had sent Yi a couple of months ago.

'I was having such a good time taking the tests in Putien,' I said, pulling my shirt on. 'You should have seen the girl sitting next to me. Short skirts and really nice white legs.'

'Slow down there, my friend. You sat next to a pretty gal for the whole three days? Did she smile at you?' Mo Gong was a diehard romantic.

'She did whenever she had difficulty answering a question,' I said.

'And did you give it to her?'

'No way.'

'Well, Da, that's stupid. Otherwise we could be on our way to visit her today. Wouldn't it have been lovely? Success plus women. It's your loss.'

We all burst into laughter. Mo Gong seemed sincerely sad about it.

'Don't worry, you'll have plenty to choose from. We'll help you find the best,' Sen said.

'You guys never sent me a letter back,' I said to Yi.

'We didn't know you were into the letter-writing business.'

'What do you mean?'

'I don't know? What do *you* mean?' He laughed, not knowing what this was about.

'Well, I sent a letter to you a while ago.'

'A letter to Yi and nothing to us?' Sen joked. 'What was it about?'

'Yeah, what was it about?' Yi asked.

'Well, that's another thing I wanted to talk to you guys about. I wrote the letter because I was concerned about a rumour. Remember the money?'

'Oh, yeah, the money,' Siang said. 'You know, Da, someone was trying to smear my dad's reputation. The shoe factory's money was returned to the treasurer's office a few days after it was stolen. No one confessed to anything, but the case was over.'

'Who returned the money? And how?' I asked.

Siang shook his head innocently. 'Someone broke into the office at night and put the money back. Not a cent missing and there was no word. The investigation was over a long time ago.'

'I'm really glad.'

My friends were quiet. It was time to change the subject.

I spent the whole day shooting birds in the thick woods, eating fruit, and smoking. Sen had brought a bottle of liquor that we passed around. Mo Gong was a little woozy after a few greedy gulps. We sent him to pick up the fallen birds. At one point, he stumbled into wet mud, and almost sank into a mudhole. We had to pull him out. Then he rolled on the ground till dried leaves stuck all over his body, and started dancing around like an aborigine, singing weird tunes that sounded like Japanese folk songs. I threw more leaves on him and he danced even more madly. Sen passed the bottle to him and he finished it off. Totally drunk, he started to laugh so heartily that it began to sound like crying. Then he collapsed on the floor, still in a fit of uncontrollable laughter. We had to kick him to stop his craziness. Then we carried him to the middle of a wooden bridge, and dropped him into the Dong Jing River. He continued laughing until he sank beneath the water.

We applauded, expecting to see him jump up like a fish for air. But one minute passed, then two. We looked at each other.

'Don't worry. He's fooling us this time.' Sen was calm.

'He could never hold his breath for that long,' I said.

'He's a better swimmer than you are.'

'But he could be dead. He's drunk, remember.'

'Even a drunk is always 30 per cent clear-headed. Don't let him fool you,' Yi said.

'The guy is dying! Do something! I'm going down there.' I took off my shirt and jumped into the water. My actions brought them all to the edge.

Suddenly, Mo Gong shot up like a fish and let out a wild cry. 'I got you!'

'See, I told you,' Sen said.

Mo Gong swam to the edge. 'I saw it all. Da was the most worried about me. Not you guys. If I'd come up and saw you still there on the bridge, smiling, I woulda quit being your friends. I really liked that, Da. Your shorts are soaking.'

We splashed water all over him and forced him into the river again.

The day's fun ended on a sad note. Siang, in his carelessness, missed a bird and the tiny bullet went into the shoulder of a woman who was passing by. She hadn't even been aware of it. There'd been a sharp sting and a small pearl of blood appeared. We all went to apologize. The woman grabbed Siang's collar and threatened to kill him with the bamboo pole she was carrying.

When she calmed down, we asked her whether it hurt. She shook her head.

Sen came over and made a deal with her. He gave her a hundred yuen; the woman was nodding and bowing to him as she left, almost singing.

'That's sick, Sen.'

'Hey, we won the money. You know, like we promised that day.'

'How much?'

'Thousands.' There was a gleam of devious delight in their eyes. My friends were getting dangerous.

Jin's mood waxed and waned daily. Some days he thought he had scored well, other days he thought he had drilled holes in the boat and was sinking. For the moment, he threw himself into farm work. On a good day, he would hum and whistle, digging the field in readiness for the autumn bean season. He was the amicable old Jin everyone liked. On a bad day, he would stay in bed really late, the quilt over his head, thinking of all the questions he had missed. He used the abacus in his head and crunched the total score of his tests. But the more he crunched, the lower his scores got. He made himself miserable. We called it the Cousin Tan factor.

In the evening, I sat with him in our backyard and chatted. Mum and Dad had give me the job of encouraging him. They didn't want to see him turn into a nut. I would pull out our bamboo abacus and play with my estimate of his scores as he remembered them. When he said 70 per cent, I threw in a modest 5 per cent mark-up. In the end, the total looked fine. He was surprised by my estimate, and wondered how I did it. I told him he was too hard on himself, then I'd go to our kitchen and pour some locally brewed liquor for him. Resistant at first, he would drink it nonetheless. It would loosen him up and we would sit talking with the rest of the family in the moonlight, late into the night.

I was the opposite. My own estimate of my scores kept going up. Everyone in the family laughed at me. It was a pure gut feeling, but they believed me and were glad for me. No one stopped me from climbing my ladder of dreams.

On the farm, Jin was given a nickname of Fang Jin. It came from a well-known historical satire. Fang Jin lived hundreds of years ago. He was a poor farmer who dreamed of one day passing the government civil service test held every four years to elect officials. The top scorers sometimes ended up marrying the emperor's daughter. Lesser ones became governors of provinces and counties. Fang Jin starved himself and studied all day in his humble shack. He had taken the test five times and failed every time. By the time he took the sixth test, he was in his forties, bony, frail, and sick-looking. To everyone's surprise, he scored so high the emperor picked him to be the governor of the county. The job promised wealth and fame. But when the messengers from the emperor arrived at his humble residence with trumpets and drums and firecrackers, Fang Jin did not appear to receive the honour.

The whole town started searching for him. He was now their hero. As darkness fell, they finally found him. He was running down the dirt street barefoot, shouting, 'Fang Jin won! Fang Jin won!' The people happily joined him in shouting the slogan, but he went on and on, much to the frustration of the messenger, who couldn't return until the honorand had received the order in person. They tried to calm him down, but Fang kept right on shouting. A local doctor was brought in. Fang Jin had gone crazy upon hearing the good news, the doctor said.

Jin accepted the nickname good-humouredly. It actually made him calmer.

A month later, rumours began to circulate that the papers had all been graded and the scores were in. The scores were low across the board. All the test-takers gossiped among themselves. Jin at this point didn't care any more. It only made me pray harder each night, hitting my head against the soft pillows in obeisance to all the gods I assembled in my head to whom I read off my list of wishes. The list got longer each day and the list of promises to the gods grew more generous. I went from one little piglet for each god to five piglets and two cows as sacrifices if all the items in my list came true. And I knew that if that happened, I would probably have to bankrupt our family, returning all our worldly possessions back to where they came. But that didn't stop me. I figured we could always deliver the sacrifices slowly, or even make out an I.O.U. with the gods on them. When all was repaid, we would add on a handsome interest. They would have no problem with that.

Dad wasn't one to sit around waiting for our scores to arrive. He wanted to know *now*, so he put up his antenna and whispered into the ears of all his patients, whose numbers had expanded into the hundreds. Word spread from the patients to their families, then rippled into their circle of friends, who might know someone on the Board of Education at Putien, the agency in charge of grading all the tests. Within two days, a young man showed up at our door with the name of a clerk working at the board in Putien. He was a close friend of a close friend of a family member of a patient's sister-in-law's aunt. Dad immediately dispatched a young teacher from Yellow Stone High, whose job was to scout the scores for all the high school graduates. His name was Chung. Carrying a letter from Dad, he rode his bike to Putien to get the scores from this distant friend.

We waited and waited. Chung didn't return home that day. At midnight he sent a note from Putien to say that he was still waiting, staying at a hotel at the school's expense until the next day. Our hearts were in our mouths. My family, usually noisy, was quiet. We were worried.

Next day at breakfast, my sisters asked me again what I thought my scores might be. I hiked it up another twenty points. They laughed till tears filled their eyes. I knew they wanted to believe it. Their love for me was genuine, and their hope for me was as high as the clouds hanging in the blue sky.

During the course of the morning, word leaked out about the score line. This was a line the government drew to cut off the successful applicants from the unsuccessful ones. It was based on how many slots were open for college enrolment that year: if there were only one hundred openings, the cut-off line would be set after the top one hundred scores. Everyone above that line was guaranteed a place in college, while the rest of the applicants wouldn't be considered at all. This year's cut-off point was 300 out of the total 500 points possible.

The news sent chills down our spines. We all must have done terribly.

At lunch, the whole family sat around the table without any real appetite. Jin picked at his food, and our sisters yammered on about irrelevant things. Dad asked me how I felt about the cut-off line. He didn't say outright that I probably needed to adjust my own estimate in order not to get hurt when the scores were disclosed, but I knew that was what he was thinking. I stood firm, but this time I didn't increase up my estimate the regular 3 per cent. Jin smiled absentmindedly, but I knew he was troubled. Mum was not at the table. I had a good idea where she was. She was talking to her gods. She had been talking to them, and would be talking to them, for as long as she lived. She had been orphaned at a young age, and Buddha and all the other local gods were her parents. It was love in the purest sense.

Just after midnight, the messenger, Chung, ran into our house, sweat covering his red face. He was breathless from the three-hour ride that he had just cut to two. We surrounded him, watching his heaving chest with great anxiety.

'Water,' he croaked.

'The scores first,' Dad said.

'I'm really thirsty.'

'The scores.' Dad's voice had never been that loud with a friend before.

Chung smiled.

We stood by, our hearts in our throats.

'Jin first.'

Chung swallowed. 'Three hundred and fifty.'

There was an odd lull. He was in. His face first turned ashen, then red. He was speechless.

'How about Da?'

'You want to know?'

'Yes, yes. What is it?'

'Three hundred and eighty!'

I felt the blood shoot up to the very top of my head. All the muscles in my arms twitched uncontrollably.

'I'm not finished yet. According to the record, Da has one of the highest liberal arts scores in the province of Fujian, including the big cities of Fuzhou, Amoy, Chuangzhou, and Nan Ping – out of hundreds of thousands of test-takers.'

There were no joyful shouts nor happy dances, only tears. It was a moment of triumph and happiness for the whole Chen family. Mum was in Dad's arms; my sisters were sniffing and holding each other. Jin and I shook hands wildly.

A dirt-poor country boy, beating all the city brats. I couldn't believe it. It was about forty points higher than my highest estimate. I could kowtow for ever.

I wanted to run down the street of Yellow Stone and shout like the ancient Fang Jin, only it would be 'Goodbye Yellow Stone, hello Beijing! And I'm not crazy!'

Twenty-five

Mum asked me to walk to her brother's house to tell Cousin Tan the news. I took the narrow road through the green fields. The fresh sea wind made the young rice dance, and woke up my dizzy mind, still dazed with the intoxicating news. I took a deep breath and started running. I was in shock and needed time alone to think. My eyes stared into the distance as my mind wandered off into dreamland. Which university would pick me? Should I go with one that had a good name, or one with a good English department? Which city? Shanghai or Beijing? As I ran, I felt as if I were sitting in the Fujian–Beijing express train, with the scenery flying by and the wind blasting my face. I wondered what Tienanmen Square looked like.

Cousin Tan was holding court at his house with a few of his classmates from AU. I heard carefree laughter as I entered. They were having tea. I wanted to drop the bomb and have the AU boys running for cover. Tan stood up as I came through the door. Smart guy, he sensed something.

'Did you hear anything?' he asked.

I stood there, trying to catch my breath.

'Is it bad news?' he asked anxiously.

I shook my head. I didn't want to seem too eager to impress a bunch of AU guys, all of whom were proudly wearing their white-and-red school badges.

'Jin got three hundred and fifty,' I said.

'Well, that's very high.' Tan knitted his intellectual brows together with disbelief. 'How about you?'

I took another deep breath.

'You didn't make it?' He started to smile and reach out his noncalloused hands to press his subtle condolence. I knew that look.

'My score was three hundred and eighty.'

All his cronies stood up.

'What did you say?' Tan didn't believe his ears.

'Three hundred and eighty,' I repeated.

Silence.

'You've got to be kidding,' Tan said absentmindedly, making a readjustment in his mind. 'I'm sure AU would consider you for their famous English department.'

'Give me a break, Tan,' one of his classmates said. 'This fellow doesn't want to go to a college isolated on a little island in the corner of China. It's okay for a bunch of older guys to study finance there, but for English, he should and *could* go to big cities like Beijing or Shanghai.'

'I'll think about all the options,' I said diplomatically. 'I'm sure AU would be an excellent choice also.' I didn't want to hurt his pride. After all, I still loved and respected my cousin. He had paved the road for Jin and me and had given us hope when we were just another landlord's family, waiting to be wasted by communism.

I said goodbye to them and told them I wanted to go and take a long nap.

They laughed and saw me to the door, slapping my shoulder in congratulation. Cousin Tan affectionately pinched the back of my neck. Coming from a bunch of college men, I considered it the red-carpet treatment. I was one of the boys now. Within a single moment, I had arrived.

I took the same route back home to avoid being stared at in the street. By now, Yellow Stone would be like dry hay aflame with the breaking news about the Chen brothers. Having one child in a family going to college was an eye-opener, but two at the same time? The town wouldn't be able to sleep for a long while. The shock would be reverberating through the people by now. It couldn't be happening. Some people in Yellow Stone wouldn't be able to take such an insulting assault on their turf. Two landlord's children, hitting the jackpot at the same time? No way. There would be hostile letters of protest, ghost-written and sent anonymously to the Board of Education, filled with big fat lies, aiming to try and stop us. There would be people gritting their teeth at this very moment, swearing to poke a hole in our balloon and let our dream be just another dream. I knew it was coming and that we should appear modest and undeserving in public.

'Sorry I scored that high, I didn't mean to. I swear I won't do it next time.' What a twisted world we lived in. I couldn't be happy when I was supposed to be, and I couldn't be sad when I was supposed to, like when my grandpa had died. I couldn't wait to pack up my bamboo mat and mosquito net and shake the dust off my feet.

Mum shut the front door early and prepared a simple dinner. We moved our dining table to the backyard. Everyone was whispering as we set the table and prepared the food. My sisters had left work early. The young rice plants could wait, but the celebration could not.

We sat close together around the table, all seven of us. It was a little crowded, and we kicked each other under the table and fought with our chopsticks for the last bite as we had when we were children. We whispered and laughed quietly, lest there were ears listening outside the walls. It was okay to let people know when you were suffering, but not when you were celebrating. They turned jealous, and evil things are bred from the seeds of jealousy.

Dad smiled like a carefree lion, smoking his pipe, while my mum still sniffled over the shock of the news. It shook her up in a very pleasant way. They both confessed that it was the best day of their lives. They were so happy and proud. It made their decades of suffering worthwhile. Our sisters poked us with challenging questions, like which pretty girls we would consider as brides. We went through a list with mock interest: none of them seemed perfect. The appealing ones didn't have the cows necessary for a

308

dowry, while the ugly ones had plenty. They giggled and giggled over our silly discussion.

We dreamed and sat there, just staring at a perfect Yellow Stone sunset.

Dia showed up the next day at my house.

'Praise Buddha, you blew the top off. I heard the news from the guy down the street. How the hell did you do it?'

He hugged me. I picked him up to throw him on the floor.

'Come on, Da, don't be so childish. You're a college guy now. We don't have to wrestle each time we see each other.'

I dropped him to the floor. He rubbed his neck in fake pain and shook his head. 'You're never gonna change, are you?'

'Nope.' I sunk my left foot into his soft stomach. He laughed like a kid.

'Better not.'

'How did you do?'

'How did I do?' Dia got on his feet and he dusted his shirt. 'I shamed my family, many generations of them. All the dead Dia men must be kicking each other's ass, blaming one another for having born this Dia.'

'How did you do, serious?'

'Two hundred and three, along with a nice little note from the commune Education Board saying something like, don't be hurt and to try again. For crying out loud, it sounded like a jail number instead of a score.'

'That wasn't too bad. It was only a hundred points off; take it again next year.'

'Not a chance. College doors might be open, but the Dia men are all brain dead. We smoke too much, have always smoked too much. The nicotine poisoned our brains and now I'm the last in line to hold the empty bag for life. Next thing you know, the Dia men are gonna be walking around with only one ball. You know the nicotine shrinks the other. Fuck the smoke, I'm sick of it.' He pulled out his usual bag of tobacco and pinched some leaves to roll a big one when he suddenly realized something. 'I forgot my smoking paper. Could you go find some from your dad.'

'You just said you were sick of smoking.'

'That was then, now is now. I need a smoke to calm down.'

I ran off and returned with some Flying Horse. He threw them back at me. 'These are as tasteless as wax. Give me the newspaper.' He tore the corner off a daily, rolled his thick one, and was an instant chimney.

'So what do you intend to do?' I asked him.

'The army.'

'The army?'

'Mum signed me up as soon as she heard my score.'

'You like the idea?'

'Yeah, I'm ready to leave home and be a man.'

'We all are. I'm proud of you, maybe you'll be a general some day. I like the way you hold your tobacco roll, there's something very official about it.'

'Oh, shut up. You know I'm very proud of you. I don't even have to say it. By tomorrow, I'll be known in my backward village as the man who slept under the same roof with Da the Great, and that should go on my tombstone if I were to die today.'

We were given an application form to fill out, along with a list of slots open to Fujian students for all the colleges. The slots for English majors were pathetically few. From the top down, there was only one for Beijing First Foreign Language Institute, and two for Beijing Second Foreign Language Institute. There was one opening for Shanghai Foreign Language Institute and a few more at other cities like Nanking, Fuzhou, and twenty at Amoy University. There were other tempting slots in foreign trade and international journalism, both of which required a strong English performance.

The school counsellor advised me that my score put me in the top 2 percent of all applicants. Any college I picked could be mine. My brother's score also qualified him for a leading university. He had his mind set on finance, and his university choices were all near home. He wanted to be close to the family. But they fully supported my choice, Beijing Language Institute, the top spot on that year's roster. I was the bird that had to fly far and high and they wanted me to reach for the sky because I thought I could.

And now they were beginning to think that I could, too.

I turned in my application at the commune headquarters, an office near the commune jail in which the principal of my elementary school had once wanted to put me.

The lady clerk smiled at me when she saw my name and choice.

'You're the star they have been talking about. I have heard your story. I want my son to do just as well as you did. Would you mind meeting him?' she asked.

'Sure.'

She stood up, went to the back room, and brought out a two-year-old toddler.

'Shake hands with him, son.' She grabbed her son's chubby, sticky hand, and I shook it. The kid was a little shy. I pinched his rosy cheek.

'Thank you. I hope he remembers meeting you.'

I felt flattered. Overnight, I had become the model son to all mums.

As I headed out, she stopped me. 'Here, I got something for you. Take these and burn them.'

There were a dozen badly written, lying letters of protest against Jin and me.

I ran behind the headquarters building and found a seat beneath a tree. I went through all the letters quickly. The most ridiculous accusation was a claim that Jin and I had cheated by swapping answers in the public toilets during the exam. Yeah, right. Jin and I had taken the tests forty miles apart from each other. Others claimed we were from a landlord's family and didn't deserve to be in college, old clichés, and other garbage. One letter said that my brother had poor eyesight and that I hung out with bad company. That was true, but did it matter?

Obviously not because the clerk had handed everything over to me. I was grateful for her gracious gesture. I tore the letters into little pieces and dumped them down a manhole, then went back and thanked the clerk. She smiled. I bent over, picked her son up from the floor where he was crawling, and played with him for a while. I tickled his tummy and got a big smile. Then I gave him back to the lovely woman.

Two days later, we got a notice from the county that said we had to have a complete physical examination. I didn't eat or sleep too well that night. Maybe my eyes would be too weak or my legs too short. I had no muscles and was all bones. My belly-button was too deep, my nipples too far apart, and my ribs heaved like an accordion. Why would our country want to invest four years of college in such a shaky person?

We went on the commune's muddy tractor. There were no showy flowers pinned on our chests, or anything like that. We arrived at Putien County Hospital a little late because we had had to fill the gas tank, and the driver had stopped to push a fallen tree to the side of the narrow road, then had brawled for a good ten minutes with the farmer who owned the tree.

The nurse rushed us through a minor check, then asked us to take off all our clothes.

'Our clothes?'

'Yeah, now.'

My brother and I squirmed uncomfortably. We finally stood there in our underwear, the last shred of our male dignity hanging loose.

'What's the matter? Come on, drop it, I don't have all day. There's a hundred female applicants waiting for me.'

That sent us flying. We faced the wall and dropped our protection. We stared at each other with goosebumps crawling over our body like ants. It was the first time we had seen each other naked. The nurse's cold hands ran over a few things. Then she took off her plastic gloves with a disgusted look, tossed them into a garbage can, and washed her hands.

We had passed.

'I guess nothing's missing,' Jin said, pulling up his shorts.

'I guess so. Mum and Dad made us right and whole.'

We laughed and were out of the exam room in a second.

The wait began as the college admissions people flew in from all the major cities to interview the applicants from Fujian. They were stuck there for the next few days until all the slots were filled. The Board of Education fed them local delicacies, put on performances to cheer them up, and passed buckets of fresh fruit around during

312

their break. They even threw a banquet for them at the end of the process.

Jin and I gave our sisters a break and took over the farm work. Jin was a lot of fun to work with. He showed me how to hold a plough straight behind a buffalo and how to dig a neat furrow. I dug up human manure from the bottom of a manhole and dumped it into buckets, which he pulled up. Then we both carried them several miles to the fields where the manure was spread as fertilizer. Jin walked faster than I, and stopped and rolled a cigarette for me. When I caught up to him, we sat by the road under the summer sun, wiped our sweat, and smoked the rolls. Then we moved on again.

It was hard labour, but we were lighthearted. We dreamed, boasted, argued and even sang as we dragged our tired feet, heading home as the moon shone on our backs. Jin was totally another person, no longer the distant, older brother who had always loved me, but had never got the chance to say so. The manhood in Yellow Stone had been too confining for him to show brotherly affection, but now it was as if a part of him had been freed. He saw me as an equal and respected me. We had sweated together and were victorious in the end. We had never been this happy before.

Not surprisingly, Jin got some generous proposals of marriage from the beauties of Yellow Stone and beyond. There were nurses, teachers, sales clerks, secretaries, and actresses. Jin showed no interest. He wanted to consider marriage only after college. But Mum, Dad, and our sisters were having a terrific time going through the list, studying them as if for real. They even broke into serious arguments over the merits of their personal choices. Some of the girls on the list shied away whenever they passed our house, acutely aware that they were being scrutinized.

One night a pretty little girl no more than seven or eight ran to our house and said that her dad was inviting me to her house to watch television. There was a special programme on that night. The invitation came from out of the blue. The girl turned out to be the youngest daughter of the party secretary of our commune. He was the only person in Yellow Stone to have a nine-inch, black-and-white TV, which he proudly placed on top of a table in the front yard. In the evenings, he would invite the town's small group of dignitaries to watch the nightly programmes, starting at seven and ending at eleven. An invitation from him to witness the magic of his nine-incher was like being given his personal seal of approval. The next day the whole town would know who was there and why.

Mum was obviously flattered by the invitation and asked me to take a long bath, put on my best white shirt, and a new pair of sandals. I had dinner early, then strolled over the bridge to his walled estate. There were about fifty people sitting, standing, and squatting outside the gate. They were there in the hope that the party secretary might be in a generous mood and let them in. If not, they would be perfectly content sitting outside the wall all night long, listening to the TV as though it were a radio.

The crowd parted as I strolled through the throng. The party secretary stood at the door, fanning away flies with a dried coconut leaf. His pot-belly was barely covered by his shorts. He welcomed me enthusiastically.

'There is a drama at nine tonight that I thought you might want to see,' he said.

'Thank you for the invitation. I love drama.'

'I thought you would.'

I entered the door; inside was another world. There were flowers in pots, a tea table, and lush sofas scattered around a stand where the TV proudly sat, precious modern magic. It was the first time I had ever seen a television.

The party secretary showed me to a prominent seat as all present stood up to meet me. I bowed to them like a spineless sucker. The party vice secretary, the head of the commune's women's group, the head of the Young Leaguers, and a few good-looking ladies were there. I was embarrassed by the attention. These guys had hanged my dad by his thumbs a few years ago, had locked my sister up for selling our clothing ration coupons, had shortened my grandfather's life and made his last days in this world a living hell. Now they all smiled and shook hands with me, praising me for the high scores. It felt strange, but extraordinarily good.

I sat down. A pretty girl, the eldest daughter of the host, carried over a cup of steaming tea on an elegant tray and served me with a sweet smile. I took the tea with a humble heart, outwardly trying to be nonchalant. She sat beside me and explained the high technology of the nine-inch black box. I felt uneasy chatting with her. It was a challenge to conduct a civil conversation without spilling my tea.

The TV blinked all night, the reception was spotty, and when thick clouds passed overhead, blurring it even more, the audience had to guess at what was happening on screen. It was a milestone in my book, nonetheless. The daughter kept pouring me tea, and I kept running to the bathroom. I left with the rest of the crowd when the TV screen turned white with busy little dots. At home, Mum had waited up to question me about how I had been received. She wanted all the details. I gave her a full and complete report, and she smiled with satisfaction.

Twenty-six

I went to the post office every morning and sorted the mail with the clerk. This chubby lady was a one-woman show: she was the phone operator, mailman, telegram person, and the counter clerk, who sold stamps and sealed packages, and was also the mother of the two kids who played on the dirt floor and watched the door for her. Whenever the truck arrived, the eldest kid would shout that the mail was in from Putien. His mum would come out, and I would help her carry it in. When she was out on her bike delivering the mail, her mother-in-law took over watching the children and the switchboard. No matter how shabby, the post office was a crucial message centre: it held my hopes and dream.

I sat on the doorstep, played with the kids, and looked for the green post office truck from Putien each morning. Whenever it came, my heart would race and my head would begin to throb with anticipation. One fine autumn day, the kid yelled as usual, and his mum and I carried in an unusually large load. She threw me the stack of mail, the sorting of which had become my routine, and I clawed through them carefully and quickly.

A large registered envelope dropped out of the sack. The return address looked familiar.

Beijing Language Institute.

It was addressed to Comrade Chen Da.

I jumped up and screamed at the clerk. She handed me a pair of scissors and I slit open the envelope.

In one simple sentence, the letter informed me that I had been admitted into Beijing Language Institute's English department, and that I was expected to report on campus within a month.

I ran home as fast as I could.

Mum, Dad, and the whole family were at hand to congratulate me. We studied the letter and the information they had sent about the department and the college. The picture of the college was a treasure.

My dream had come true. I would be off to Beijing to study English. I would be the first one in the history of Yellow Stone High to do so. Now I had a future, a bright one. In a few years, I would be fluent in English, could go to work for the Foreign Ministry and would converse in that fine language with fine people in an elegant international setting. Other things would follow, and I would be able to take care of my wonderful family and give them all that had been denied them.

Though I had never set foot outside my county and Putien was the largest city I had ever been to, my mind had wings, and it had travelled far away.

I made a list of people to visit before I left. Professor Wei was at the top. She had been away travelling with her sister since I took the test, but now she was back.

I took two ducks and visited her one afternoon. She opened the door and made me tell her what had happened. I said we should talk inside. She said she couldn't wait another second.

Beijing Language Institute, I said.

She said she couldn't believe it.

She jumped up and down like a small child, and said she was so glad she wanted to hug me and thank me for being such a good student.

We hugged and she rested her head on my shoulder. I felt her tears wet my white shirt. She was having a good time.

I promised to write and report all my progress to her. She looked at me and shook her head slowly, still incredulous. Her hands cupped her delicate, refined face, as she stood in her doorway waiting until I disappeared into the woods.

Of course her mean dog was still angry at me. He seemed to be

317

saying, *I'm the only one in town to see through you. You are nothing but a country boy and will always be a country boy.* I made peace with myself and agreed with the dog for the first time. I would always be a country boy, no more, no less.

Dad gave me another list of people to visit, the older generation, his friends and those relatives with whom we had lost contact during the tough times. I visited them all, and was received warmly and with respect.

My four buddies reappeared from nowhere one day and had two bikes on hand. They took me to a fancy restaurant in Putien, one that we used to look at from a distance as we smelled the fine aromas wafting from the ventilation window, trying to guess the price of each smell.

We boasted and talked about the old days. Mo Gong took off his old leather shoes and said that I would need them in a cold city like Beijing. We went to a photo studio and froze our memory into a black-and-white picture.

Meanwhile, we were getting worried about Jin's admission. He was a little older than the usual college student, and we suspected that someone might have been making trouble for him. With his score, he should have received letters from the colleges by now. The whole family was sort of caught between us two. I was in the celebrating mood, while he still waited in agony. There had been cases where applicants with high scores had been left out by clerical error. He began to go to the post office just as I had, waiting every day. He, too, played with the kids and helped the lady clerk with her routine.

Finally, two days before I was about to leave, his letter came.

It was a moment of great happiness for all of us. Mum and Dad, who were hardened by many years of suffering and deprivation, rarely revealed their emotions, but now I saw Dad collapse into a chair, bury his face in his shaking hands, and weep. Mum sat down also and let loose a torrent. Everyone was sniffling.

Thirty years of humiliation had suddenly come to an end. Two sons had been accepted into leading universities within the same year. Mum and Dad had never dreamed of such a day. They had thought we were finished. Kicked around in school, I had almost dropped out many times. Jin had been forced to quit school at the age of twelve to become a farmer with nothing to look forward to but blisters on his tender hands, being spat upon by the older farmers, and back-breaking work that had taken away ten prime years of his life. There had been years of no hope, no dreams, only tears, hunger, shame, and darkness.

I held my brother's shoulders as he sobbed. But it was soon over. He was the first to wipe his eyes and smile broadly at everyone. All the tears were done with.

During the next two days, Jin threw himself into packing for me as I went around bowing and thanking everyone in the neighbourhood. My heart was full of gratitude to everyone, even the meanest people on the street who used to slight us. I bade goodbye to them all. They were touched and shook my hand firmly. They said they would try to take care of my parents while Jin and I were gone. I thanked them again.

On the day of my departure, we got up early. Mum prepared all the cows and pigs I had promised the gods and Buddha. She made them with flour and water and painted them red. I kowtowed a thousand times and thanked them for making my dream come true.

Mum gave me an embroidered silk bag filled with dust from the incense holder and a pinch of soil from Yellow Stone. She asked me to bring it with me to Beijing and to spread it on the ground there when I arrived. It would ensure protection from the gods and Buddha at home. I hid the bag safely in the middle of my wooden trunk.

After breakfast, I checked my train ticket for the last time. Dad, my sisters, and Jin had borrowed bikes and were coming to Putien to see me off at the bus station. I hugged Mum at the door again and again. She cried, but a smile shone through her tears. She pulled me once more into her arms, then gently pushed me away and nodded. Only at that moment as I looked at her, did I realize that she was the most beautiful woman in the whole world and that I was going to miss her when I was thousands of miles away in Beijing.

As I hopped up on to the back seat of the bike, our neighbours came out to wave goodbye to me. The cigarette man, Liang, was old now. He wobbled to the edge and smiled and bowed to me. The doctor was also there, waving his cane in my direction. Some neighbours stood at my mum's side, comforting her. I took a long last look at the cobbled street of Yellow Stone, the Dong Jing River, and the Ching Mountain, looming tall in the background.

Goodbye, Yellow Stone. I am for ever your son.

We rode on our four bikes, chatting and laughing on the way to the bus station. I had never seen Dad so happy and carefree. He joked and told stories about my childhood. We arrived at noon. My bus was already boarding.

Jin was coming with me to Fuzhou to see me off at the train station, because I had never seen a train before. Without his guidance, it would be Da in Wonderland, running after the train as it left. I had never been on a bus before, either. The only motor vehicle I had ridden on was the commune's noisy tractor.

Together Jin and I threw my heavy wooden trunk on to the overloaded luggage rack on top of the shaky, dusty bus. Then we squeezed into a crowded seat that was marked for four people but actually had six occupying it. My sisters came up to the bus and hugged me tearfully, then Dad climbed up the steps. He stumbled, and I sprang out of my seat to meet him. He was a big man and gave me a bear hug. I was surrounded once more by the same warmth I used to feel as a small kid hiding under his padded cotton overcoat. He took my face in his hands and bit his lower lip until it turned pale.

'I want to get some fruit for you, son. You wait.'

He stumbled down from the bus and ran towards a fruit stand a few yards away. His back was hunched over, and his steps were slower than he wanted them to be. He climbed over the guardrail that separated the passengers from the onlookers and almost fell.

When he came back, the engine had already started. Dad walked in front of the bus to stop it. The driver was yelling at him. He ran to the window where we sat, and passed four pears to me. He was out of breath and looked very tired. His eyes were wet, but

320

there was a smile on his wrinkled face. I couldn't help the tears that rolled down my cheeks as we pulled away from the crowded station. Dad stood there waving to me. I craned my neck until I could see him no longer.

I love you, Dad. I am your son for ever.

Acknowledgements

I thank the following people for being there for me as I was in the process of bringing this memoir to life:

My beautiful wife, Sunni, who told me to write this book, taught me how to write it, and worked tirelessly as a brilliant first editor for it, our third child. This is our book!

Victoria, our daughter, for letting me grow with you. Michael, our son, for your great-grandpa's smiling eyes.

My literary agent, Elaine Koster: you are a dream, a class act, and a dear friend. You are a superagent. Thank you for loving the book with passion, and making it all happen.

Bill Koster: thank you for sharing her vision.

William Liu and Alice Liu for loving me like a son. Without the half-days off during many tumultuous months, this book could not have been written.

My dear sister, Ke Ke, for your blind confidence. I can't wait to see your book in print.

My brother, Jin, my sisters, Si and Huang, for loving your little brother abundantly. In abundance, I love you all.

Cindy, my niece, for those wild flowers that were the essence of a summer day.

For all my friends mentioned in the book, wherever you are, the book speaks for itself. I miss you all.

To Tom, Doris, Jeff, Diane, Joe, Ken Holland and the rest of the Hudson Valley Writers' Association. Thank you for stirring the ashes, and for believing in me first.

Jean-Isabel McNutt, at Random House: you are a true poet and your craftsmanship overwhelms me.

And the rest of the Random House team who laboured over the book with love and enthusiasm.

My American editor and publisher, Ann Godoff, editor-in-chief, publisher, and president of the Random House Trade Group: never a day goes by without me thanking God for you. You are an extraordinary editor and a visionary, someone who comes along only once in a long while. You've made my dream come true!

And lastly, my UK editor, Victoria Hipps, thank you for your artistic vision, ever increasing enthusiasm, and editorial brilliance that made this book shine.

CHILD OF HAPPY VALLEY

Juanita Carberry
with Nicola Tyrer

'Honest, entertaining ... shocking' James Fox, author of *White Mischief*

Juanita Carberry spent her childhood in the 1920s and 1930s on a beautiful Kenyan coffee farm. Brought up by her father's black servants and white governesses, much of her time was spent riding and with the tame wild animals, including chimps and cheetahs, who lived on the estate.

Yet life was far from idyllic. Beaten and tormented by her sadistic governess and father, sent to European finishing schools when yet not at teenager, and passed off as her stepmother's younger sister at wild 'White Mischief' parties, Juanita soon discovered the seamier side of adult life.

At the age of fifteen Juanita became involved in the Lord Erroll affair: she is the only person to whom Delves Broughton confessed to the murder of Lord Erroll. This is Juanita's story: a colourful and passionate memoir, which reveals the darkness behind glittering White Mischief society.

'This devasting matter-of-fact memoir shows that it was worth giving the last word on [Kenya's Happy Valley] to an eyewitness who observed the goings' on with the cold, clear eyes of a child' Hugh Massingberd, *Daily Telegraph*

'I knew when I heard Juanita's story, which she gives here in full, that the quest [for the truth behind the Erroll murder] was over' *James Fox*

'Fascinating' *Scotland on Sunday*

'Juanita Carberry's memories of the people, landscape and wildlife of Kenya illuminate her account of what was to be one of her last – and most scandalous – chapters of colonial history' *Express*

ON GOLD MOUNTAIN

Lisa See

'Weaves together fascinating family anecdotes, imaginative details, and the historical details of immigrant life ... Enviably entertaining'
Amy Tan, author of *The Joy Luck Club*

In 1867, Lisa See's great-great-grandfather arrived in America, where he prescribed herbal remedies to immigrant labourers who were treated little better than slaves. His son Fong See later built a mercantile empire and married a Caucasian woman, in spite of laws that prohibited unions between the races. And Lisa herself grew up playing in her family's antiques store in Los Angeles' Chinatown, listening to stories of missionaires and prostitutes, movie stars and all-Chinese baseball teams.

Out of these stories and years of research she has constructed a sweeping chronicle of a Chinese-American family on 'Gold Mountain', the Chinese name for the United States. Encompassing racism and romance, entrepreneurial genius and domestic heartache, secret marriages and sibling rivalries, *On Gold Mountain* is a powerful history of two cultures meeting in a new-world, beautifully written and abounding with intimate recognitions.

'Astonishing ... as engagingly readable as any novel ... comprehensive and exhaustively researched.'
Los Angeles Times Book Review

'Lovingly rendered ... a vivid tableau of a family and an era.'
People

OTHER BIOGRAPHIES AVAILABLE FROM ARROW

❑ Child of Happy Valley	Juanita Carberry	£6.99
❑ A Safe Place	Lorenzo Carcaterra	£6.99
❑ Sleepers	Lorenzo Carcaterra	£6.99
❑ My Dark Places	James Ellroy	£6.99
❑ Haywains and Cherry Ale	Joan Kent	£5.99
❑ Lamplight on Cottage Loaves	Joan Kent	£5.99
❑ To War With Whitaker	Countess Ranfurly	£7.99
❑ The Man Who Listens to Horses	Monty Roberts	£6.99
❑ On Gold Mountain	Lisa See	£7.99

ALL ARROW BOOKS ARE AVAILABLE THROUGH MAIL ORDER OR FROM YOUR LOCAL BOOKSHOP AND NEWSAGENT.
PLEASE SEND CHEQUE/EUROCHEQUE/POSTAL ORDER (STERLING ONLY) ACCESS, VISA, MASTERCARD, DINERS CARD, SWITCH OR AMEX.

```
┌─┬─┬─┬─┬─┬─┬─┬─┬─┬─┬─┬─┬─┬─┬─┬─┐
│ │ │ │ │ │ │ │ │ │ │ │ │ │ │ │ │
└─┴─┴─┴─┴─┴─┴─┴─┴─┴─┴─┴─┴─┴─┴─┴─┘
```

EXPIRY DATE .... SIGNATURE ....
PLEASE ALLOW 75 PENCE PER BOOK FOR POST AND PACKING U.K.
OVERSEAS CUSTOMERS PLEASE ALLOW £1.00 PER COPY FOR POST AND PACKING.
ALL ORDERS TO:
ARROW BOOKS, BOOKS BY POST, TBS LIMITED, THE BOOK SERVICE, COLCHESTER ROAD, FRATING GREEN, COLCHESTER, ESSEX, CO7 7OW, UK.
TELEPHONE: (01206) 256 000
FAX: (01206) 255 914

NAME: ....

ADDRESS ....

....

Please allow 28 days for delivery. Please tick box if you do not wish to receive any additional information ❑
Prices and availability subject to change without notice.